Every Day
in God's Word
Volume 4

by

Jo Krueger

Wrider Publishing

Published by Wrider Publishing, printed through Amazon KDP.

Layout and design by Rachel Burkum. www.rachelburkum.com

Edited by Jo Krueger and Rachel Burkum.

Scriptures taken from the Holy Bible: Easy-to-Read Version™ (ERV™) © 1987, 2004 by Bible League International and used by permission.

Dedication

Every Day in God's Word, Volume 4, is dedicated to all of my readers – especially those who share their thoughts with me. These are the people who read a devotion and let me know that they were blessed and that the message was "just what they needed that day."

God has blessed me so many time with these words of encouragement, and they truly were "just what I needed that day."

May God bless you all as you read His Word and stay close to Him every day.

- Jo

Special Thanks

This book would not be possible if it were not for my dear friends (and family) who have taken the time to put their spiritual thoughts down on paper. Thank you for supporting me and for sharing how God has touched your lives. The names of these authors are listed below.

Thanks also to my husband, Hank, for putting up with me as I struggled to get this book together, and to my daughter, Rachel, whose design skills and proofreading have made the book beautiful and easy to read.

And my personal thanks to God who has constantly prompted me to keep writing and sharing about Him.

Contributing Authors

- Suzanne Austin-Hill
- Jody Bethards
- Rachel Burkum
- Pam Davis
- Lynette Denton
- Jennifer Forrester
- Jim Godsey
- Valerie Godsey
- Bonnie Hall
- Donna Howard
- Debbie Klahn
- Bob La Forge
- Norma Mezoe
- Mary Rosebush
- Gayle Thorn
- Lily Woods

Introduction

Writing these devotion books has been a wonderful experience, full of blessings. Sometimes it's stressful as I try to write and collect enough devotions to fill a new book. Meeting the year-end deadline isn't always easy. But readers like you make it all worth it.

I have continued to put together these books for you. Yes, YOU! God has laid it on my heart to persevere in this ministry. Each time someone comments about enjoying a particular devotion, or tells me they've bought another book, it's a reminder from God that I'm doing His work, and that it's indeed important.

So, thank you. Thank you for picking up this book. Thank you for using this tool to spend time in God's Word... *Every Day*. May you be as blessed reading the following pages as much as I am blessed through this project.

- Jo Krueger

Be Filled with Joy by Jo Krueger

Today's Reading: Philippians 4:4-7

Paul was arrested for telling people about Jesus, and taken to Rome. The last few verses of Acts, chapter 28, tell us during that time Paul stayed in his own rented house in Rome. What did he do while he was there? He continued telling people about Jesus. Paul could have been discouraged and upset about his circumstances. But instead, he thanked God for the opportunity to share the Gospel with the people he met.

Paul expressed this positive attitude in our Bible reading for today. In verse 1 he said, *"Always be filled with joy in the Lord. I will say it again. Be filled with joy."* Paul chose to be filled with God's joy. Because of that, he didn't have to worry about anything. He depended on God to be with him every day and to give him strength to do God's work.

Today is the beginning of a new year. You have no idea what will happen to you this year. Many things that happen will be out of your control. But you can control your attitude. You can be joyful throughout this year, even when bad things happen to you.

Start the new year off right. Choose to be filled with God's joy every day of this year. Happy New Year!

Prayer: *Dear God, thank You for a new year of service to You. Help me to be filled with Your joy, and share that joy with others. In Jesus' name. Amen.*

Blind Guide by Gayle Thorn

Today's Reading: Matthew 15:13-14

There are many people in the world today who try to tempt us to follow them. They do this through their words and actions. They want us to think like they think. They want us to dress like they dress. They want us to listen to the kinds of music and watch the kinds of TV programs and movies that they watch.

In our Bible verses for today, Jesus calls these people blind guides. Jesus was warning the Jewish people about their leaders. *"Jesus answered, 'Every plant that my Father in heaven has not planted will be pulled up by the roots. Stay away from the Pharisees. They lead the people, but they are like blind men leading other blind men. And if a blind man leads another blind man, both of them will fall into a ditch.'"*

We need to be alert so we don't blindly follow someone. Before we follow a person, we need to find out where that person is headed and what they are doing to get there. Maybe that person is doing things that God doesn't approve of. If we follow them, we would be like a blind person following a blind guide dog. We would be headed for certain disaster!

As you go through this new year, you need to be careful to keep your eyes on Jesus and only follow Him. You need to know and study God's Word, the Bible, and obey it.

Prayer: *Heavenly Father, I want to follow Jesus. Help me to keep my eyes on Him and follow His example. In Jesus' name. Amen.*

Look to God by Suzanne Austin-Hill   **Today's Reading:** Psalm 121:1-8

My last name is Hill. So my husband and I are "The Hills." I smile when I read a Bible verse that says something about "the hills." Today's Bible verses are some of my favorites. Verses 1-3 say, *"I look up to the hills, but where will my help really come from? My help will come from the Lord, the Creator of heaven and earth. He will not let you fall. Your Protector will not fall asleep."*

Bible scholars suggest that this psalm was written by a person who was traveling to Jerusalem and camped in the hills around Jerusalem. At night, that could be dangerous place. Wild animals or robbers could attack. So the people camping there might have been wondering, "Who will protect us?" The writer of this psalm answers that question. He says if you want to feel safe, look to God, our Creator. Only He can truly help us in any situation.

The world we live in today can be a scary place. We might wonder who will protect us and how we will stay safe. There are good people who can help us in certain situations – doctors, police officers, firefighters, or even people whose last name is Hill! But only God can help us in all situations we will face in life.

Ask God to be with you and protect you as you serve Him and obey His Word every day!

Prayer: *Loving Father, I want to always look to You first for my safety and protection. You are all that I need. Thank You. In Jesus' name. Amen.*

All New by Gayle Thorn   **Today's Reading:** Romans 6:1-11

Verse 4 of our Bible reading says, *"So when we were baptized, we were buried with Christ and took part in his death. And just as Christ was raised from death by the wonderful power of the Father, so we can now live a new life."*

New life in Christ is more than just a "fresh start." New life in Christ isn't just starting again to build our lives on the same old foundation. With Christ, new life means building our life on a new foundation. That new foundation is Jesus! A new life means using a new way of thinking, a new way of behaving and a new way of speaking.

When we allow Jesus to take control of our lives, a new life isn't the only new thing He gives us. Jesus also gives us a new song (Psalm 40:3), a new name (Revelation 2:17), and a new body (1 Corinthians 15:44). And the Holy Spirit comes to live with us. Jesus said that when His Holy Spirit is living in us, we have a whole new world. We are new from the inside out and from top to bottom!

I hope you have given your life to Jesus and decided to begin your new life with Him. Every day will be filled with God's blessings, and you will be able to look forward to living forever with Him.

Prayer: *Heavenly Father, I am sorry that I have been stubborn and held onto my old life for so long. Forgive my sins and make me a new person through Your Son, Jesus. In His name. Amen.*

God's Love and Peace by Donna Howard   **Today's Reading:** Psalm 136:1-26

My husband and I were returning home after our grandson's baseball game. The brilliant orange sun lit up the western horizon. I felt at peace. However, a few minutes later, dark clouds streaked through the sunset taking away its beauty and my peace. I tried to focus on the beautiful sunset as much as I could, and I soon felt at peace again. The clouds were still there, but they no longer affected me.

Sometimes the events in our lives are like that. Things are going well, and we feel at peace. Then suddenly a hardship or sadness comes into our life. Then we feel depressed and alone. But when we concentrate on God, things change. His great love gives us peace. Our Bible reading today is a psalm of praise. The writer begins and closes the psalm with the same thought. *"Praise the Lord because he is good. His faithful love will last forever"* (verse 1). Then he lists things that he can praise God for – things that happened to him and things that happened in the past to his people, the Israelites.

We can know without a doubt that God loves us. When we focus on Him, the feelings of discouragement and sadness go away. We can feel happy and at peace once again. When you are facing problems in life, think about God and His never-ending peace.

Prayer: *Dear God, thank You for the assurance that Your love will continue forever. And thank You for the peace that it brings into my life. In His name. Amen.*

Death by Gayle Thorn   **Today's Reading:** John 5:24-30

Death may not be a topic that we like to talk about. But we will all die physically someday. However we don't have to die spiritually. Physical death happens when the body's functions stop and the earthly body is separated from the soul. Spiritual death happens when we are separated from God forever.

While physical death may seem scary to us, Christians shouldn't feel threatened by it. Why? Because Christians know that when their earthly body stops working, their soul will go on living with God. Verse 24 of our Bible reading for today says, *"I assure you, anyone who hears what I say and believes in the one who sent me has eternal life. They will not be judged guilty. They have already left death and have entered into life."* And then Jesus said in verses 28-29, *"Don't be surprised at this. A time is coming when all people who are dead and in their graves will hear his voice. Then they will come out of their graves. Those who did good in this life will rise and have eternal life. But those who did evil will rise to be judged guilty."*

Jesus died and then came to life again to end the hold that death has over us. If we believe that Jesus died so that we don't have to, we will not experience spiritual death and be separated from God forever. Thank God today for His wonderful plan of salvation.

Prayer: *Dear God, I know that true strength comes from You. Fill me with Your strength and use me today. In Jesus' name. Amen.*

Attitude of Gratitude by Lynette Denton   Today's Reading: 1 Thessalonians 5:12-22

American poet Maya Angelou said, "Let gratitude be the pillow upon which you kneel to say your nightly prayer." Instead of having the attitude that the world owes us something, we should remember all the ways God has blessed us.

It is good to begin and end our prayers with gratitude. Gratitude is a big word, but it is really a humble word. It simply means being thankful for what you have. You can be thankful by making a list of all the ways God has blessed you – basic needs such as food, shelter, clothing, friends and family and extra blessings such as a job, Christian friends, a teacher or a pet. The more you develop an attitude of thankfulness, your list will grow.

Paul wrote a letter to the Christians in Thessalonica to teach and encourage them. As he closed out his letter, he listed some things that those people should be doing such as being patient, living in peace, doing good for others, being full of joy and always praying. Then Paul says in verse 18, *"Whatever happens, always be thankful. This is how God wants you to live in Christ Jesus."*

When we start off our day with gratitude, it sets the mood for a good day and gives us joy. It's a great way to end our day, too. Thanking God for what He has done for us gives us peace and rest.

Prayer: *Dear Lord, please help me each day to be grateful for all the wonderful things You have done for me. In Jesus' name. Amen.*

Celebrate! by Gayle Thorn   Today's Reading: Psalm 18:46-50

In verse 46 of our Bible reading for today, King David said, *"The Lord lives! I praise my Rock, the God who saves me. How great he is!"* We should all do what King David urges us to do. We should praise and exalt God at all times.

Are you having a good day? Celebrate! Did someone just give you an unexpected gift? Celebrate! Have you received an answer to prayer? Celebrate! Has your day not been going well? Celebrate! Did someone forget your birthday? Celebrate! Did you lose your job? Celebrate! Are you still waiting for the answer to the prayer you have been praying for months? Celebrate! No matter what is happening in your life today, you can celebrate and thank God.

Celebrate by being a light that shows Jesus to people. Celebrate by rejoicing that God is alive and in control of every situation. Celebrate by praising God for the joy of good circumstances and for what you learn from bad experiences. Celebrate by being thankful that God is always there to share your happiness in good times and to give you strength and comfort in bad times.

Whether your circumstances today are good or bad, happy or sad – celebrate! Celebrate the Lord!

Prayer: *Heavenly Father, I celebrate You, Your Son, Jesus, and the presence of the Holy Spirit in my life. In Jesus' name. Amen.*

JAN. 9 :	John 2: 1-11	
JAN. 16 :	Deut. 1: 26-46	
JAN. 18 :	Deut. 2: 1-7	
JAN. 21 :	Deut. 3: 21-29	
Feb. 11 :	John 4: 46-53	Hello:
Feb. 17 :	Deut. 4: 1-14	
Feb. 25 :	Deut. 5: 22-33	
Feb. 29 :	Deut. 6: 1-19	Here is the
MAR. 12 :	Deut. 7: 1-11	fourth book
MAR. 20 :	Deut. 8: 1-10	where some
Apl. 16 :	Deut. 11: 8-28	of my
Apl. 30 :	Deut. 12: 1-14	devotionals
MAY 14 :	Deut. 9: 1-21	appear along
May 25 :	Deut. 15: 1-18	with the
May 27 :	Deut. 13: 1-11	author and
June 13 :	Deut. 16: 1-17	16 others.
June 20 :	Deut. 17: 14-20	
June 28 :	Deut. 18: 1-22	Listed to the
July 5 :	Luke 5: 1-11	left are
Aug 23 :	Deut. 32: 1-47	the dates
ept. 6 :	Matt. 8: 1-5	with the
ept. 8 :	Joshua 1: 1-9	Scriptures
Sept. 16 :	Joshua 3: 1-17	where you
Sept 24 :	Joshua 2: 1-24	can find
ct. 15 :	Joshua 4: 1-24	the ones
ct. 26 :	Joshua 6: 1-27	i wrote.
Oct. 30 :	Joshua 8: 1-35	Blessings—Bonnie
nov-15 :	Joshua 10: 1-25	

Pray about It by Bonnie Hall

In John, chapter 2, we read about Jesus' first miracle. It was not a healing or a calming of a storm. Instead, it involved responding to His mother's request. Here is what happened when Jesus and his family were at a wedding. *"At the wedding there was not enough wine, so Jesus' mother said to him, 'They have no more wine.' Jesus answered, 'Dear woman, why are you telling me this? It is not yet time for me to begin my work'"* (verses 3-4).

But Jesus responded to His mother's request. Jesus told the servants to fill the large wine pots with water. They did, and when they dipped out the water, it was no longer water. It was wine! And not just ordinary, everyday wine – it was the best wine! Through this miracle, Jesus showed His greatness and His followers believed in Him.

Sometimes I have a simple request, and I feel I shouldn't bother God about it. But I go ahead and pray for it. Then God answers my prayer by granting me the request, by reminding me that it is something that is not good for me, or by telling me I need to be patient and wait. When God answers my prayers, my belief in Him is strengthened, and I grow closer to Him.

Be sure to share your requests with God today!

Prayer: *Father, thank You for always paying attention to my prayers and knowing what is best for me. In Jesus' name. Amen.*

Depend on Him by Gayle Thorn

Psalm 37 is another wonderful song written by King David. As you read through this psalm you will realize that verse 40 contains an amazing promise for us. *"The Lord helps good people and rescues them. They depend on him, so he rescues them from the wicked."*

Do you love that promise? It's comforting to know that God is always here to rescue us from wickedness and the bad attitudes and behavior of sinful people. So why do we continue to experience bad and wicked things? Maybe we have overlooked something in that verse. Do you see the four little words in the middle of the verse? *"They depend on him."* People who want God to defend them against evil must give their lives totally to Him – 100%.

If we want God to rescue us and defend us, we must run to Him and give Him control over what's happening to us with all the bad people and their bad attitudes and wicked actions. So we must choose every day to hide in the safety and protection of God's arms.

Are you hiding in the safety of God's arms today? Or are you trying to handle the bad people all by yourself? God has promised to rescue us if we depend on Him for our help and strength.

Prayer: *Father, please be my refuge and safe place. Protect me from people who would like to harm me. In Jesus' name. Amen.*

God's Plan (1) by Jennifer Forrester

Today's Reading: Acts 1:6-8

The book of Acts in the New Testament tells us about the start and the growth of God's church. But God's church didn't just happen. From the beginning, God had a specific plan for His church.

In our Bible reading today, Jesus shared that plan with His followers before He left the earth to go and be with God. Jesus told them that they would be His witnesses who would tell other people about Him. *"But the Holy Spirit will come on you and give you power. You will be my witnesses. You will tell people everywhere about me – in Jerusalem, in the rest of Judea, in Samaria, and in every part of the world"* (verse 8).

God's plans for the church started in the city of Jerusalem on the Day of Pentecost. On that day Peter preached to a large group of people. *"Those who accepted what Peter said were baptized. On that day about 3000 people were added to the group of believers"* (Acts 2:41).

God wants you to be a witness and tell other people about Jesus, too. But where do you start? You probably don't live in Jerusalem, but you do live in or near a town or city. Start with the people who live around you. Talk to your friends and family members. Look for opportunities today to share God's love and tell someone about Jesus.

Prayer: *Dear God, show me someone who needs to know about Your love today. In Jesus' name. Amen.*

God's Plan (2) by Jennifer Forrester

Today's Reading: Acts 8:1-4

In chapters 6 and 7 of Acts, we learn about a man named Stephen. Stephen loved God and preached about Jesus. But some Jewish people did not accept his message. They became so angry with Stephen that they wanted to kill him. So these people took Stephen outside Jerusalem and stoned him to death.

Our Bible verses for today tell us that after Stephen was killed, some Jews began to do bad things to Christians in Jerusalem. These Jews *"went into their houses, dragged out men and women, and put them in jail. All the believers left Jerusalem. Only the apostles stayed. The believers went to different places in Judea and Samaria "* (verses 2 and 3).

Judea was the area surrounding Jerusalem. When this persecution started, many Christians were afraid and moved out of Jerusalem to other places in Judea. Wherever these people went, they shared the Good News about Jesus. In that way, the church spread outside of Jerusalem – just like Jesus had told His followers before He left the earth.

Are you excited to tell others about Jesus? Maybe you can share about Jesus with people outside the town where you live. Ask God to help you find someone who needs to know about His wonderful gift of salvation.

Prayer: *Heavenly Father, thank You for Your gift of salvation through Your Son, Jesus. In His name. Amen.*

God's Plan (3) by Jennifer Forrester   **Today's Reading:** Acts 8:5-25

We have seen that according to God's plan, the church spread from Jerusalem throughout the area of Judea. Then the Christians started sharing about Jesus with people in Samaria, an area north of Judea.

Our Bible verses tell us that *"Philip went to the city of Samaria and told people about the Messiah"* (verse 5). He *"told the people the Good News about God's kingdom and the power of Jesus Christ. Men and women believed Philip and were baptized"* (verse 12). When the apostles in Jerusalem heard about this, they sent Peter and John to Samaria, too.

Wherever Philip, Peter and John went, they witnessed about Jesus. Then more people became Christians, and the church continued to grow bigger. You, too, can reach outside your area with God's message. Share about Jesus with people you meet when you travel. Send a text message or an e-mail to your friends and relatives who live far away. Tell them what Jesus has done for you and how they can know Him as their Savior.

Be like Philip, Peter and John today. Spread the Good News about Jesus so that others can live forever with Him.

Prayer: *Dear Loving Lord, thank You for salvation through Jesus. Wherever I go, I want to tell people about Him. Help me to be a bold witness like Philip, Peter and John. In Jesus' name. Amen.*

God's Plan (4) by Jennifer Forrester   **Today's Reading:** Acts 1:6-8

Christians shared about Jesus in Jerusalem, Judea and Samaria. Then the last part of God's plan for His church was for people to go to *"every part of the world"* (verse 8b). The rest of the book of Acts tells us how the twelve apostles, Paul and other people spread the Good News of Jesus throughout the entire world.

Paul made three trips around the Roman Empire to tell Jews and non-Jews about Jesus. Paul was a missionary — someone who is sent to share God's message with others. Paul faced many hard times while he traveled for Jesus, but God was always with him and protected and encouraged him.

We, too, have a responsibility to share Jesus with the whole world. But maybe you are thinking, "I can't travel everywhere in the world. How can I share Jesus with people in other places?" One way is for you to support missionaries who are serving in other countries. You can pray for them every day and support them financially.

Also, you may be able to go on a short-term mission trip to another country or a mission in your own country. Take some time today to think about how you can be a missionary for Jesus. Let God help you be a part of His wonderful plan to show Jesus to the whole world.

Prayer: *Father, I want the whole world to know about Jesus. Show me how I can be a witness to others today. In Jesus' name. Amen.*

Difficult People by Gayle Thorn   **Today's Reading:** Proverbs 22:10

Improving our relationships with difficult people starts in our own minds. We must change our attitude and our behavior toward them. We must stop criticizing them and looking at their flaws. We must being thinking about their positive qualities. We must begin treating them with love and respect – the way God expects us to treat them. We must pray for them and for ourselves. Once we make these changes, God will begin working in us and in them. Then the difficult people in our lives may become less difficult.

Sometimes being with difficult people isn't good for us, and we need to put some space between us and them. In our Bible verse for today Solomon said, *"Get rid of the proud who laugh at what is right, and trouble will leave with them. All arguments and insults will end."* If someone in our life is continually mocking, ridiculing, insulting or criticizing other people, we need to remove that person from our lives. They can't help us become more like Jesus. They will only drag us down. And when we are with them, we can become tempted to do and say the same sinful things they do and say.

Ask God to help you in your relationships with difficult people. He will show you what to do.

Prayer: *Dear Lord, help me to know if someone in my life is causing me to say or do things that displease You. In Jesus' name. Amen.*

God is in Front by Bonnie Hall   **Today's Reading:** Deuteronomy 1:26-46

Deuteronomy, chapter 1, tell us about the Israelites' journey to the land God had promised to them. Moses told the people that with God's help they could overtake their enemies in the land. But the people were afraid, so they suggested that Moses send some spies into the new land to see what it was like.

But when the spies returned, the Israelites still didn't want to go into the new land. They were afraid of the strong people who lived there. But Moses told the people, *"Don't be upset or afraid of those people. The Lord your God is in front, leading you. He will fight for you just as he did in Egypt. You saw what happened in the desert. You saw how the Lord your God carried you like a man carries his child. He brought you safely all the way to this place"* (verses 29b-31). But God was not happy with the Israelites and their disobedience and their lack of trust. So God caused them to wander in the wilderness for 40 years.

There may be times in our lives when we are afraid like the Israelites were. We may be facing a new job, family problems, financial difficulties or the loss of a loved one. That is when we need to remember that God is in front of us, leading us to a place of safety and peace. Don't be like the Israelites — trust God and His plan for our lives!

Prayer: *Father, sometimes I become afraid as I face problems every day. Help me to look to You and trust You. In Jesus' name. Amen.*

Snowflake by Bob La Forge

Today's Reading: Acts 2:42-47

One snowflake by itself is frail and vulnerable. The slightest bit of heat or pressure will melt it. But if you put enough snowflakes together, you can stop a city for several days.

A Christian is a lot like that. When we are off by ourselves we can easily fail because of a difficult job or the demands from people. The pressure from broken relationships or the world's temptations can cause us to cave in. But when we surround ourselves with other Christians, we can hold each other up and guide each other away from the wrong influences that would cause us to sin.

That's how it was in the early church in Jerusalem. Those people stuck together and helped each other. Verse 42 of our Bible reading for today says, *"The believers spent their time listening to the teaching of the apostles. They shared everything with each other. They ate together and prayed together."* And what was the result? The news about Jesus spread, and the church grew.

Fellowship with other Christians helps us to reset our priorities and rest. We may find ourselves devastated by some sin, but when we lean on other Christians, we can stop the sin. Our best defense is to stand strong with other Christians on God's Word and His promises.

Prayer: *Father, help me to understand that I need to depend on You and my brothers and sisters in Christ. In His name. Amen.*

God is with You by Bonnie Hall

Today's Reading: Deuteronomy 2:1-7

In Deuteronomy, chapter 2, Moses continues to tell us about the Israelites' journey in the wilderness. Moses wanted these people to do exactly what God wanted them to do. He reminded them about all the wonderful things God had done for them in the past. *"Remember that the Lord your God has blessed you in everything you have done. He knows about everything that happened on the trip through this great desert. The Lord your God has been with you these 40 years. You have always had everything you needed"* (verse 7).

As I think about that verse, I remember what has happened to me over the past 40 years – when my 2-month-old son was very sick in the hospital, when my other son was severely bullied in school, when I suffered several health crises and then when my husband passed away unexpectedly. During those times I held onto every word I read in the Bible, and I asked God every day to guide and protect me. Through these times I learned that God was with me and that He provided everything I needed.

You may be going through some hard times today. You may find it difficult to know what you should do next. Don't give up. Remember that God is with you and will comfort and guide you.

Prayer: *Lord, I don't know what will happen to me today, but I know that You are with me and will provide for me. In Jesus' name. Amen.*

Be Perfect? by Gayle Thorn   Today's Reading: Matthew 5:43-48

God is perfect. God NEVER sins. God never lies. God never makes mistakes. God never says the wrong things.

God is ALWAYS kind. God is always gentle. God is always forgiving. God is always dependable. God is always available. God is always loving.

In verse 48 of our Bible reading for today, Jesus said, *"What I am saying is that you must be perfect, just as your Father in heaven is perfect."* How can we possibly be perfect like God is? The truth is, we can't be perfect, and God knows we won't be perfect. When Jesus gave this command, He was talking about love. God expects us to be perfect about loving other people. He wants us to love them in the same way that He loves them. We are not to pick out favorite people to love more. We are not to leave anyone unloved. We are to love every person completely and unconditionally – just the way God loves all of us!

When we perfectly love people and God, we are truly obeying God. Look around at the people you will meet today. It may be easy to love your friends and family members. But what about people whose skin is a different color or people who show that they don't love God? Work toward perfectly loving all people the way God loves you!

Prayer: *Heavenly Father, show me people today that I don't love the way You love me. Help me to love them and share Your love with them. In Jesus' name. Amen.*

Clean Up in Aisle 3 by Jo Krueger   Today's Reading: Romans 3:21-26

One day I was shopping in a grocery store. There was a large display of pickle jars in the middle of an aisle. Near me was a mother with a small boy. For some reason, the boy took off running and charged right into the display. Pickle jars went everywhere, and most of them burst open. Thankfully, the little boy was not hurt, but the mother was horrified. She thought that she would have to pay for the damages. But the store manager assured her that the store had insurance for things like that. The mother was so relieved! Soon the pickles were cleaned up and the mother went on her way.

Jesus is like the store's insurance. The Bible tells us that all people sin and that the punishment for sin is eternal separation from God. But our Bible verses today give us some good news. *"All have sinned and are not good enough to share God's divine greatness. They are made right with God by his grace. This is a free gift. They are made right with God by being made free from sin through Jesus Christ"* (verses 23-24).

When Jesus died on the cross and rose from the dead three days later, He accepted the punishment for our sins. If we accept His free gift of salvation, we don't have to be afraid that we will ever be separated from God. Thank God for His gift of salvation today!

Prayer: *Father, thank You for sending Jesus to die for my sins. I am excited to live forever with You. In Jesus' name. Amen.*

God will Fight for You by Bonnie Hall   **Today's Reading:** Deuteronomy 3:21-29

In Deuteronomy, chapter 3, Moses gives a summary of the Israelites' journey. He explained to them how God had led them and how He had given them the land He had promised to them years before.

Moses reminded the people how successful they had been in defeating those enemies that stood in their way. Then in verses 21 and 22, he told them what he had told Joshua. *"Then I told Joshua, 'You have seen all that the Lord your God has done to these two kings. The Lord will do the same thing to all the kingdoms you will enter. Don't fear the kings of these lands, because the Lord your God will fight for you.'"* Moses reminded the Israelites again and again to trust God and not be afraid because God would fight for them.

You are probably not facing an army of your enemies today but you may run into people who are hard-hearted or want to control your life. When that happens, we often try to take care of things ourselves. Then we become frustrated and discouraged. Just as God led Moses and the Israelites through the many challenges of the wilderness, He will help us through our problems.

You don't know what will happen to you today. But you can know that God will fight for you and that you don't need to be afraid.

Prayer: *Dear Loving God, please be with me today and help me to not be afraid. In Jesus' name. Amen.*

The Benefits of Prayer by Gayle Thorn   **Today's Reading:** Hebrews 4:13-16

Verse 16 of our Bible reading says, *"With Jesus as our high priest, we can feel free to come before God's throne where there is grace. There we receive mercy and kindness to help us when we need it."* We go before God's throne when we talk to Him through prayer. This verse tells us that there are benefits to prayer. Two of these benefits are receiving God's mercy and kindness.

But what are some other benefits that we get when we regularly spend time praying to God? Prayer gives us the opportunity to have God help us make positive changes in our lives, to show Him that we trust His ability to solve our problems and to show God that we trust Him to be just and fair.

Prayer also gives us the opportunity to trade worry and fear for peace and security. When we doubt God, prayer helps us to have confidence in God's willingness to do what is best for us. Prayer also gives us the opportunity to love other people by asking God to do what is best for them.

The key to receiving these benefits is for us to pray regularly and to pray sincerely. I hope that you will talk to God today. Then you can begin enjoying the many benefits of prayer.

Prayer: *Heavenly Father, thank You that I can come before Your throne in prayer. And thank You for all the wonderful benefits that You give me when I spend time talking with You. In Jesus' name. Amen.*

Mathematical Signs (1) by Jo Krueger   **Today's Reading:** 2 Peter 1:3-9

Today and for the next few days we will look at some mathematical signs and how they relate to God's Word. Probably the first sign that we were taught in math class was the addition or plus sign (+). We learned that 1 + 1 = 2 and 2 + 2 = 4. When we add things together we get a larger amount than we started with.

In our Bible verses today, Peter talked about Christians qualities that we need to have. In verse 5-7 he said, *"Because you have these blessings, do all you can to add to your life these things: to your faith add goodness; to your goodness add knowledge; to your knowledge add self-control; to your self-control add patience; to your patience add devotion to God; to your devotion add kindness toward your brothers and sisters in Christ, and to this kindness add love."*

The more of these qualities that we have in our life, the better we can serve God and share Jesus with others. Peter said that if we have these things, we will never fail to be useful to God. And these qualities will help us produce good fruit that will lead others to Jesus.

Do you have these qualities in your life? If not, then you need to ask God to help you add them to your life. Some may be easy to add and others may require more work. But God will be with you as you seek to serve Him better every day.

Prayer: *Dear Lord, I want to serve and love You every day. Help me to have these qualities in my life. In Jesus' name. Amen.*

Mathematical Signs (2) by Jo Krueger   **Today's Reading:** John 3:22-30

Yesterday we talked about the plus sign. Today we will talk about the minus or less sign (–). Sometimes people think that less is bad. They don't want to have less money or fewer friends or be less important than another person.

Our Bible reading today tells us about John the Baptist. John's work was to prepare the way for the coming of Jesus. He told the Jewish people to repent of their sins and get ready for the Messiah, God's "chosen one," to come. Many people followed and listened to John. But then Jesus began His ministry on earth. John knew that he had to become less important so that Jesus would be most important. In verse 30 John talked about Jesus, *"He must become more and more important, and I must become less important."*

John was humble. His goal was to do what God wanted him to do, even if that meant he had to become less important. John told his followers that they needed to stop following him and follow Jesus instead. Sometimes in our ministry in the church we may need to step aside and allow another person to become more important than we are. That's when we ask God to help us be humble and obedient.

Be like John as you serve God today. He will be pleased with you and bless you for your humility.

Prayer: *Dear God, I want to be obedient and humble as I serve You each day. In Jesus' name. Amen.*

Mathematical Signs (3) by Jo Krueger   **Today's Reading:** Matthew 18:21-35

The multiplication or times sign (x) is the next mathematical sign that children learn in school. Multiplication is kind of like a fast way of adding. 4 + 4 + 4 + 4=16, but 4 x 4 also equals 16.

In our Bible verses for today, Jesus told His disciples a story about forgiveness. He told the story after Peter asked Him a question. Peter asked Jesus how many times he needed to forgive someone who did something wrong to him. He wondered if seven times was enough. Jesus answered Peter in verse 22. *"I tell you, you must forgive them more than seven times. You must continue to forgive them even if they do wrong to you seventy-seven times."*

Then Jesus told a story about a man who had been forgiven but was unwilling to forgive someone else. Jesus ended the story by saying that if we don't forgive other people, God will not forgive us. Sometimes it is hard to forgive someone. And if they keep hurting us over and over again, it is even harder to show them forgiveness. But Jesus said that we need to continue to forgive them. Remember that when you show forgiveness to others, God will forgive your sins.

Ask God to help you have a loving and forgiving heart today toward people who hurt you.

Prayer: *Thank You, God, for forgiving my sins. Show me how I can forgive other people. In Jesus' name. Amen.*

Mathematical Signs (4) by Jo Krueger   **Today's Reading:** Acts 2:42-47

Our next mathematical sign is the division sign (÷). Dividing something means that it is separated into smaller groups. 20 ÷ 5 = 4 means that 20 is divided into 5 groups with 4 in each group.

After the church was established in Jerusalem on the Day of Pentecost, the new Christians stayed close to one another. They ate together, worshiped God together and helped each other. Verses 44-45 tell us what else these Christians did. *"All the believers stayed together and shared everything. They sold their land and the things they owned. Then they divided the money and gave it to those who needed it."*

Acts, chapter 2, tells us that many of the people who listened to Peter preach were from out of town. If they obeyed Peter's words and were baptized, they may have stayed in Jerusalem for a while to fellowship with the other Christians. If these people did not have enough food or a place to stay, the Jerusalem Christians may have used their money and possessions to help these people and others in need.

Today there are many ways we can help other Christians. We can share money, clothes and food with needy people. Be willing to give and share so that people will have their needs satisfied.

Prayer: *Father, You have given me so much. Help me to share my money and possessions with other Christians. In Jesus' name. Amen.*

Mathematical Signs (5) by Jo Krueger   **Today's Reading:** 1 John 4:1-6

Two mathematical signs that complement each other are the greater than (>) and less than (<) signs. These signs are used to compare two amounts. 5 > 4 and 4 < 5 are examples of how these signs are used. Often something that is greater than something else is also better.

There are two forces that are in the world. Sometimes we call them "good" and "evil." The "good" is Jesus, and the "evil" is the devil. People choose to follow either Jesus or the devil. In our Bible verses John talks about false prophets in the world who follow the devil. They try to get people to believe lies about Jesus. We can see today that many people follow these false prophets and live for the devil.

But in these verses, John reminds us that Jesus is much greater than the devil. Verse 4 tells us, *"My dear children, you belong to God, so you have already defeated these false prophets. That's because the one who is in you is greater than the one who is in the world."* When we follow Jesus, He lives in us and helps us obey Him. We don't need to be afraid of these false prophets and their message because Jesus is greater than the devil (the one who is in the world).

I hope you are following Jesus today. You can depend on Him to be with you as you reach out to other people with His message of salvation.

Prayer: *Dear God, You are so great! Please help me to depend on Jesus and Your Word today. In Jesus' name. Amen.*

Mathematical Signs (6) by Jo Krueger   **Today's Reading:** Philippians 2:1-11

The past few days we have looked at several mathematical signs. The last sign we will talk about is the equal (=) sign. The equal sign is used to show that two things are the same. 3 + 4 = 2 +5 is an example. 3 + 4 = 7 and 2 + 5 = 7, so they are equal.

Many people in the world today talk about equality. They want men to be equal with women and all races to be equal. But the very most important equality involves God and Jesus. God and Jesus are equal. Verses 6-7a of our Bible reading for today tell us about that. *"He was like God in every way, but he did not think that his being equal with God was something to use for his own benefit. Instead, he gave up everything, even his place with God."* Jesus is like God in every day. That means He is equal with God.

It is very important for us to know that Jesus is equal with God. Why? Because if Jesus is equal with God, that means He is without sin. And because Jesus is without sin, He was able to die in our place and accept the punishment for our sins. Also, because Jesus is equal with God, we know that His words in the Bible are true and that we should obey them.

Because Jesus is equal with God, we should love and obey Him every day. Ask Him to show you how to live for Him today.

Prayer: *Dear Lord, thank You for Your Son, Jesus. Thank You that He was willing to die on the cross for me. In His name. Amen.*

Deceit by Gayle Thorn   **Today's Reading:** Proverbs 6:12-14

God made King Solomon to be a very wise man. In verses 12-14 of our Bible reading, Solomon tells us some important things that we need to know. *"Some people are just troublemakers. They are always thinking up some crooked plan and telling lies. They use secret signals to cheat people; they wink their eyes, shuffle their feet, and point a finger. They are always planning to do something bad."* This is an accurate description of deceit.

Deceit is more that just not telling the truth. Lying is one kind of deceit, but there are other kinds of deceit, too. If you make a promise and then break that promise, that is deceit. If you say you will do something, but you don't do it, that is deceit. If you have kept important information from someone, that is deceit. If you live one way on Sunday but act like a completely different person the rest of the week, that is deceit. If you look for ways to get out of something that you are responsible for doing, that is deceit.

Be careful to examine your words and actions today. Have you been deceiving someone through the things you do or say? If so, ask God to forgive you and to remove the deceit from your life. Then ask Him to give you the strength to do what is right every day.

Prayer: *Dear Father, help me to remove all the deceit from my life and to obey You fully. In Jesus' name. Amen.*

Jesus, Not You by Rachel Burkum   **Today's Reading:** Romans 8:12-17

Have you ever heard the phrase, "You do you"? It means you do whatever you want, or whatever feels good to you. Our culture tells us that we should do anything we think is right for our own goals. There is no one true way to do thing – we can decide for ourselves. But what does the Bible say about this?

If you read today's Bible verses, Paul is very clear about how we should live. *"If you use your lives to do what your sinful selves want, you will die spiritually. But if you us the Spirit's help to stop doing the wrong things you do with your body, you will have true life"* (verse 13). If we follow our sinful desires, we will die spiritually. This means our relationship with God is broken and we have no hope of eternal life. When we put God first in our lives, only then will we have the true life that Paul was talking about.

1 Corinthians 15:34a says, *"Come back to your right way of thinking and stop sinning."* Paul doesn't teach us to do whatever feels good or whatever we think is best. He tells us to stop sinning! Period! There is no debate. There is no "gray area" where we get to choose what is right or wrong. God has set His rules in place to protect our hears and souls. If we don't follow Him, we are lost.

Don't "do you," today. Instead, do what Jesus wants.

Prayer: *Dear God, I know You put rules in place for my own good. Please help me to always do what You want me to do. In Jesus' name. Amen.*

The Infield by Gayle Thorn

Today's Reading: 1 John 4:11-18

Imagine that you have crossed a racetrack to the center infield. Then the race begins. Cars are speeding around the track, so it isn't possible or safe to cross the track. You can see the people on the other side of the track. You can remember what it is like to be on the other side. You might even have moments when you wish that you were on the other side again but you must stay where you are.

In the same way, you have "crossed the track" when you asked God to forgive your sins and send the Holy Spirit to live in you. You are then on the "infield" with God to stay forever. You can see people that are still living apart from God. You can remember what it was like when you were sinning and living away from God. And sometimes you might even be tempted to be on the other side of the track again.

However, once you are with God, that is where you should stay. Verse 13 of our Bible reading says, *"We know that we live in God and God lives in us. We know this because he gave us his Spirit."* You can be confident that God is always with you because His Holy Spirit always lives in you. God won't give up on you or send you back across the track. God loves you and wants you to obey Him and be with Him forever.

Prayer: *Dear God, I feel so safe with You. Help me to rely on Your Holy Spirit to lead me each day. In Jesus' name. Amen.*

The Sun (1) by Jo Krueger

Today's Bible Reading: Genesis 1:1-31

Did you watch a colorful sunrise or an impressive sunset today? Did you feel the warmth of the sun today and thank God for making it? Often we take the sun for granted. It comes up and goes down every day, but we don't really think about how important it is. Today we will begin a series of devotions about the sun. We will look at seven places in the Bible that talk about the sun.

Verses 16-18 of our Bible reading tell us, *"So God made the two large lights. He made the larger light to rule during the day and the smaller light to rule during the night. He also made the stars. God put these lights in the sky to shine on the earth. He put them in the sky to rule over the day and over the night. They separated the light from the darkness. And God saw that it was good."* The sun is called the "larger light." Other translations say it is the "greater light."

The sun is a necessary part of our lives. The sun's gravity holds our solar system together. It gives us heat and light. And the sun helps plants to grow and thrive. God made the sun and put it just the right distance from the earth. If it were closer, we would burn up; it if were farther away, we would freeze to death.

Take some time today to think about the sun. Thank God for making the sun and the many ways it helps us throughout our lives.

Prayer: *God, You are awesome! Thank You for making the sun to help us live each day. In Jesus' name. Amen.*

The Sun (2) by Jo Krueger   **Today's Reading:** Deuteronomy 4:15-20

Yesterday we talked about the importance of the sun. Although the sun is necessary for our existence here on earth, it is not something that we should worship. Sun worship has been a part of many cultures through the years, and even today, many people in India worship the sun. When God gave His people, the Israelites, a list of rules to obey, He made sure that they knew they were not to worship the sun.

In our Bible verses, Moses told the Israelites that God did not want them to sin and destroy themselves by worshiping false gods like other people worshiped. Verse 19 says, *"And be careful when you look up to the sky and see the sun, the moon, and the start — all the many things in the sky. Be careful that you are not tempted to worship and serve them. The Lord your God lets the other people in the world do this."* God wants us to worship only Him, the Creator, and not the things that He has created.

There are many temptations in the world today to worship things other than God. Modern people often worship their physical beauty or their wisdom. Some people worship their money or their possessions. And yet others may worship their family members. Anything that we make more important than God becomes our object of worship.

Think about God today. Make Him the center of your life and your worship.

Prayer: *Thank You, God, for who You are. Help me to make You the center of my worship. In Jesus' name. Amen.*

The Sun (3) by Jo Krueger   **Today's Reading:** Joshua 10:1-14

Because God is the Creator, He can use things He has created to help people on earth. One example of this is found in Joshua, chapter 10. The people of the city of Gibeon made a peace agreement with the Israelites. So when they were being attacked by five Amorite kings and their armies, they sent a message to Joshua and asked that the Israelites help save them.

So Joshua took his best fighting men and went up against the five armies. On the day that God helped the Israelites defeat these enemies, something very strange happened. Joshua told the sun and moon to stand still! *"So the sun did not move, and the moon stopped until the people defeated their enemies. This story is written in the Book of Jashar. The sun stopped in the middle of the sky. It did not move for a full day. That had never happened before, and it has never happened again"* (verses 13-14a).

What did it mean that the sun stopped? It meant that God kept the sun from setting. Instead, God changed the rotation of the earth so that the sun would give light, thus allowing the Israelites more time to defeat their enemies. This may be hard to understand, but it truly was a wonderful miracle from God.

Praise God today for His wonderful power, and thank Him for showing us His love through the miracle of salvation.

Prayer: *Lord, only You can do such wonderful miracles. Thank You for Your power and love. In Jesus' name. Amen.*

The Sun (4) by Jo Krueger   **Today's Reading:** Psalm 148:1-14

Psalm 148 is a psalm about praising God. In fact, it not just a song about praising God; it is a command for us to praise God! In this psalm, the writer tells many things in nature to praise God. And he concludes by reminding the readers that they, too, should praise God. Verses 3-6 say, *"Sun and moon, praise him! Stars and lights in the sky, praise him! Praise him, highest heaven! Waters above the sky, praise him! Let them praise the Lord's name, because he gave the command and created them all! He made all these continue forever. He made the laws that will never end."*

These verses talk about the sun, the moon, the stars, other lights in the sky and water praising God. But how can these things in creation praise God? Can they bow down and worship Him? Can they clap their hands and sing a song of praise? No! These things praise God by doing exactly what they were meant to do. So when the sun, moon and stars shine brightly and water gives moisture to the earth, they are praising God.

So how can you praise God? You can praise God by doing exactly what God meant you to do – love Him, thank Him, accept His Son as your Savior, and then share that message with other people. God made you and wants you to love and obey Him every day. Look for ways to show your praise to God today!

Prayer: *Heavenly Father, thank You for making me and showing me how I can praise You every day. In Jesus' name. Amen.*

The Sun (5) by Jo Krueger   **Today's Reading:** Jonah 4:1-11

In our Bible verses today, God used the sun to teach Jonah a lesson. Jonah was upset that God had saved the city of Nineveh from destruction. He complained to God and made himself a small shelter outside the city. God made a large gourd vine to cover Jonah and keep him cool. That made Jonah very happy. But then God made a worm to eat the gourd, and the plant died. Next, God made the hot sun to shine on Jonah and sent a hot east wind to blow on him. Jonah became very hot and weak and asked God to let him die.

Verses 9-11a tell us, *"But God said to Jonah, 'Do you think it is right for you to be angry just because this plant died?' Jonah answered, 'Yes, it is right for me to be angry! I am angry enough to die!' And the Lord said, 'You did nothing for that plant. You did not make it grow. It grew up in the night, and the next day it died. And now you are sad about it. If you can get upset over a plant, surely I can feel sorry for the big city like Nineveh.'"*

Jonah did not care about the people in Nineveh who did not worship God and would be destroyed. Are you like Jonah? Do you ignore people in the world who need to know about Jesus? Think about people you know who are not Christians. Ask God to help you reach out to them today and share the Good News about His Son, Jesus.

Prayer: *Dear God, so many people do not know You. Help me to tell them about Your love and Your plan of salvation. In Jesus' name. Amen.*

The Sun (6) by Jo Krueger   **Today's Reading:** Luke 23:1-49

Today our Bible verses are about another miracle that God performed with the sun. Jesus' enemies did not believe that He was God's Son, so they arrested Him and nailed Him to a cross. This was the saddest day that ever existed on earth. And God caused several very strange things to happen when Jesus died.

"It was about noon, but it turned dark throughout the land until three o'clock in the afternoon, because the sun stopped shining. The curtain in the Temple was torn into two pieces. Jesus shouted, 'Father, I put my life in your hands!' After Jesus said this, he died" (verses 44-46). When Jesus died, God cause the sun to stop shining. Some people have suggested that this was an eclipse of the sun. But this doesn't seem to have been an eclipse. Instead, God caused the sun to stop shining as a symbol that this was the darkest of all times, spiritually.

The good news for us is that three days later, Jesus rose from the grave. He did this to show that He was truly God's Son and that He would give eternal life to people who follow Him. The darkness of the day that Jesus died was overcome with the light of His resurrection.

Praise and thank God today for His plan of salvation and the promise of living with Him forever.

Prayer: *Thank You, God, for Jesus and that He died for my sins. Help me to follow You each day. In Jesus' name. Amen.*

The Sun (7) by Jo Krueger   **Today's Reading:** Revelation 21:22-27

The past several days we learned some things about the sun and have seen the miracles that God performed with the sun. Today we will talk about a time when there will no longer be any sun.

We are used to seeing the sun every day, and we often take it for granted. So it is hard to imagine life without the sun. But when we live in the New Jerusalem with God, there will be no sun. In our Bible verses, John described what the New Jerusalem will look like. In verse 23 John says, *"The city did not need the sun or the moon to shine on it. The glory of God gave the city light. The Lamb was the city's lamp."*

There will be no sun in the New Jerusalem to give light. Instead, the light will come from Jesus, the Lamb, and God's glory. The city will be made of precious jewels and gold. There will be no gates on the city, and there will never be anything unclean of sinful there. Can you imagine how awesome that will be?

I hope you are excited to think about the time when you will live forever in the New Jerusalem with God and Jesus. God has prepared a wonderful place for His children – a place that is beyond what our minds can imagine here on earth. There will be no pain or tears or sadness, and we will spend eternity praising and loving God. That will truly be wonderful!

Prayer: *God, thank You for loving me, giving me the gift of salvation and preparing a place for me to live forever. In Jesus' name. Amen.*

Everything is New by Norma Mezoe   **Today's Reading:** 2 Corinthians 5:11-21

David truly rejoiced in his salvation. He was always ready to witness about God's goodness to him. But before accepting Jesus as His Savior, David had a life that was lived according to his own will and desires. One of those desires was an affair that threatened to destroy his marriage.

During that crisis, David and his wife counseled with a minister. Dave humbled himself before God and asked Jesus to be his Lord and Savior. David's life and marriage were renewed with that commitment. In our Bible reading today, Paul talked about people like David. *"From this time on we don't think of anyone as the world thinks of people. It is true that in the past we thought of Christ as the world thinks. But we don't think that way now. When anyone is in Christ, it is a whole new world. The old things are gone; suddenly, everything is new!"* (verses 16-17).

Perhaps we haven't had the same kind of salvation experience that David had. Some of us may have grown up in a home where becoming a Christian seemed like the natural thing to do. No matter how we came to know the Lord, we can rejoice and praise Him. Not only do we choose to love and serve God, but God has chosen us to be His sons and daughters.

Thank God today for making everything new in your life!

Prayer: *Loving Father, thank You for the gift of salvation and for making everything new in my life. In Jesus' name. Amen.*

Dreams by Gayle Thorn   **Today's Reading:** 1 Kings 3:1-14

Dreams can sometimes be funny, strange or scary. Some dreams seem so real that we remember every detail. At other times we don't remember anything about our dreams when we wake up.

In the Old Testament we learn that God spoke to Jacob, Joseph and Daniel through dreams. And in our Bible reading for today, God spoke to King Solomon in a dream. God asked Solomon what he wanted. In verse 9 Solomon gave his reply. *"So I ask you to give me the wisdom to rule and judge them well and to help me know the difference between right and wrong. Without such great wisdom, it would be impossible to rule this great nation."* Because Solomon didn't ask for things like wealth and fame, God gave him wisdom *and* wealth and fame.

God may speak to us today through our dreams, too. If you should ever wonder if God spoke to you through a dream, remember to follow John's advice in 1 John 4:1. *"... test the spirits to see if they are from God."* How do you do that? Compare your dream to what the Bible teaches. Pray and ask God to help you understand the truth. Seek advice from your pastor or other mature Christians.

We can know for sure that God speaks to us through His Word, the Bible. However God speaks to you, be sure to listen and obey!

Prayer: *Dear Heavenly Father, help me to always listen to You and obey You. In Jesus' name. Amen.*

Alike but Different by Donna Howard   **Today's Reading:** Romans 3:21-26

A friend told me about her two young daughters' visit to their grandparents' farm. After the visit, the older girl said to her little sister, "Now you know the difference between boy cows and girl cows, don't you?" The younger girl quickly replied, "Yes! The boy cows have hairy knees."

We may laugh at that or not even understand it, but it is a fact that God chose to make many different kinds of animals as part of His creation. And within that creation, He often made male animals to look different than the females. God also made each person on earth to be unique. Even twins that look exactly alike may be very different in many ways.

But our Bible verses remind us that there is one way that all people are alike. Verses 23-24 say, *"All have sinned and are not good enough to share God's divine greatness. They are made right with God by his grace. This is a free gift. They are made right with God by being made free from sin through Jesus Christ."* All people disobey God and need to find a way to have their sins forgiven. That one way is Jesus! He was different from people in one special way – He never sinned.

That's why Jesus is the only way to have our sins forgiven. Will you accept Jesus' sacrifice for you and make Him the Lord of your life today?

Prayer: *Father, I know that I have sinned and that I need to accept Your wonderful gift of salvation. In Jesus' name. Amen.*

God Heard My Prayer by Bonnie Hall   **Today's Reading:** John 4:46-53

Our Bible verses for today tell us about a man from Capernaum who had a sick son. *"The man heard that Jesus had come from Judea and was now in Galilee. So he went to Jesus and begged him to come to Capernaum and heal his son, who was almost dead"* (verse 47). Jesus saw that the man had faith that He could heal his son. So Jesus told the man to go home – that his son had been healed. When the man arrived home he learned that his son had been healed at the exact time when Jesus had said that his son would live.

Once my son was sick, too. He was only two months old and in the hospital. The doctor said that the next 48 hours would decide if my son would live or die. There was a shortage of nurses, so I stayed awake all night, making sure that my son was okay and praying that God would heal him. The next morning I went home to sleep. I continued to pray that my son would get well. When I got back to the hospital, I learned that my son was resting comfortably and that he would be okay.

I was so thankful that God had heard my prayers and healed my son. I am sure that's how the man in our Bible story felt, too. I know that God has heard all of my prayers throughout my life and answered them according to His will.

Turn to God today. He will listen to you and be there to help you.

Prayer: *Dear Lord, thank You for always listening to my prayers and helping me. In Jesus' name. Amen.*

Hebrews 10 (1) by Jo Krueger   Today's Reading: Hebrews 10:1-18

The writer of the book of Hebrews wrote to Jews who had become Christians. But some of these Jews wanted to follow the teaching of the Old Testament instead of the teachings of Jesus and His followers. The author told these Jews to only follow Jesus. Then he talked about several things that Christians should do. For the next few days we will take a closer look at what we can learn from Hebrews, chapter 10.

The Most Holy Place was the part of the Temple where God lived. One day every year, the high priest went into the Most Holy Place to make a sacrifice for the sins of the people. When Jesus died, the curtain in front of the Most Holy Place was torn into two pieces. This showed that Jesus had become the final sacrifice for sins.

Verses 11-12 tell us, *"Every day the priests stand and do their religious service. Again and again they offer the same sacrifices, which can never take away sins. But Christ offered only one sacrifice for sins, and that sacrifice is good for all time. Then he sat down at the right side of God."* After Jesus died, the priests didn't need to make any more sacrifices for the people. Jesus was the perfect sacrifice.

Jesus died for you! If you are not a Christian, you need to study the Bible and learn how you can follow Him. If you are already a Christian, thank God that Jesus was willing to become our sacrifice.

Prayer: *Father, I love You! Thank You for Jesus and His one-time sacrifice for my sins. In Jesus' name. Amen.*

Hebrews 10 (2) by Jo Krueger   Today's Reading: Hebrews 10:19-23

The Jewish high priest was the only person who could enter the Most Holy Place where God lives. No other person could enter that place and make sacrifices. But when Jesus died, everything changed – Christians could have their sins forgiven through the blood of Jesus. They did not need to have a high priest make a sacrifice for them.

In our Bible reading we can find several things that Christians should do. First, we should *"come near to God with a sincere heart"* (verse 22). We can do this because Jesus removed our sins and made us clean. Second, we should remember the hope that we have. *"We must hold on to the hope we have, never hesitating to tell people about it. We can trust God to do what he promised"* (verse 23). This hope is that Jesus will come again to take us to be with Him forever. Third, we should tell other people about this hope.

Think about your life today. Maybe you have not allowed Jesus to remove your sins. Maybe you have forgotten that Jesus will come again. Maybe you are not telling other people about Jesus. Now is the time for you to change. Decide to begin obeying these verses today. God will be with you and give you strength to follow Him each day.

Prayer: *Dear God, thank You for making a way for us to be saved through Jesus. In His name. Amen.*

Hebrews 10 (3) by Jo Krueger
Today's Reading: Hebrews 10:24-25

Our Bible reading today is very short, but these two verses are important for Christians. These verses tell us that some of the Christian Jews had stopped meeting together to worship God. *"We must not quit meeting together, as some are doing. No, we need to keep on encouraging each other. This becomes more and more important as you see the Day getting closer"* (verse 25). The writer of Hebrews told them to meet together and strengthen each other. Why? So that they could be strong when they had to face hard times and persecution.

Today many Christians around the world face difficult situations. Some Christians face death because they follow Jesus. To stand strong during these times, we need to have encouragement from other Christians. Acts 2:42 tells us that the early Christians met together to listen to teaching, to share with each other, to eat together and to pray together. Today we can receive this kind of encouragement from our worship services, Bible studies, fellowship dinners and prayer meetings. If we continue to do these things with other Christians, we will have the courage to stand strong for God.

You can look for ways to be with other Christians today. Fellowship with your brothers and sisters in Christ and encourage them to always keep on standing strong for God.

Prayer: *Father, thank You for other Christians who encourage me. In Jesus' name. Amen.*

Hebrews 10 (4) by Jo Krueger
Today's Reading: Hebrews 10:26-31

When my children were young, I explained our family rules to them. If they did something wrong, but did not know about a rule, I would tell them the rule and not punish them. But if my children knew about the rule and still disobeyed me, I would punish them.

When we become Christians, we learn from the Bible how we can please God. We can't say, "I don't know what God wants me to do," because we can read the Bible and follow His instructions. So if we know what God wants us to do and still disobey Him, He is not happy with us and we may suffer some kind of punishment here on earth.

We read in the Old Testament that God punished the Jews when they disobeyed His law. But our Bible verses today are talking about people who have become Christians. The writer says that when a Christian turns away from Christ, he is not showing respect for the new agreement through Jesus' death. *"So think how much more punishment people deserve who show their hate for the Son of God — people who show they have no respect for the blood sacrifice that began the new agreement"* (verse 29a).

Study the Bible so you can know what God wants you to do. Then be sure that you obey Him and do things that please Him.

Prayer: *Dear Gracious God, I love Your Son, Jesus. Thank You for sending Him to die for me. In His name. Amen.*

Hebrews 10 (5) by Jo Krueger   **Today's Reading:** Hebrews 10:32-39

No one has ever done really bad things to me just because I am a Christian. But there are many Christians around the world today who are severely persecuted. Sometimes their enemies take away their homes and possessions or threaten them with physical harm or even death. I am amazed that these persecuted Christians remain strong and encourage other Christians to continue following Jesus. They do this because they know that something better – eternal life with God – will happen later.

Sometimes I may face small persecutions in my life. Maybe someone makes fun of me for reading my Bible or going to church. Or maybe some of my friends leave me because I will not join them in their sinful activities. Our Bible verses today remind us to be patient and to keep our courage and joy when we are persecuted. *"So don't lose the courage that you had in the past. Your courage will be rewarded richly. You must be patient. After you have done what God wants, you will get what he promised you"* (verses 35-36).

It is hard to have courage and joy when facing persecution. But if we continue to have faith in God, He will help us through those bad times. Depend on Him and His Word to keep you strong in your faith.

Prayer: *Loving Father, I want to always follow You, no matter what happens to me. In Jesus' name. Amen.*

Don't Forget by Bonnie Hall   **Today's Reading:** Deuteronomy 4:1-14

In our Bible reading Moses warned the Israelites to obey God's laws. God had given the people laws so that they would be safe and make good choices. God also had shown them again and again that He would take care of them. In verse 9 Moses said, *"But you must be careful! Be sure that as long as you live you never forget what you have seen. You must teach these things to your children and grandchildren."*

One summer my young sons learned that it was important to follow our family rules. We lived just a few miles away from a very busy interstate highway. The closer you got to the interstate, the more traffic there was. So we made a rule that they could only ride their bikes close to our house. We explained to the boys that we were trying to keep them safe. One day I said they could ride their bikes and reminded them, "Don't forget our rule." But they decided to race each other, and soon they were surrounded by a lot of scary traffic. When I went to check on them, I couldn't find them. So I got in the car and drove until I found them. I think they learned a good lesson that day about obeying the rules and staying safe.

We can read God's rules for us in the Bible. God wants us to know these rules and obey them. Why? Because He loves us and wants us to be safe! Don't forget that God always knows what is best for you!

Prayer: *Dear Father, thank You for loving me and helping me be safe and make wise choices in life. In Jesus' name. Amen.*

Facing Death (1) by Norma Mezoe   **Today's Reading:** Hebrews 9:27-28

Nellie was an elderly woman that I knew about. She was battling a terminal illness. As her strength slowly went away, she continued to hold on to the bitterness that had filled her life. Then Nellie appeared to be close to death.

When I read verse 27 of our Bible reading for today, I knew that I had to contact Nellie. *"Everyone must die once. Then they are judged."* I felt God's gentle voice speaking to my heart, urging me to write to Nellie and tell her that God loved her. So I wrote her a letter, telling her about my friend, Jesus, who always is with me to help me through my problems. I told Nellie about God's love for her and how Jesus had suffered, died and rose again so she could have the opportunity to live with Him forever. *"So Christ was offered as a sacrifice one time to take away the sins of many people. And he will come a second time, but not to offer himself for sin. He will come the second time to bring salvation to those who are waiting for him"* (verse 28).

Nellie died a few days after I mailed the letter. I do not know if she was able to read the message. But I felt I had obeyed God in writing to her, and I was at peace. God had shared His will with me and had given me the desire to obey.

Do you know someone who needs to know about Jesus? Don't wait! Share the saving message of the Gospel with them today.

Prayer: *Father, I pray for people like Nellie who have not yet decided to follow Jesus. Help me to share with them about You. In Jesus' name. Amen.*

Facing Death (2) by Norma Mezoe   **Today's Reading:** Hebrews 6:16-21

The rich man in today's Bible reading seemed concerned only for himself. His thoughts seemed to be about the pleasures in life. He had no concern about the future. This rich man wanted to acquire more possessions and wealth. *"But God said to that man, 'Foolish man! Tonight you will die. So what about the things you prepared for yourself? Who will get those things now?'"* (verse 20).

Contrast that man's life to the life of David Livingstone. He was from a very poor family, and at age 11 he had to quit school and go to work in a cotton mill. After working all day, Livingstone attended a night school and eventually became a medical doctor. During those years, he became a Christian and committed his life to Christ.

Dr. Livingstone served as a missionary to Africa and was there until his death. While in Africa, Livingstone explored and tried to locate the source of the Nile River. It is said that he died while praying on his knees.

What a contrast between the rich man who lived only for himself and Dr. Livingstone who dedicated his life to serving God and helping others. I hope you are humble and living a life of service to God. Ask Him to help you stay focused on Him.

Prayer: *Dear God, help me to keep my life focused on You and what You want me to do for others. In Jesus' name. Amen.*

Facing Death (3) by Norma Mezoe

Today's Reading: Psalm 116:12-19

My mom was ill for 12 years. During that time, I stood by helplessly as her illness caused her body to fail and robbed her of the ability to think and to remember. Even though Mom couldn't remember my name, she always had a smile when I visited her.

I carried Mom's little New Testament and Psalms Bible with me and read to her often from the Psalms. She seemed to be listening to the words as I read. Perhaps she understood more than I realized.

Then Mom's condition worsened, and I sensed that she would soon die. I sat by her bedside on Thanksgiving Day, stroking her forehead and holding her hand. Then suddenly I realized that Mom was not breathing. While I sat beside her, Mom's soul had slipped from her worn body and gone home to be with her Savior.

I was comforted when I read verse 15 from our Bible reading. *"Very dear to the Lord are the lives of his followers. He cares when they face death."* I knew that God had been with my mom as she was dying, and I knew that God was with me, too – comforting me and filling me with His peace. Share these words with someone you know who is facing the death of a loved one, and remind them that they are not alone.

Prayer: *Father, help us to realize that for a Christian, death is victory, not defeat. Thank You for Your peace and comfort. In Jesus' name. Amen.*

Facing Death (4) by Norma Mezoe

Today's Reading: Revelation 21:1-8

Janet's husband is an invalid, unable to even turn himself over in bed. She takes care of his needs day and night, but she seldom complains. Janet's 22-year-old granddaughter, Rachel, was recently diagnosed with a rare terminal illness. Rachel's life span is expected to be short. And, Janet has health problems, too. She copes with her own pain as she cares for her husband's needs. But despite these trials, Janet still faces each day with a smile. Often I have heard her praising God and thanking Him for His goodness.

Even though Janet faces the possibility of losing two of her loved ones, she knows that God is with her and that someday all of earth's trials will be gone. Verses 3b-4 of our Bible reading for today talk about what it will be like to live forever with God. *"Now God's home is with people. He will live with them. They will be his people. God himself will be with them and will be their God. He will wipe away every tear from their eyes. There will be no more death, sadness, crying, or pain. All the old ways are gone."*

Janet knows God's promises and is comforted to know that one day all her tears will be wiped away. She also knows that God gives her strength each day. What about you? Are you facing hard times and struggling each day? Depend on God's grace and comfort now and His promises of a better life in heaven.

Prayer: *Dear Lord, thank You for Your compassion and mercy. Help me to depend on You and Your strength each day. In Jesus' name. Amen.*

Facing Death (5) by Norma Mezoe   **Today's Reading:** Acts 7:54-60

Stephen was a man who was chosen by God to serve in various ways. He was one of the seven men who were appointed as deacons in the early church in Jerusalem. As a deacon, his job was to distribute food to needy people, including widows in the church.

Later Stephen was speaking with some Jewish religious leaders. He reminded them about the history of the Jewish people. Stephen accused their ancestors of persecuting the Old Testament prophets who told about the coming of Jesus. He also accused them of helping crucify Jesus.

As Stephen spoke to these men, they became very angry. Our Bible reading tells us that they dragged Stephen out of the city and began to stone him. *"As they were throwing the stones at him, Stephen was praying. He said, `Lord Jesus, receive my spirit!' He fell on his knees and shouted, `Lord, don't blame them for this sin!' These were his last words before he died"* (verses 59-60).

Even as Stephen was facing terrible pain and was dying, he was thinking about other people and praying for them. He had led a life of service to God and was faithful to the end. Thank God today for men and women who, like Stephen, faithfully serve Him every day.

Prayer: *Dear Father, help me to serve You like Stephen and to remain faithful to the end of my life. In Jesus' name. Amen.*

Facing Death (6) by Norma Mezoe   **Today's Reading:** Mark 15:25-39

Today we will close out our series of devotions about facing death by talking about Jesus' death. The night before Jesus died, Jesus shared the Passover meal with His disciples and reminded them of His love for them. After the meal, Jesus humbled Himself and washed the feet of His 12 disciples.

Later, Judas betrayed Jesus, and He was arrested in the Garden of Gethsemane. After several trials, Jesus was beaten and ridiculed and finally hung on a cross outside the city of Jerusalem. The final hours before Jesus' death were a very dark time for Him. During that time, God turned away from Him because He was taking on the sins of the world.

Verses 37-39 of our Bible reading tells us, *"Then Jesus cried out loudly and died. When Jesus died, the curtain in the Temple was torn into two pieces. The tear started at the top and tore all the way to the bottom. The army officer who was standing there in front of the cross saw what happened when Jesus died. The officer said, `This man really was the Son of God!'"*

Jesus' purpose for leaving heaven and being born of a virgin had been fulfilled. But soon He rose from death and gave us all the opportunity to live forever with Him. Thank God today for His wonderful plan of salvation!!

Prayer: *Thank You, God, for sending Jesus to die for me so I can have the gift of eternal life. In Jesus' name. Amen.*

Constant Rhythm by Bob La Forge   **Today's Reading:** 1 Timothy 4:1-10

A metronome is a device with a pendulum that swings back and forth at a set speed. Each time the pendulum passes the center, it makes a clicking noise. Musicians use a metronome to create a constant rhythm as they play an instrument or sing. Without a metronome, the music might become too slow during the difficult parts or too fast in the easier parts. Then the music would sound terrible and everything would be out of sync.

As Christians, we have a metronome that keeps our lives steady during difficult times and helps us to stay on course during the easier times. This metronome is our fellowship with God. We need daily fellowship with Him through our Bible reading and prayer. Throughout the day, we need a constant rhythm of prayer and worship. Then when our life becomes overwhelmed with problems, we will not lose our focus on God.

In our Bible verses for today, Paul instructed Timothy on how to be a good worker for God. In verses 6b-7 Paul said, *"You will show that you are made strong by the words of faith and good teaching you have followed. People tell silly stories that don't agree with God's truth. Don't follow what these stories teach. But teach yourself to be devoted to God."* We, too, need to be devoted to God. Be sure that you spend time today reading His Word and talking to Him through prayer.

Prayer: *Dear Father, thank You for times of fellowship with You. In Jesus' name. Amen.*

Obey God's Laws by Bonnie Hall   **Today's Reading:** Deuteronomy 5:22-33

Chapter 4 of Deuteronomy tells us about Moses encouraging the Israelites to obey God's laws. Then in chapter 5, Moses begins by reminding them how God spoke to them through the fire on the mountain, and repeating some of God's commands. Often we call these commands the Ten Commandments. These commandments help us keep in fellowship with God and get along with other people.

Then Moses told the Israelites that if they obeyed these commands, they would live a good life in the land that God had promised to them. After this, God spoke to Moses about the commands. In closing (verses 32-33) Moses said to the Israelites, *"So you people must be careful to do everything the Lord commanded you. Do not stop following God! You must live the way the Lord your God commanded you. Then you will continue to live, and everything will be fine with you. You will live a long life in the land that will belong to you."*

These commands are good for us to obey today, as well as Jesus' teachings that we find in the New Testament. As it was with the Israelites, if we obey God, then things will go well with us. Sometimes it is hard to obey God. That's when we need to rely on His Holy Spirit to lead us in the right way. Be sure that you choose to obey God today!

Prayer: *Dear Lord, thank You for Your love and Your commands. Help me obey You today. In Jesus' name. Amen.*

Caught in a Tree by Pam Davis

Today's Reading: 2 Samuel 18:9-18

When I was a young girl, we had an apple orchard in back of our house. Once my older sister was brave enough to climb one of the apple trees. While up in the tree, my sister saw a caterpillar. She was scared and quickly started back down. But she became caught in the tree and scraped her arms, legs and chest on the rough bark.

Our Bible verses for today tell us about a man who was also caught in a tree. But his story did not end so well. His name was Absalom, and he was one of King David's sons. But Absalom disobeyed God and tried to take the throne from his father. So David send his army after Absalom and his men. David's army defeated Absalom's army and 20,000 men were killed that day. Verse 9 tells us, *"It so happened that David's officers found Absalom. Absalom jumped on his mule and tried to escape, but the mule went under the branches of a large oak tree. The branches were thick, and Absalom's head got caught in the tree. His mule ran out from under him, so Absalom was left hanging above the ground."* Then one of David's soldiers killed Absalom. Absalom's disobedience brought about destruction and sadness, especially for David who grieved for his son.

God is pleased with us when we obey Him. But when we don't obey Him, we may bring sadness to ourselves and our loved ones. Be sure to obey God today!

Prayer: *Father, I want to always please You by obeying You. Help me to stay close to You today. In Jesus' name. Amen.*

Be a Volunteer by Mary Rosebush

Today's Reading: 1 Peter 4:7-11

Through my many years working for a Christian organization, I have experienced hundreds of wonderful volunteers. These people were of all ages and possessed many different talents. Some came to help us one time; others came back again and again. But there is one thing that I noticed in all of these people – they loved God and wanted to serve Him. That's what motivated them to stuff thousands of newsletters, shampoo our carpets, do yard work or build movie sets.

In our Bible reading for today, Peter talked about loving God and serving others. In verse 10 he said, *"God has shown you his grace in many different ways. So be good servants and use whatever gift he has given you in a way that will best serve each other."* Often we can volunteer our time and use the talents God has given to us. But other times, volunteer opportunities may not require any special skills – such as helping with mailings at a mission, sweeping the floors at church or feeding homeless people at a food kitchen.

You can start today to look for ways to volunteer to help other Christians. Call a church or a mission in your area and ask if they can use a volunteer. Or volunteer to serve as a helper with missionaries who in other countries. God will give you the strength to do the work, and He will be praised through your efforts.

Prayer: *Dear God, show me how I can show my love by serving other Christians today. In Jesus' name. Amen.*

Protection by Rachel Burkum   **Today's Reading:** Ephesians 6:11-18

At my job, I have to park in a staff parking lot that is quite a ways from the building where I work. In the winter time I park my car and get ready before I open my car door. I make sure my coat is zipped up, my gloves are on and I have my scarf or hat on, too. There have been days when I have forgotten one or two of these items, and by the time I reach the building, I feel like I am frozen!

I try to make sure I protect myself from the weather when I walk to or from my car. But that's not the only protection I need during the day. I also need protection against the devil and temptations to sin. In today's Bible reading, we learn about the "armor of God." While we live on earth, we are in the middle of a spiritual war. To protect ourselves, we need spiritual armor. This includes the belt of truth, chest protection (breastplate) of right living, footwear of the Good News and the shield of faith. *"Accept God's salvation as your helmet. And take the sword of the Spirit – that sword is the teaching of God"* (verse 17). How do we put on this armor? We read God's Word, talk with Him, work on our relationship with Him and try to follow His commands. If we focus on this, we will be prepared for the world.

We need to protect our bodies from the heat and cold. But let's always remember to be spiritually prepared, too. Are you close to God today?

Prayer: *Dear God, I want to be close to You. Please help me put on Your spiritual armor every day. Thank You for Your protection. In Jesus' name. Amen.*

Do What is Right and Good by Bonnie Hall   **Today's Reading:** Deuteronomy 6:1-19

In chapter 6 of Deuteronomy, Moses tells the Israelites what they need to do as they finish their journey to the land God had promised to them. Moses reminded the people of how God had helped them on their journey and that they needed to always be careful to obey God and not forget Him. He also instructed them to teach these things to their children so that future generations would obey God and stay close to Him.

What Moses said to the Israelites in these verses is good for us to remember today, too. In verse 5 Moses said, *"You must love the Lord your God with all your heart, with all your soul, and with all your strength."* And in verse 18 he said, *"You must do what is right and good – what pleases the Lord. Then everything will go well for you, and you can go in and take the good land that the Lord promised your ancestors."* God hasn't promised us a new land like He did for the Israelites, but He has promised us a home in heaven with Him forever.

Just like the Israelites, we will face good times and bad times in our life. But through it all, we need to continue to do what is right and know that God is with us. Whatever you face today, remember to obey God and depend on Him to help you stay strong.

Prayer: *Dear Loving God, thank You for being with me today to help me and encourage me. In Jesus' name. Amen.*

Be a Blessing by Norma Mezoe   **Today's Reading:** Philippians 2:1-5

The morning had been extremely stressful. My husband, Gene, suffered from dementia, and he was experiencing depression. All morning he was crying and taking his frustrations out on me. In the afternoon Gene had a doctor's appointment, and I dealt with more anger and crying as we drove to and from the clinic.

As we returned to our hometown, I stopped at the post office to get our mail. Gene received a card from his cousin. When he read the words she had written, his attitude changed immediately, and he expressed gratitude that she had taken time to send the card.

Perhaps Gene's cousin felt a nudge from the Lord to send the card. Because she took the time to write a note and send the card, Gene received a much-needed blessing. In verses 3 and 4 of our Bible reading for today, Paul talked about doing things for other people. *"In whatever you do, don't let selfishness or pride be your guide. Be humble, and honor others more than yourselves. Don't be interested only in your own life, but care about the lives of others, too."*

Maybe today you will feel an inner voice urging you to make a phone call, write a note or visit someone in the hospital or nursing home. Don't put it off. Obey God's prompting and be a blessing to others.

Prayer: *Father, help me to be obedient to You and to show that I care about the lives of other people. In Jesus' name. Amen.*

You are a Christian! by Jo Krueger   **Today's Reading:** 1 John 5:6-15

I saw something online today that prompted me to write this devotion. The post said, "Take this Bible quiz of 30 questions. If you get 16 or more right, you are a Christian!" Needless to say, I didn't take the quiz. Why? Because I already know that I am a Christian!

Now, there's nothing wrong with taking a Bible quiz or increasing your Bible knowledge. But answering Bible trivia questions correctly doesn't make you a Christian. And I feel sorry for people who believe everything they read on online and think that Bible knowledge alone makes them a Christian.

Verse 13 of our Bible reading says, *" I write this letter to you who believe in the Son of God. I write so that you will know that you have eternal life now."* We don't need to go through life wondering if we are saved or not. We can *know* that we are saved.

So who is saved? Peter answered that question in Acts 2:38. *"Change your hearts and lives and be baptized, each one of you, in the name of Jesus Christ. Then God will forgive your sins, and you will receive the gift of the Holy Spirit."* If we have obeyed Peter's words and continue to follow God, we can know that we are saved.

So I encourage you to be very careful. Make sure that the Bible alone is your guide and that what you read always agrees with God's Word.

Prayer: *Dear Lord, thank You for Your Word which leads me to salvation through Jesus. In His name. Amen.*

Hannah's Prayer by Donna Howard   **Today's Reading:** 1 Samuel 1:1-28

Hannah was sad, and she cried. Why? Because she had no children. But Hannah loved God and prayed to Him. When she went to Shiloh with her husband to worship God and make sacrifices, she prayed and asked God for a son. Verse 11 of our Bible reading says, *"She made a special promise to God and said, 'Lord All-Powerful, you can see how sad I am. Remember me. Don't forget me. If you will give me a son, I will give him to you. He will be yours his whole life, and as a Nazirite, he will not drink wine or strong drink, and no one will ever cut his hair.'"*

While Hannah was praying, Eli, the priest, saw her and thought she was drunk. But Hannah was not drunk. She told Eli she was praying to God. Eli told Hannah that God would give her what she had asked for. God remembered Hannah's prayer, and she became pregnant and gave birth to a son. *"She named him Samuel. She said, 'His name is Samuel because I asked the Lord for him'"* (verse 20b).

When Samuel was still young, Hannah took him to Shiloh and left him there with Eli to serve God, just as she had promised. Hannah prayed and believed that God would answer her prayer. When we pray, we should believe that God will hear our prayers and answer them. As you pray today, believe that God knows what is best for you and will bless you.

Prayer: *Thank You, Father, for listening to my prayers and blessing me according to Your will. In Jesus' name. Amen.*

Jesus' Blood (1) by Jo Krueger   **Today's Reading:** 1 Peter 1:18-21

Some Christian pictures show Jesus on the cross. These pictures are not pretty pictures because when Jesus was crucified on the cross, He bled. Blood was a necessary part of God's Old Testament system of sacrifices and it is also part of His wonderful plan to give us salvation. Today and for the next few days we will talk about the importance of Jesus' blood.

Some people today do not like to think about blood. There are churches that no longer sing songs about Jesus' blood. But blood is very important to God and His plan to save us. The Bible talks about blood more than 700 times. Verses 18-19 of our Bible reading for today say, *"You know that in the past the way you were living was useless. It was a way of life you learned from those who lived before you. But you were saved from that way of living. You were bought, but not with things that ruin like gold or silver. You were bought with the precious blood of Christ's death. He was a pure and perfect sacrificial Lamb."*

Over the next few days we will continue to see what Jesus' blood does for us. Remember that He was willing to suffer and die so that you can have your sins forgiven. Praise God for the sacrifice of Jesus' precious blood that gives you the promise of eternal life.

Prayer: *Dear God, thank You that Jesus came to earth to die on the cross for me. In Jesus' name. Amen.*

Jesus' Blood (2) by Jo Krueger   **Today's Reading:** Hebrews 9:16-22

Yesterday we began a series of devotions about Jesus' blood. Today we will talk about Jesus' blood being important to us because it gives us forgiveness, and we will look at Bible verses that tell us about God's plan for salvation. According to God's plan, blood is necessary so our sins can be forgiven.

Today's Bible verses tell us about Moses and the first agreement between God and the Israelites. God required that an animal be sacrificed so sins could be forgiven. *"The law says that almost everything must be made clean by blood. Sins cannot be forgiven without a blood sacrifice"* (verse 22). When Jesus came to earth, died on the cross and rose again, God made a new agreement with people. According to this agreement, God accepted Jesus' death as the sacrifice for our sins. And Jesus accepted the punishment for our sins. If we believe in Jesus and obey God's Word, God will forgive our sins and give us eternal life with Him.

It is hard for me to think about Jesus' death and that He had to suffer and die so that my sins could be forgiven. I am humbled and thankful when I think that Jesus was willing to do this for you and me! Share the news about Jesus and God's agreement with someone today. Tell them about God's forgiveness and His great gift of salvation!

Prayer: *Dear Lord, thank You for what Jesus did for me and that I have forgiveness through His blood. In Jesus' name. Amen.*

Jesus's Blood (3) by Jo Krueger   **Today's Reading:** John 6:47-58

Jesus' blood is important to us because it gives us eternal life. In our Bible reading for today, Jesus explained to His followers that they must eat His body and drink His blood. Verses 53-54 say, *"Jesus said, 'Believe me when I say that you must eat the body of the Son of Man, and you must drink his blood. If you don't do this, you have no real life. Those who eat my body and drink my blood have eternal life. I will raise them up on the last day.'"*

Jesus was not telling His followers to eat His physical body and drink the blood from His body. Jesus was telling them to believe that He was truly God's Son and follow and obey His teachings. In our verses Jesus called Himself *"the bread that gives life"* (verse 48). God provided a special bread called manna for the Israelites while they were traveling in the wilderness. We all need bread (food) to stay alive. In the same way, we need Jesus if we want to live forever with Him. Every time we eat the Lord's Supper, we remember that Jesus gave His body and His blood when He died on the cross. And we also remember that after Jesus died, He rose again. Through His resurrection, Jesus gives us the promise of living with Him forever.

I am excited to think about living forever with Jesus in a wonderful place that He has prepared for me. I hope that you are excited, too!

Prayer: *I love You, God, and I thank You for salvation through Jesus. I am excited to think about living forever with You. In Jesus' name. Amen.*

Jesus' Blood (4) by Jo Krueger   **Today's Reading:** Ephesians 2:12-18

Another reason that Jesus' blood is important to us is because it brings us close to God. Verse 13 of today's Bible reading says, *"Yes, at one time you were far away from God, but now in Christ Jesus, you are brought near to him. You are brought near to God through the blood sacrifice of Christ."* Jesus' blood cleanses us and removes our sins. When our sins are removed, we can have a close relationship with God.

When I was young, my mother and I went out of town for a week to visit a relative. All week I missed my father so much! I can still remember the happiness I felt when I saw him again. We met in a parking lot. When I saw my father, I ran as fast as I could and jumped into his waiting arms. I knew that I wanted to always be close to him.

God, our heavenly Father, wants us to be close to Him by reading His Word and talking to Him through prayer. When we are close to God, we can feel His love and peace. But sometimes we do things that draw us away from God. During those times we should always remember that God is waiting for us to repent and to be close to Him again.

Accept the forgiveness that Jesus offers you through His blood and stay close to God today!

Prayer: *Merciful Father, thank You for salvation through Jesus' blood. Please keep me close to You today. In Jesus' name. Amen.*

Jesus' Blood (5) by Jo Krueger   **Today's Reading:** 1 John 1:5-10

Jesus' blood is also important to us because it cleanses us. Verse 7 of our Bible reading for today says, *"We should live in the light, where God is. If we live in the light, we have fellowship with each other, and the blood sacrifice of Jesus, God's Son, washes away every sin and makes us clean."*

Several years ago, my husband and I decided to put our house up for sale. But first we knew that we needed to clean out our basement. We cleaned all day and at the end of the day, I was very dirty. There were cobwebs stuck in my hair, and my hands and face were covered with dirt and scratches. I couldn't wait to get in the shower and be clean again.

In our last devotion we talked about being close to God. If we want to be close to God every day, we must first allow Jesus' blood to make us clean. Verse 9 tells us how this happens. *"But if we confess our sins, God will forgive us. We can trust God to do this. He always does what is right. He will make us clean from all the wrong things we have done."*

When we become a Christian, we are clean. But because we are living on earth, we will continue to sin. Praise God that we can confess our sins and allow Jesus' blood to cleanse us every day!

Prayer: *Dear God, I know that I need Jesus to make me clean every day. Thank You for His sacrifice on the cross. In Jesus' name. Amen.*

Jesus' Blood (6) by Jo Krueger   **Today's Reading:** Revelation 12:10-12

Today is the last day we will look at verses that talk about Jesus' blood. Our Bible reading for today tells us that Jesus' blood is important because it helps us defeat the devil. Verse 11 talks about Christians who will have the final victory over the devil. *"They defeated him by the blood sacrifice of the Lamb and by the message of God that they told people. They did not love their lives too much. They were not afraid of death."* This victory will happen because Jesus became the sacrifice for our sins. When we allow Jesus to cleanse us and remove our sins, we will share in this victory over the devil.

Every day we are in a battle with the devil. The devil attacks us and tries to get us to turn away from God. The devil knows our areas of weakness and wants us to stop serving and loving God. But because of Jesus' sacrifice, we have the gift of God's Holy Spirit. The Holy Spirit helps us to resist the devil and stay close to God. James 4:7 reminds us, *"So give yourselves to God. Stand against the devil, and he will run away from you."*

The Holy Spirit will be with you today to lead you and help you defeat the devil. And reading your Bible and praying will help you to stand strong and live for God every day!

Prayer: *Dear Loving God, I want to depend on Your Holy Spirit to help me stay close to You today. In Jesus' name. Amen.*

Amore's Door by Debbie Klahn   **Today's Reading:** Matthew 27:33-54

Amore is our cat. She is a 15-year-old "tuxedo" cat with a black heart-shaped patch on her chest. My sister, Annie, adopted her on February 14th so that's why we named her Amore, which means love.

We live in Florida, and Amore loves to go on our screened-in porch and sleep with the sun on her face. We left the door slightly ajar, so Amore could go into the porch. She could open the door, but not close it, so that became a problem with keeping the house cool. Amore would beg us to go out several times every day so we had to get up and let her out. Finally we decided to put in a pet door. Amore learned to use the door, and now she comes in and out as she pleases. She has access to her favorite place in the sun any time she wants, and this makes her happy.

For many years the Jewish people did not have direct access to God. They had to go through a priest. Our Bible verses tell us that when Jesus died on the cross, *"the curtain in the Temple was torn into two pieces"* (verse 51b). This showed that from then on, people would have direct access to God.

We should be happy because we can pray to God any time and tell Him our praises and our requests. Just as Amore has access to the porch where she can lie in the sun, we have access to God and can spend time in His presence.

Prayer: *Faithful Father, thank You for always being there to hear our prayers and help us. In Jesus' name. Amen.*

Amore's Impatience by Debbie Klahn   **Today's Reading:** Galatians 5:16-26

Amore, our cat, is very impatient. When she is hungry, she wants to eat NOW. Often she decides early in the morning that she wants to eat. She will jump on us as we sleep and demand that we feed her or give her water. Sometimes she cries when she wants food. If we ignore her, she will jump up on furniture and push things off to get our attention.

Amore's impatience reminds me of my relationship with God sometimes. I do not like to wait. I decide I need something, and I want it right now. I have a problem, and I want God to fix the problem now. When God does not answer my prayer exactly when I want the answer, I may get upset or act like a child and throw a fit. Amore needs to learn she must wait until we get up in the morning to be fed. And I need to learn to wait for God's answers.

In our Bible reading for today, Paul talked about "fruit" (good things) that the Holy Spirit will help us have in our lives. *"But the fruit that the Spirit produces in a person's life is love, joy, peace, patience, kindness, goodness, faithfulness, gentleness, and self-control"* (verses 22-23a). One of those good things is patience. With the help of the Holy Spirit, I am learning to be patient and to wait for God's help.

Be patient today as you wait for God to respond to your prayers.

Prayer: *Heavenly Father, help me to be patient and to wait for Your answers. In Jesus' name. Amen.*

God's Love and Protection by Bonnie Hall   **Today's Reading:** Deuteronomy 7:1-11

One of my sons had a problem with some of his friends. Nothing he tried seemed to help solve the issue. Finally I had to stand up and confront the people who were causing the problem. Many people were surprised that I had the strength and courage to do that. But I love my son and I was willing to do anything to help and protect him.

In our Bible verses for today, Moses reminded the Israelites that they should obey God. He talked about how God had brought them out of slavery in Egypt and brought them to a new land. He explained that God was willing to do anything to help and protect them. Then in verses 7 and 8 Moses explained why God did this. *"Why did the Lord love and choose you? It was not because you are such a large nation. You had the fewest of all people! But the Lord brought you out of Egypt with great power and made you free from slavery. He freed you from the control of Pharaoh, the king of Egypt. The Lord did this because he loves you and he wanted to keep the promise he made to your ancestors."* God took care of the Israelites because He loved them!

God loves us, too, and He wants to help and protect us every day. But He also wants us to obey and follow Him. Be sure that you are following God today and relying on His strength and power to help you.

Prayer: *Dear Lord, thank You for loving me so much and for always protecting me. In Jesus' name. Amen.*

God Wants Us by Bob La Forge   **Today's Reading:** Hebrews 12:1-3

God could have done very well without any of us! He did not need to create us, but He did. Then Adam and Eve sinned in the Garden of Eden and caused a great separation between us and God. He could have let us struggle forever in our loneliness and pain. But He wanted to have a close relationship with us, so He made a plan to bring us back to Him.

God's plan was for His Son, Jesus, to be born of a virgin and become a man. But Jesus did not receive adoration and gratitude. Instead He was accused of having demons, rejected by His family and then denied, mocked and tried as a criminal. Was that enough to stop God's plan? Jesus' response was to pay the highest cost by suffering on the cross for the sins of the world.

Verse 2a of our Bible reading for today tells us about Jesus. *"We must never stop looking to Jesus. He is the leader of our faith, and he is the one who makes our faith complete. He suffered death on a cross. But he accepted the shame of the cross as if it were nothing because of the joy he could see waiting for him."* Through Jesus, God opened His arms to welcome us into a personal relationship with Him.

God loves us and wants us to be His sons and daughters. Worship Him with a thankful heart today.

Prayer: *Dear Loving Father, thank You for wanting to love me and live with me forever. In Jesus' name. Amen.*

Child-like Faith by Valerie Godsey   **Today's Reading:** Mark 10:12-14

When I was a child, God was honored in my home. My parents were believers, but they were not church attenders. So as a little girl, I was *sent* to church, not *taken* to church. I loved Sundays! I remember my short walk from my house to the little white church with the tall steeple.

I was excited as I entered the church and hurried downstairs to the musty basement for Sunday School. I don't remember the names or faces of my teachers, but I do remember they taught me that Jesus loved me. Because of those Sunday School teachers, I have always had a child-like faith that has strengthened and comforted me throughout my life.

Our Bible reading tells us about a time when children were brought to Jesus. Perhaps Jesus' disciples thought that the children bothered Jesus because they told the people to stop bringing their children to Him. But in verse 14b Jesus responded, *"Let the little children come to me. Don't stop them, because God's kingdom belongs to people who are like these little children."*

If you have been a Sunday School teacher, you have pleased God. And if you are looking for a way to serve, consider teaching children about Jesus. You will make an everlasting difference in their lives!

Prayer: *Heavenly Father, show me how I can serve You and lead others to Jesus. In His name. Amen.*

Love for God by Jennifer Forrester   **Today's Reading:** Genesis 22:1-14

Today and the next few days we will look at different kinds of love mentioned in the Bible – love for God, love for friends, love for family, love for Jesus and God's love for us.

In our Bible verses for today, we read that God asked Abraham to offer his son, Isaac, as a sacrifice. Abraham and his wife, Sarah, waited many years to have a son. They were so happy when Isaac was born. But then God asked Abraham to kill Isaac.

Abraham loved Isaac, but most of all, he loved God. That's what made him take Isaac up on the mountain and prepare to kill him. *"When they came to the place where God told them to go, Abraham built an altar. He carefully laid the wood on the altar. Then he tied up his son Isaac and laid him on the altar on top of the wood"* (verse 9). But God stopped Abraham from killing Isaac. Through this, Abraham showed God how much he loved Him. And Abraham also showed he had faith that God would take care of him.

How much do you love God? Probably God will not ask you to sacrifice your child, but He may ask you to be missionary or give your time and money to help other people. Think about your love for God today.

Prayer: *God, I do love You and want to show You how much I love You. Help me to always be faithful to You. In Jesus' name. Amen.*

Love for Friends by Jennifer Forrester   **Today's Reading:** 1 Samuel 20:1-17

In the book of 1 Samuel we find an example of two men who were good friends. King Saul's son, Jonathan, and David were best friends. But it was difficult for them to be close friends. Why? Because Saul was jealous of David and wanted to kill him.

Our Bible verses tell us that David and Jonathan met and talked about their situation. David wanted Jonathan to find out why his father was trying to kill him. Jonathan promised that he would find out how Saul felt. In doing this, Jonathan was risking his own life. Why would Jonathan do this? Because he loved his friend, David. *"Jonathan loved David as himself, and because of this love, he asked David to repeat this agreement for himself"* (verse 17).

Good friends are a blessing from God. It is wonderful to have a good friend that you can always trust. A true friend loves you despite your faults and loves you even when you are grouchy or discouraged. And a good friend always helps you obey God and avoid temptations.

Think about your best friend today. Call them and thank them for being your friend. Or do something nice for them. Most of all, thank God for giving you friends who love and encourage you.

Prayer: *Father, thank You for blessing me with good friends. Show me how I can encourage and love my friends every day. In Jesus' name. Amen.*

Love for Family by Jennifer Forrester   **Today's Reading:** Luke 15:11-24

In chapter 15 of Luke we read a wonderful story about a father who loved his son. But the son was not happy. He wanted to take his share of the family wealth and go away. So the father gave his son his part of the inheritance. *"A few days later the younger son gathered up all that he had and left. He traveled far away to another country, and there he wasted his money living like a fool"*(verse 13).

The son spent all his money and had nothing to eat. He thought about his nice home with his family and all the food they had to eat. Soon he realized that he have been very foolish, so he decided to go home. He hoped that his father would give him a job as a servant.

Every day the father was watching and waiting for his son to come home. *"While the son was still a long way off, his father saw him coming and felt sorry for him. So he ran and hugged and kissed him"* (verse 20b). The father gave his son some new clothes and shoes and celebrated his return with a big party.

Why did the father do this for the son who had left him? Because he truly loved his son. These verses show us that God loves us. And they also show us that He wants us to show love for our family members. What can you do today to show your love for your family?

Prayer: *Dear God, thank You for my family. I want to show them how much I love them. In Jesus' name. Amen.*

Love for Jesus by Jennifer Forrester   **Today's Reading:** John 21:15-19

Peter was one of Jesus' special disciples. Peter followed Jesus and learned from Him for about three years. Peter even said one time that he was willing to die for Jesus. But the night that Jesus was arrested, Peter was scared and said three times that he did not know Jesus.

Jesus was crucified, and three days later He rose from the dead. After that, Jesus met with His followers several times before He returned to heaven. Our Bible verses today tell us about a time when Jesus appeared to Peter and some of His other disciples by Lake Galilee.

Jesus and Peter had a discussion. Three times Jesus asked Peter, *"Do you love me?"* The first two times Peter replied, *"Yes, Lord, you know that I love you."* When Jesus asked Peter a third time, *"Peter was sad because Jesus asked him three times, 'Do you love me?' He said, 'Lord, you know everything. You know that I love you!'"* (verse 17b). Peter had denied Jesus three times, and now Jesus gave Peter three opportunities to say that he truly loved Jesus.

God wants us to love Jesus. How can we show our love for Him? We can obey Jesus and try to be like Him. I hope you will find ways to show your love for Jesus to others today!

Prayer: *Heavenly Father, I truly love Your Son, Jesus, and I want to always follow and obey Him. In His name. Amen.*

God's Love for Us by Jennifer Forrester   **Today's Reading:** John 3:16-21

The greatest example of love is God's love for us. Today we will close this series of devotions by looking at a few of the ways God shows us His love.

The book of Genesis tells us that God created the world. Every day we can look around us and see the wonderful things God has made for us. God made the sun to keep us warm and to give us light. He made plants so we can have food to eat. And God made animals to help us and make us happy.

God also shows His love by answering our prayers and providing what we need every day. In Matthew, chapter 6, Jesus told His followers that they didn't need to worry. Why? Because God loved them and provided just exactly what they needed each day.

But the greatest way God shows His love for us is found in our Bible verses for today. Verse 16 says, *"Yes, God loved the world so much that he gave his only Son, so that everyone who believes in him would not be lost but have eternal life."* God loves us so much that He was willing to send His Son, Jesus, to die for our sins. Because Jesus died for us, we have the opportunity to accept God's free gift of salvation.

Thank God today for His wonderful love and His gift of eternal life through His Son, Jesus.

Prayer: *Dear Lord, thank You for loving me so much that You were willing for Jesus to die on the cross. In His name. Amen.*

A New Home by Bonnie Hall   **Today's Reading:** Deuteronomy 8:1-10

In our Bible reading for today, Moses once again reminded the Israelites about God's love and provision as they journeyed through the wilderness to their new home. Verses 4 through 7 are a summary of what God did for them. *"These past 40 years, your clothes did not wear out, and your feet did not swell. You must remember that the Lord your God teaches and corrects you as a father teaches and corrects his son. You must obey the commands of the Lord your God. Follow him and respect him. The Lord your God is bringing you into a good land — a land with rivers and pools of water. Water flows out of the ground in the valleys and hills."*

As I look back over the past 40 years of my life, I can see how God has taken care of my family and me, too. We survived a terrible tornado and suffered through health issues. My sons grew up and went out into the world to work and start new families. There were times of desperation and need, and we also faced great sorrow. But God was always with us to make sure that we were taken care of.

And just as the Israelites were happy to reach the new land God had promised to them, I happily look forward to my new home in heaven. In that new home there will be no more pain, sorrow, challenges or hurt. And God will be there with me forever. I hope you are looking forward to heaven, too!

Prayer: *Dear God, thank You for always taking care of my family and me. And thank You for the promise of heaven. In Jesus' name. Amen.*

Life Isn't Fair by Rachel Burkum   **Today's Reading:** Matthew 5:43-48

"But that's not fair!" I have heard this phrase countless times. People think they deserve something more or better. If someone mistreats them or they don't get what they think they should, people will automatically complain that it's not fair.

I have one response for those people. Life isn't fair! We think for life to be "fair," we should get all the good things we see other people get – rich people, powerful people or smart people. If they succeed, so should we, right? And if anyone does something wrong against us, we should be angry, right?

Our Bible reading today gives us a different perspective. Verse 45b talks about God. *"He lets the sun rise for all people, whether they are good or bad. He sends rain to those who do right and to those who do wrong."* That is actual fairness. God does not treat some people more special than others. He loves us all, and treats everyone the same . . . even our enemies. It is not "unfair" when we experience hard times or when other people seem to have an easy life. The world has sin in it, and therefore it is not perfect. We cannot expect life to be perfect until Jesus comes again. What we *can* expect is for God to help us through the hard times if we trust and follow Him. If we have given our lives to Christ, we have hope. And that hope is salvation and eternal life when Jesus returns.

Prayer: *Father, thank You for loving me. I know this world is not perfect, and life doesn't feel fair. But You are holy, and I trust You. In Jesus' name. Amen.*

Jackpot by Jo Krueger   **Today's Reading:** Ecclesiastes 5:10-17

I just heard on the news about a person who won a lottery jackpot of a half million dollars. Wow – that's a lot of money! Every day in the United States millions of people stand in line for hours to buy a lottery ticket. And some people buy a new ticket every day. This shows me just how "money-centered" our world is.

Our Bible verses from Ecclesiastes were written by King Solomon thousands of years ago. Some people think he may have been the wealthiest person who ever lived. Solomon had everything he could ever want – gold, a beautiful palace to live in, jewels, possessions and opportunities to experience many things.

Even though Solomon had great wealth, he said in verse 10a, *"Those who love money will never be satisfied with the money they have. Those who love wealth will not be satisfied when they get more and more."* Then in verse 12 he added, *"Those who work hard all day come home and sleep in peace . . . the rich worry about their wealth and are not able to sleep."*

We might dream about having great wealth, but Solomon truly experienced it. His conclusion was that wealth brings sadness, sorrow, trouble, sickness and anger (verse 17). So don't focus on gathering more money and possessions. Instead, focus on God and serving Him with all your heart.

Prayer: *Help me, Father, not to focus on money and possessions. Instead, help me to focus only on You. In Jesus' name. Amen.*

Red Sails by Gayle Thorn   **Today's Reading:** Matthew 16:1-4

There's an old saying that goes like this: "Red sky at night, sailor's delight. Red sky in the morning, sailor's warning." This saying talks about how the color of the sky could predict the weather that is coming.

Jesus may have been referring to this saying when he responded to the Jewish Pharisees and Sadducees who asked for a sign from heaven. In verses 2 and 3 of our Bible reading Jesus said, *"When you people see the sunset, you know what the weather will be. If the sky is red, you say we will have good weather. And in the morning, if the sky is dark and red, you say that it will be a rainy day. These are signs of the weather. You see these signs in the sky and know what they mean. In the same way, you see the things that are happening now. These are also signs, but you don't know their meaning."* What was Jesus saying here? He was telling the Jewish leaders that they had a better understanding of the weather than they had of the signs that God's plan was being fulfilled.

It is good for us to learn about the weather and many other things on earth. But it is much better to learn about God, His salvation and His plan for our lives. Are you reading the Bible and attending church and Bible study so you can learn more about God? Are you praying every day and asking God to teach you about His plan for your life? Think about these questions today!

Prayer: *Heavenly Father, please guide me and teach me today. In Jesus' name. Amen.*

Get the Mail Delivered by Jo Krueger   **Today's Reading:** Matthew 28:18-20

My husband and I have been watching a TV program about the Pony Express. The Pony Express was a horse-based mail service in the United States that ran from 1860 to 1861 between Missouri and California. During the 18 months that the Pony Express was in operation, they reduced the time to get a message from the east coast to the west coast to about 10 days. Riders rode as fast as they could with the mail pouch in order to deliver it to the next rider. Even though the riders sometimes faced robbers or Indian attacks, they knew it was important that the mail be delivered.

When Jesus was ready to leave the earth, He spoke one last time to His followers and gave them some last-minute instructions. These instructions talked about the importance of His message and that the message needs to be delivered to everyone. In our Bible reading Jesus said, *"So go and make followers of all people in the world. Baptize them in the name of the Father and the Son and the Holy Spirit. Teach them to obey everything that I have told you to do. You can be sure that I will be with you always. I will continue with you until the end of time"* (verses 19-20).

Just as the Pony Express riders needed to get the mail delivered, we need to deliver God's message of salvation to everyone we meet – our friends, our relatives and the people we meet each day.

Prayer: *Lord, give me strength to share Your message of salvation with the world. In Jesus' name. Amen.*

Show Me the Way by Donna Howard   **Today's Reading:** Psalm 25:1-7

My husband and I enjoy taking walks. One of our favorite trails is narrow in some places and wide in other places. The trail meanders through the trees which line both sides. However, the trail ends in a big open circle in the middle of the woods. So when we get there, we need to make a decision. Should we continue off the path and perhaps get lost in the woods? Or should we turn around, stay on the path and return to our starting point? We have found that it is best if we stay on the path. That way we are sure of a safe trip home.

The same is true of our spiritual path in life, too. Through the Bible, God has outlined the path that we should take. If we go off that path, we can easily become ensnared in the sinful traps of the world. David knew that he needed to stay on the path that God had laid out for him. In verses 4 and 5 of our Bible reading for today, David said, *"Lord, help me learn your ways. Show me how you want me to live. Guide me and teach me your truths. You are my God, my Savior. You are the one I have been waiting for."* David knew that he could trust God to lead him in life. He knew that God would never let him down.

Are you sometimes tempted to go off the spiritual path that God has for you? Stay close to Him through prayer and Bible reading and ask Him to show you the way.

Prayer: *Lord, show me Your ways and help me to always follow You so I can arrive safely in heaven. In Jesus' name. Amen.*

Distractions by Jo Krueger   **Today's Reading:** Mark 1:35-39

Last week a woman came to my church who was on furlough from being a missionary in a foreign country. It was so good to see her again and learn about her work. She started talking about prayer, and I asked her if her prayer life changed when she was on the mission field.

The woman shared that she had learned to shut out all distractions so she could focus on her prayer times with God. She said in the country where she serves most people do not have TVs, computers or cell phones. It was easier for her to focus on God when there were no TV shows to watch or cell phones to answer. When she returned to America, she decided to not watch as much TV or spend as many hours on her phone and computer.

Our Bible verses for today tell us about a time when Jesus was very busy teaching and healing people. *"The next morning Jesus woke up early. He left the house while it was still dark and went to a place where he could be alone and pray"* (verse 35). Jesus wanted to get away from the distractions of the world so that He could pray and talk with God.

I hope that you will be able to spend some quiet time alone with God today. Focus on Him and His Word!

Prayer: *Dear God, help me to eliminate some of the distractions in my life so I can focus on You. In Jesus' name. Amen.*

Spiritual Basics by Bob La Forge

Today's Reading: Acts 2:42-47

About eight years ago, I started playing the violin. My goal is to play music composed by Bach, Vivaldi and Handel. But in order to reach that goal, I must first practice the basics of playing scales on the violin. Playing scales teaches my fingers where they should go to play the proper notes. I can never expect to play great musical compositions unless I first build a foundation on the basics.

In the same way, we need to be faithful to the basics. What are some spiritual basics? We need to have a daily time for prayer, Bible reading and worship. We need to belong to a fellowship of Christians where we can support and encourage each other. We need to love our neighbors, co-workers and family members. And we need to share the Good News about Jesus with people who are not saved. When we do these basic things, we will resist the temptation to sin, and develop the character of God. Then God can use us in greater ways for His glory. Verse 46 of our Bible reading tells us what the early Christians did. *"The believers shared a common purpose, and every day they spent much of their time together in the Temple area. They also ate together in their homes. They were happy to share their food and ate with joyful hearts."* God used these Christians to do great things for His kingdom.

Get back to the basics of prayer, Bible reading and Christian fellowship today!

Prayer: *God, help me to develop the spiritual basics so that I can do greater things for You. In Jesus' name. Amen.*

It's True! by Gayle Thorn

Today's Reading: Luke 24:1-12

Verses 6 and 7 of our Bible reading say, *"Jesus is not here. He has risen from death. Do you remember what he said in Galilee? He said the Son of Man must be handed over to the control of sinful men, be killed on a cross, and rise from death on the third day."* It's true! Jesus did rise from the dead!

The first people to see Jesus alive, three days after His crucifixion and burial, were some women. But they weren't the only ones to see Jesus. More than 500 people over a period of 40 days saw Jesus teaching and showing proof of His resurrection (1 Corinthians 15:6).

Some doubters today think that these people were hallucinating. But it seems doubtful that more than 500 people could have the same hallucination. It also seems doubtful that 500 people would have risked shame and possible execution for claiming that Jesus was alive. So I believe those people really saw Jesus alive – walking, talking, eating and giving them encouragement – before He was taken up into heaven.

Do you doubt Jesus' resurrection? If so, I encourage you to read the Bible and learn the truth. You will come to the same conclusion as these 500 people. It's true! Jesus did rise from the dead!

Prayer: *Heavenly Father, thank You for Jesus, His resurrection, His forgiveness and the promise of eternal life. In Jesus' name. Amen.*

Jesus Suffered by Gayle Thorn   **Today's Reading:** Zechariah 12:1-12

Let's take a moment to read verses 10-11a of our Bible reading. *"I will fill David's family and the people living in Jerusalem with a spirit of kindness and mercy. They will look to me, the one they stabbed, and they will be very sad. They will be as sad as someone crying over the death of their only son, as sad as someone crying over the death of their firstborn son. There will be a time of great sadness and crying in Jerusalem."* In these verses God is speaking. "They" is talking about the Israelites and "I" refers to God. He said that the Israelites had stabbed Him or caused Him pain because of their sin and rebellion. The rest of the verse indicates that someday the Israelites will recognize their sin and be sad and repent.

But I think there is a deeper meaning to this verse. When Jesus was dying on the cross, He was stabbed with a spear. This caused Him great pain. But why did all this happen? Jesus was crucified because of our sins. We are responsible for His death. How sad that we caused God and Jesus such pain!

But wait . . . there is good news! God chose to send Jesus to die, and Jesus chose to suffer for us. Why? Because they love us! Jesus' death made it possible for our sins to be forgiven, for us to have a right relationship with God and for us to live with Him forever. Praise God!

Prayer: *Heavenly Father, thank You for sending Jesus to die for my sin so that I can live forever with You. In Jesus' name. Amen.*

Only Jesus Could by Gayle Thorn   **Today's Reading:** Zechariah 9:9-10

Zechariah 9:9 predicts Jesus' triumphal entry into Jerusalem just days before His arrest and crucifixion. This verse says, *"People of Zion, rejoice! People of Jerusalem, shout with joy! Look, your king is coming to you! He is the good king who won the victory, but he is humble. He is riding on a donkey, on a young donkey born from a work animal."*

That verse is one of the many verses in the Old Testament that predicted what would happen to Jesus while He lived on earth – His birth, ministry, death and resurrection. A man named Peter Stoner once calculated the probability of someone fulfilling all of these prophecies. He figured that the probability of someone other than Jesus fulfilling just 48 of the hundreds of prophecies is 1 in a number with 157 zeros after it!

It is true that some people could have fulfilled one or two of the prophecies, but Jesus fulfilled ALL of them, including riding a donkey into Jerusalem a few days before He was crucified. Only Jesus could do that!

Wow! Jesus really is the one and only person who could – and did – fulfill the prophecy of dying for our sins so that we can have eternal life. Take a moment today to praise God and celebrate Jesus' victory!

Prayer: *Father, thank You that Jesus is able to do the impossible — fulfilling all the prophecies about Him. And thank You that He is able to forgive my sins and give me eternal life. In His name. Amen.*

Messiah by Gayle Thorn

Today's Reading: Genesis 12:1-3

Today's Bible reading contains an amazing promise made by God to Abraham (Abram). Verses 2 and 3 say, *"I will build a great nation from you. I will bless you and make your name famous. People will use your name to bless other people. I will bless those who bless you, and I will curse those who curse you. I will use you to bless all the people on earth."*

Doesn't the promise that God made to Abraham sound terrific? Wouldn't it be wonderful to have God give us the same promise? The fact is, we have been blessed because of the promise that God made to Abraham. The blessing in that promise included sending a Messiah, God's chosen one, to give us a way out of the trap of sin and back into closeness with God.

The Messiah is Jesus. When Jesus was born, lived on earth for about 30 years and later died on the cross, He took the punishment for all of the sins of the world – yours and mine included. God blessed us by giving us the freedom to choose between living a life as a slave to sin or living a life full of peace, joy and freedom from sin. We can have that when we accept Jesus as our Savior and accept His sacrifice as the punishment for our sins.

Won't you choose to accept God's blessing today?

Prayer: *Heavenly Father, thank You for the blessing that comes through Jesus, the Messiah. In His name. Amen.*

Faith that Endures by Bob La Forge

Today's Reading: Numbers 14:1-19

What if God would miraculously provide you with all your food and drink, your clothes never wore out and all of your enemies were moved far away? And then God promised a future filled with wonderful abundance. You would think that you would persevere through any hardship and always stay faithful to God.

That is what the Israelites experienced in the book of Exodus. So what was their response? They complained that the food was not good enough and that the leadership was not doing a good job. Then they rebelled and created a golden calf and worshiped it. Why? They did not have a faith that endures. They judged God by the current situation, and if they didn't like it, they shouted, "Let's go back to Egypt!" Their faith was only based on how well their circumstances were going.

Our Bible verses today tell us that only two men, Joshua and Caleb, had a faith that endured. After spying out the new land, they said, *"The land that we saw is very good. It is a land filled with many good things. If the Lord is pleased with us, he will lead us into that land. And he will give that land to us. So don't turn against the Lord! Don't be afraid of the people in that land. We can defeat them. They have no protection, nothing to keep them safe. But we have the Lord with us, so don't be afraid!"* (verses 7b-9).

Always remember how good God is, and have a faith that endures!

Prayer: *God, when I am struggling in life, help me to remember Your love and Your goodness. In Jesus' name. Amen.*

Trees by Suzanne Austin-Hill   **Today's Reading:** Acts 10:34-43

Trees are mentioned almost 300 times in the Bible. And several Bible characters are compared to the strength and endurance of trees. I think God must like trees. He placed Adam and Eve among the trees in the Garden of Eden. One of Adam's jobs was to take care of the trees and plants. Trees provided the wood for the Temple where the Israelites worshiped God. God created trees to give us oxygen to keep us alive, give us materials to build our homes, provide us with shade and give us a source of food. Revelation 22:2 tells us that the tree of life will be located in heaven.

And most importantly, God used a tree as part of His wonderful plan of salvation. When Peter was telling a man named Cornelius about Jesus, he said, *"We saw all that Jesus did in Judea and in Jerusalem. But he was killed. They put him on a cross made of wood. But on the third day after his death, God raised him to life and let him be seen openly"* (verses 39-40). Jesus was crucified on a wooden cross that was made from a tree. Although the cross was an instrument of torture and pain, it provided the way that our sins could be forgiven through the blood of Jesus.

When you see a tree today, stop and think about how it shows us God's goodness and His plan for us to live forever with Him!

Prayer: *Heavenly Father, thank You for loving the world so much that You gave us Your Son. In Jesus' name. Amen.*

Completely Accepted by Donna Howard   **Today's Reading:** Mark 5:1-20

A friend and I study the Bible together every week. One day our lesson was about the man in Mark, chapter 5, who was demon-possessed. One of the discussion questions asked us to imagine that we were that man. Verses 2b-5 describe what the man was like. *"This man had an evil spirit living inside him. He lived in the burial caves. No one could keep him tied up, even with chains. Many times people had put chains on his hands and feet, but he broke the chains. No one was strong enough to control him. Day and night he stayed around the burial caves and on the hills. He would scream and cut himself with rocks."*

At first I thought that I couldn't identify with the man since I have never suffered anything like demon-possession. But then I saw myself standing before Jesus with all my sins uncovered. I was very much like the demon-possessed man! Full of shame, I fell to my knees and asked God to forgive me and heal my life. Just as Jesus looked at the demon-possessed man with compassion, I knew that God had compassion for me, and I felt completely accepted.

Are you feeling the pain of guilt and shame in your life because of sin? If so, confess your sin to God and ask Him to forgive you. You will feel the blessing of His love and acceptance.

Prayer: *Dear Lord, thank You for loving me so much that You sent Jesus to die on the cross. Help me to be strong and to overcome the sin in my life. In Jesus' name. Amen.*

Rock Solid by Gayle Thorn

Today's Reading: Deuteronomy 32:4

Rock was the primary building material in Bible times. It was strong, and it never changed its shape or shifted its position. Rocks made the perfect foundation for homes and for large buildings such as the Temple.

Today's Bible verse talks about a very special rock. This verse is part of a song of praise that Moses sang about God to the Israelites. It says, *"The Lord is the Rock, and his work is perfect! Yes, all his ways are right! God is true and faithful. He is good and honest."*

Jesus is our rock. He is strength. He is immovable. He is unchangeable. When we build our lives on God's Son, Jesus, and make Him the foundation of our lives, Jesus gives us His strength. Nothing can separate us from Him. No one can take Him away from us. Jesus will always be there to love us and protect and defend us. He will forever be our refuge, a place where we can go when we are hurting or afraid. Jesus is the only foundation on which we can build our lives that is truly rock solid.

I hope you are building your life on the rock solid foundation of Jesus today. If not, go to God and ask Him to forgive you and help you build your life on His Son, Jesus.

Prayer: *Heavenly Father, thank You for the solid foundation my life has in Jesus. In His name. Amen.*

Healing Power by Pam Davis

Today's Reading: Luke 8:43-48

What's your problem? Have you ever had a doctor ask you that question? I know I have. We go to the doctor when we are sick or in pain. Often we do not understand why we are not feeling well. Most of the time the doctor is able to help us, but sometimes they are not able to find out the source of our problem. That is what happened to the woman in our Bible verses for today. She had been sick for many years, but the doctors had done nothing to help her.

The woman had heard about Jesus and His wonderful miracles of healing, and she had faith that Jesus could help her, too. So one day when Jesus was surrounded by other people, she went close to Jesus and touched the bottom of his coat. Verses 46-48 tell us, *"But Jesus said, 'Someone touched me. I felt power go out from me.' When the woman saw that she could not hide, she came forward, shaking. She bowed down before Jesus. While everyone listened, she told why she touched him. Then she said that she was healed immediately when she touched him. Jesus said to her, 'My daughter, you are made well because you believed. Go in peace.'"*

Imagine how happy the woman was! She had faith that Jesus could help her, and He did. Jesus can help us, too, whether we have a physical problem or a spiritual problem. Reach out to Him today and allow His healing power to strengthen you.

Prayer: *Father, thank You for the example of this woman's faith. Help me to reach out to You when I need help. In Jesus' name. Amen.*

Ecclesiastes (1) by Jo Krueger   **Today's Reading:** Ecclesiastes 1:1-3

The book of Ecclesiastes is a short Old Testament book. It is a book of Hebrew poetry, along with Job, Psalms, Proverbs and Song of Solomon. We do not know for sure who wrote this book. However, throughout the book, the writer calls himself the "Teacher." Many people think that King Solomon wrote the book of Ecclesiastes. The writer talks about being a king of Israel and having great wisdom and wealth. Those things certainly describe King Solomon.

As you read the book of Ecclesiastes, you will realize that the writer is trying to find answers to his questions. In verse 3 of our Bible reading today, the writer asks the question, *"Do people really gain anything from all the hard work they do in this life?"* At the end of Ecclesiastes, the writer answers that question by telling us what is most important in life.

Reading through the book of Ecclesiastes will help us learn several important lessons that we should follow as Christians. Tomorrow we will start to look at these lessons.

Take time today to thank God for the many lessons you can learn as you read through the Bible. And ask Him to help you apply these valuable lessons to your Christian life.

Prayer: *Heavenly Father, thank You for Your Word, the Bible. Help me to read and study it every day. In Jesus' name. Amen.*

Ecclesiastes (2) by Jo Krueger   **Today's Reading:** Ecclesiastes 1:4-11

Our Bible verses for today remind us that there *"is nothing new in this life"* (verse 9b). People are born, and they die. The sun comes up in the east and sets in the west every day. The wind blows from the south and then from the north. The rivers flow into the oceans. Our daily routines become tiresome and are filled with seeing and hearing bad things.

People don't really change either. You may watch the news on TV and think that things in the world now are worse than ever. But people are still doing the same sins they have been doing for thousands of years – stealing, causing war, lying, cheating, murdering and abusing people.

It may be depressing to think that things in the world are not getting better. But there is some really good news! The Bible tells us that Jesus is always the same – He never changes. He is the same today as He was yesterday and as He will be in the future. That means that no matter how bad the world becomes, we can always depend on Jesus to be our Lord and Savior.

As you look around today and see bad things happening, remember that you can always depend on Jesus. He is always ready to share His love and blessings with you, and that will never change.

Prayer: *Father, I am so thankful that Jesus never changes. Thank You for sending Him to die on the cross for my sins. In His name. Amen.*

Ecclesiastes (3) by Jo Krueger

Today's Reading: Ecclesiastes 2:24-26

Every day God gives us many wonderful blessings. He sends sunshine to keep us warm and to make the plants and trees grow. God gives us air to breathe, water to drink and food to eat. And God gives us our families and friends to love us and encourage us. But often we take these things for granted and forget to thank God for them.

In our Bible verses for today, the writer decided that the *"best thing people can do is eat drink, and enjoy the work they must do"* (verse 24b). That is good advice for us Christians today, too. But even more important than this, the writer realized that all these wonderful blessings come from God. *"I also saw that this comes from God"* (verse 25b).

Maybe you have daily struggles so you think that God is not blessing you. But God blesses each one of us, even when we are facing problems. God gives us wisdom, comfort and strength to help us work through our problems and then give glory to Him.

Think about the ways that God is blessing you today. Then take time to thank Him and praise Him!

Prayer: *Dear God, You do so many wonderful things for me every day. Thank You for the blessings that You are giving me today. Help me to be thankful for the way You take care of me. In Jesus' name. Amen.*

Ecclesiastes (4) by Jo Krueger

Today's Reading: Ecclesiastes 3:1-8

The verses today in our Bible reading are very familiar to many people. In the 1960s a popular American folk song was based on these verses. Sometimes these verses are read at a funeral. Verse 1 says, *"There is a right time for everything, and everything on earth will happen at the right time."*

It is very important that we recognize that God is in control of the universe. From the time we are born until the time we die, God has a plan for our lives. We don't always understand what God is doing in our lives, but we still need to trust and depend on Him.

These verses remind us that all people will face many different things in life. Some of these things are birth, death, crying, laughter, sadness, joy, love, hatred, keeping things, throwing things away, war and peace. These things are common to most people who live on earth. As we face these things, we need to allow God to work in our lives. Then our lives will have meaning and purpose, and we will make God happy.

No matter what happens to you today, remember to trust God to direct your life and show you how you can live for Him.

Prayer: *Father, thank You for working in my life today. I trust You to take care of me and show me how to live. In Jesus' name. Amen.*

Ecclesiastes (5) by Jo Krueger
Today's Reading: Ecclesiastes 4:9-12

In our Bible verses for today, the writer shows us the importance of experiencing true friendship. He says that it is good when people cooperate and work together. *"Two people are better than one. When two people work together, they get more work done"* (verse 9).

As I read these verses, I think about two people traveling together long ago. As they travel, the two of them can get more work done. They can also help each other if they stumble and fall. When they sleep at night, they can keep each other warm. And if danger comes, they can defend each other. Then the writer goes on to say that three people working together are even better than two. *"And three people are even stronger. They are like a rope that has three parts wrapped together – it is very hard to break"* (verse 12b).

I feel happy when I think about the many friends I have had through my life – from my childhood friends to the friends I have today. Some have worked with me. Many friends have prayed for me and encouraged me in my Christian life. And a few friends have protected me when I was in danger.

God has blessed you with friends. Thank Him today for the people in your life who help and encourage you.

Prayer: *Dear Loving Lord, thank You for blessing me with wonderful friends. In Jesus' name. Amen.*

Ecclesiastes (6) by Jo Krueger
Today's Reading: Ecclesiastes 5:10-17

Many people in the world today worship their money. In fact, money is something that people have worshiped for thousands of years. In our Bible reading, the writer of Ecclesiastes looks at what people think about money and wealth.

People think that wealth gives them satisfaction. But the writer says that *"those who love wealth will not be satisfied when they get more and more"* (verse 10b). Many people also think that money will solve all their problems. But having a lot of money only makes new problems for us.

Some people believe that wealth gives them peace of mind. But we can think about many people whose lives have been ruined by their wealth. The writer also says people think that money gives them security. But bad things can happen and cause us to lose our money. Finally, money is temporary – we can't take it with us when we die. Verse 15 says, *"People come into the world with nothing. And when they died, they leave with nothing. They might work hard to get things, but they cannot take anything with them when they die."*

We all need money to live, but it cannot bring happiness. True happiness can only come from loving God and having a close relationship with Him. Make sure you are close to Him today.

Prayer: *Dear God, I love You so much! I want to always have a close relationship with You. In Jesus' name. Amen.*

Ecclesiastes (7) by Jo Krueger   Today's Reading: Ecclesiastes 7:7-9

In chapter 7 of Ecclesiastes, the writer includes a list of wise teachings for us. These wise teachings are very similar to those written by King Solomon in the Old Testament book of Proverbs.

Verses 7 through 9 of our Bible reading give us some teachings that are wise and good for us to follow every day. Verse 7 talks about bribery. Bribery may seem to be the easy way to get something done. But it only makes people act foolish and stupid.

Verse 8 reminds us that when we start something, it is important for us to finish it. And this verse also tells us that it is *"better to be gentle and patient than to be proud and impatient."*

Verse 9 talks about anger. The writer says that we should not become angry quickly. Why? Because *"anger is foolish."*

I encourage you to read all of Ecclesiastes, chapter 7. The writer closes the chapter with these wise words. *"Look at what God has made. You cannot change a thing, even if you think it is wrong. When life is good, enjoy it. But when life is hard, remember that God gives us good times and hard times. And no one knows what will happen in the future"* (verses 13-14).

Prayer: *Dear Heavenly Father, help me to be wise and to obey You every day. In Jesus' name. Amen.*

Ecclesiastes (8) by Jo Krueger   Today's Reading: Ecclesiastes 8:16-17

The world is filled with people who claim that they are wise. Some of these people even say that they can understand God entirely. But that is not true. Verse 17 of our Bible reading for today says, *"I also saw that no one can understand all that God does. People can try and try to understand the things that happen here on earth, but they cannot. There may be wise people who claim to understand the meaning of these things, but they are wrong. No one can understand it all."*

Do you know how many stars are in the sky? Do you know how big the universe is? Do you know how many drops of water are in the oceans? We don't know these things, but God does!

When I think about those questions, I feel frustrated that I can't figure out the answers. I need to realize that I am not wise like God. He does not expect me to have all the answers. Isaiah 55:8-9 talks about this. *"The Lord says, 'My thoughts are not like yours. Your ways are not like mine. Just as the heavens are higher than the earth, so my ways are higher than your ways, and my thoughts are higher than your thoughts.'"* But God does expect me to learn all I can and obey His teachings in the Bible.

When you think about the world today, remember that God is wise and all-knowing. Thank Him for His Word and ask Him to help you obey it.

Prayer: *Dear God, You are so awesome. I praise You for Your great wisdom and love. In Jesus' name. Amen.*

Ecclesiastes (9) by Jo Krueger

Today's Reading: Ecclesiastes 11:9-12:1

The writer of Ecclesiastes says that he is writing today's Bible verses for young people. But I think that all people, no matter what their age is, can learn from these verses, too.

The writer of Ecclesiastes encourages young people to do whatever their heart leads them to do. But he also adds this warning, *"Do whatever you want, but remember that God will judge you for everything you do"* (verse 9b). Young people should enjoy their lives, but they must also be careful not to do things that will lead them to sin and become separated from God.

Then in verse 10, the writer reminds young people to not let their anger control them or let their bodies lead them to sin. The world is filled with so many temptations for young people today. They need to remember to be wise and not foolish. Finally, in verse 1 of chapter 12, the writer tells young people to remember God, who is our Creator, and obey His Word.

Whether you are young or old, it is good for you to carefully follow and obey God's Word every day. Live so that you won't look back on your life and realize that you have wasted the time that God has given you. Use your time to serve and honor Him!

Prayer: *Father, thank You for my life and for my salvation through Jesus. Help me to use my time wisely for You. In Jesus' name. Amen.*

Ecclesiastes (10) by Jo Krueger

Today's Reading: Ecclesiastes 12:9-14

We are finally at the end of our series of devotions from the book of Ecclesiastes, and now the writer tell us what he has learned is most important in life.

Throughout the book, the writer has looked at wealth, wisdom, success and other things we may experience in life. Now he concludes with some very wise advice. *"The most important thing a person can do is to respect God and obey his commands"* (verse 13b). He does not say that we should try to have more wealth, wisdom or success. Instead, the writer says that the most important thing we can do is to respect and obey God.

If we respect God, we will pay attention to His Word, the Bible, and obey it. When we read and study the Bible, we learn more about God and how we can follow Him. Verses 1 and 7b of Psalm, chapter 112, talk about this. *"Praise the Lord! Great blessings belong to those who fear and respect the Lord, who are happy to do what he commands. They are confident because they trust in the Lord."*

I hope you have learned some good lessons from the verses we have studied in Ecclesiastes. Even though these verses were written a long time ago, they still have important messages for us today. May God bless you as you respect and obey Him throughout your life!

Prayer: *God, thank You for Your teachings in the Bible. I love and respect You. In Jesus' name. Amen.*

God's Blessings by Bonnie Hall   Today's Reading: Deuteronomy 11:8-28

In our Bible verses today, the Israelites are again being reminded that they need to follow God's commands. Verses 13-15 say, *"The Lord says, 'You must listen carefully to the commands I give you today: You must love the Lord your God, and serve him with all your heart and all your soul. If you do that, I will send rain for your land at the right time. I will send the autumn rain and the spring rain. Then you can gather your grain, your new wine, and your oil. And I will make grass grow in your fields for your cattle. You will have plenty to eat."* If the Israelites obeyed God, things went well for them. If they stopped following God, things did not go so well.

In those verses, God was preparing the Israelites to live in the new land that He had promised to them. He wanted to make sure that they obeyed Him and received all the blessings He had for them. As I look back over the past few weeks, I see that I have not been as careful to follow God as I should. I have rushed through my times of prayer and studying the Bible, and I have started complaining when things didn't go as I thought they should. So I have repented and asked God to forgive me for moving away from Him.

God has many blessings that He wants to give to you today. Stay close to Him and obey Him. He knows what is best for you!

Prayer: *Lord, I know that You love me and want to bless me. Help me to stay close to You. In Jesus' name. Amen.*

Poison by Gayle Thorn   Today's Reading: Proverbs 27:6

If I had a friend who was doing something that was dangerous or could hurt someone else, I would feel the need to do something to help them change their behavior. Why? Because I love my friend and always want what is best for them. That's what Solomon was saying in our Bible verse for today. *"You can trust what your friend says, even when it hurts. But your enemies want to hurt you, even when they act nice."*

If a person is bitten by a poisonous sake and the bite is left untreated, the person will probably die. Often a bite mark is cut open so that the blood can wash the poison out of the person's body before it does serious damage. The cut isn't made to deliberately hurt the person, but it is a necessary wound made to save the person's life.

Sometimes it is a friend's job to "wound" his friend – not to be cruel, but to stop the friend from continuing to hurt himself. Love sometimes wounds a friend because it refuses to sit back and watch the friend's life be ruined by their poisonous and sinful actions.

Doing what you know is right isn't always easy, but it is always right! Ask God to help you as you help and strengthen your Christian friends.

Prayer: *Heavenly Father, give me the courage to always do what I know is right. In Jesus' name. Amen.*

God is Watching You by Donna Howard   **Today's Reading:** Psalm 121:1-8

On winter mornings when my husband and I take our dog for a walk, it is still dark. One morning my husband, who is a volunteer driver for elderly people, had to leave at 6:00 a.m. to take someone to the hospital. So I had to walk the dog alone. Normally that would not be a problem, but that morning the sidewalks were icy. I am 86 years old and I have poor balance, so I was afraid to go on the walk alone.

As a precaution, I put my cell phone in my pocket just in case I might need it. We live in a small town where most of the people know each other. So several people waved to me as I was walking. One couple even stopped to ask if my husband was alright. And as I walked, God brought verses 1-3 of today's Bible reading to mind. *"I look up to the hills, but where will my help really come from? My help will come from the Lord, the Creator of heaven and earth. He will not let you fall. Your Protector will not fall asleep."*

That was God's way of letting me know that He was with me. He was not asleep – He was paying attention to me and protecting me. Those verses gave me the confidence to continue on my walk and arrive home safely.

Are you going through something fearful today? Remember these verses and know that God is watching over you.

Prayer: *Father, thank You for reminding me that You are always watching over me. In Jesus' name. Amen.*

Quiet Service by Jo Krueger   **Today's Reading:** Acts 20:22-38

I just received a phone call from a former co-worker, telling me that a friend had suddenly passed away. This friend was truly a woman of quiet service. For all the years that I worked for Deaf Missions, this woman was always there to volunteer for projects. If there was a job to be done, she was willing to be there and help. She never made a big deal out of her service. She just smiled and did what she could to help out.

In our Bible reading today, Paul met with the elders of the church in Ephesus. Paul loved the Christians in Ephesus, and he knew this was the last time he would ever see them. Paul was on his way to Jerusalem, where he knew he would be arrested and taken to Rome. Paul encouraged these Christians to continue living for Jesus. He prayed with them, and they cried together. In verse 35 Paul said, *"I always showed you that you should work just as I did and help people who are weak. I taught you to remember the words of the Lord Jesus: 'You will have a greater blessing when you give than when you receive.'"* That's what my friend did – she gave of herself! And God blessed her because of it.

Look for ways today that you can lead a life of quiet service. Be willing to give of yourself and help others.

Prayer: *Dear God, thank You for my friend's example of quiet service. Help me to be like her. In Jesus' name. Amen.*

Keep Going by Rachel Burkum

Today's Reading: 1 Peter 4:12-19

We live in a "fallen" world. That means ever since the very first time someone sinned (Adam and Eve), the world has no longer been perfect. Sin creates chaos, and bad things happen. Until Jesus comes again, we must endure. Our Bible reading for today talks about suffering because we are Christians. Many people in the world may mock us or even harm us. There are Christians today who are being killed for their faith in God. But Peter reminds us we should be joyful and *"... continue to do good"* (verse 19b). We can't give up!

It can be hard to take Peter's advice. Because of sin, we experience hard times, death and countless struggles. Stress has become a part of daily life. Even if we have faith in God, that does not remove all bad things. It would be very easy for us to blame God or become bitter. We could complain all the time or give up trying to do good things. It would be easy to say, "forget it," and turn away from God.

But we have hope! In John 16:33b Jesus Himself tells us, *"In this world you will have troubles. But be brave! I have defeated the world!"* Through His death, burial and resurrection, Jesus has already overcome this sinful world! The trials you are facing? He has already overcome those, too. Peter told us to continue doing good. Jesus told us to be brave. Let's keep trusting God no matter what!

Prayer: *Loving God, I know the world is not perfect. But I also know You have already overcome all sin. Please help me to be brave and have faith. In Jesus' name. Amen.*

The Passover Meal by Norma Mezoe

Today's Reading: Exodus 12:1-20

Several years ago, I joined some members of my church to share a Passover meal. About 20 of us gathered around a table in the church basement. All of us there were excited and didn't know quite what to expect. Our minister explained why the Jewish people observed the Passover. God gave them this celebration meal to help them remember how He had helped them to escape slavery in Egypt.

During the meal, small plates of herbs were passed from member to member around the table. Later, unleavened bread and pieces of lamb were shared. As we ate this meal, our minister shared verses from our Bible reading for today. Verse 14 says, *"You will always remember tonight — it will be a special festival for you. Your descendants will honor the Lord with this festival forever."*

Finally, our church group shared the Lord's Supper together. We took the bread which represented Jesus' body and then the juice which stood for the blood that He shed when He died on the cross. During that evening, we truly felt God's presence as we worshiped Him.

We are not commanded to celebrate the Passover like the Jews were. But we do need to remember every day how God has saved us from our slavery to sin. Praise God today for salvation through Jesus!

Prayer: *Father, thank You that I can be part of Your wonderful family of believers. In Jesus' name. Amen.*

My Favorite Toys (1) by Jo Krueger   **Today's Reading:** Luke 1:26-38

When I was young, I had many toys. But I remember some toys as being very special to me. Today we will begin talking about some of those favorite toys.

In my preschool years, I had several dolls. The first doll I received, I named Mary. Of course I had heard the story of Jesus' birth over and over again, so I named the doll after Mary, the mother of Jesus. The next year I received another doll at Christmas. Then my first doll became "Old Mary," and the new one become "New Mary." My mother tried to get me to choose another name, but I wouldn't give in. And the third doll I got I named "Newer Mary." I guess I was really impressed with Mary!

Mary is a wonderful role model for us. Our Bible verses tell us about the angel Gabriel coming to Mary and telling her she would give birth to God's Son. I am sure Mary must have felt scared and confused. But what did she say? *"I am the Lord's servant. Let this thing you have said happen to me!"* (verse 38a). Mary was humble and willing to do whatever God wanted her to do, even though she didn't understand everything.

Are you like Mary? Are you ready to obey God and do His will? Ask God today to help you be His humble and faithful servant.

Prayer: *Dear God, show me how I can be humble like Mary and do Your will today. In Jesus' name. Amen.*

April 23

My Favorite Toys (2) by Jo Krueger   **Today's Reading:** Philippians 4:10-13

When I was in grade school, my friends and I had metal skates that we attached to the outside of our shoes. In the summertime, we skated all over our neighborhood. One sidewalk near my home had a small hill. To us, the hill seemed very steep, and we were scared to skate down it. We were afraid we would go too fast and not be able to stop. But my friends and I were determined to conquer that hill. So we started skating from about halfway up, and gradually added a few more feet each day until we were able to skate down the whole hill and control our speed.

Years later, I drove past that hill. My first thought was, "What happened to that hill?" There was a small rise in the sidewalk, but I certainly would not call it a hill. But as a child, that small rise seemed like an unsurmountable hill.

Often we look at something we need to do and think that it is impossible. Perhaps we need to finish college, take care of a sick parent, downsize our home or go on living without a spouse. Things often seem worse than they really are. That's when we need to depend on God to help us conquer our fears and get the job done. Paul had many hard things he had to do, but he relied on God's help and strength. In verse 13 of our Bible reading Paul said, *"Christ is the one who gives me the strength I need to do whatever I must do."*

Depend on God today to help you overcome your fears and serve Him.

Prayer: *Dear Father, thank You for always being there to help me. In Jesus' name. Amen.*

My Favorite Toys (3) by Jo Krueger   **Today's Reading:** 1 Peter 2:13-25

When I was young, most older women wore high heels. I often thought about the day when I would be old enough to wear shoes like my mother wore. Then one day I saw some child's plastic high heels in a variety store. I was so excited! I begged my mother to buy a pair for me. I remember putting the shoes on right away when we got into the car. When we got home, I unsteadily walked into the house. Finally, I was just like my mother!

People today look up to professional athletes, movie actors and politicians. They want to be rich and famous like them. But often these people live lives that are filled with problems and sinful activities. As Christians, we should not want to be like people in the world. We should want to be like Jesus.

In our Bible reading today, Peter talks about being a willing servant and showing love and respect. Then he talks about how Jesus suffered many things so that our sins could be forgiven. In verses 21-22 Peter says, *"This is what you were chosen to do. Christ gave you an example to follow. He suffered for you. So you should do the same as he did: 'He never sinned, and he never told a lie.'"* Jesus is the one we should look up to and try to be like.

Think about Jesus today. Ask God to help you be humble and obedient like Jesus.

Prayer: *Lord, I want to be like Jesus. Show me how I can be Your humble servant today. In Jesus' name. Amen.*

My Favorite Toys (4) by Jo Krueger   **Today's Reading:** Revelation 21:1-27

Another toy I had was a View-master. The View-master came with cardboard disks called reels. On each reel were 14 small 3-D pictures of people and places. I had several reels, and one had pictures of Roy Rogers. Another reel showed views of the Grand Canyon. When I put a reel into the View-master and looked at the pictures, I felt like I was actually with Roy Rogers or at the Grand Canyon. These reels gave me a glimpse of things that I might never experience in my life.

I think a lot about heaven. I wonder what it will look like, how I will feel there and who I will see. I can't look at pictures of heaven through my View-master, but I can read the book of Revelation. Revelation, chapter 21, tells us there will be no death, sadness, crying or pain in heaven. That will be so wonderful! The light in heaven will come from God's glory. The foundation of the city is made of may precious jewels. The gates are made from pearl and the streets from gold.

Verse 27 gives us more information about heaven. *"Nothing unclean will ever enter the city. No one who does shameful things or tells lies will ever enter the city. Only those whose names are written in the Lamb's book of life will enter the city."* Can you imagine how wonderful that will be? Take some time today and think about the place that God has prepared for you.

Prayer: *Almighty God, thank You for preparing a place for me to live with You forever. In Jesus' name. Amen.*

My Favorite Toys (5) by Jo Krueger

Today's Reading: 1 Thessalonians 5:1-11

One of my favorite toys when I was very young was a Jack-in-the-Box. I can remember the brightly colored pictures on the side of the metal box, the squeak as the crank was turned and the music that it played. The first few times Jack popped out of the box, I was scared and cried. But eventually I got used to it and loved to be surprised.

Life is full of surprises! Some of them are good and some of them are bad. We think that we will get a tax refund, but instead, we end up paying more taxes. Our family gives us an unexpected birthday party. Weeks before we are scheduled to retire, we are laid off from our job.

Most of us don't like to be surprised. We want to know exactly what will happen to us in the future. But some people will face a huge surprise someday. These are people who have lived a sinful lives. Jesus will come again, and they will have to face His judgment and punishment. Verses 2-3a of our Bible reading talk about this. *"You know very well that the day when the Lord comes again will be a surprise, like a thief who comes at night. People will say, 'We have peace and we are safe.' At that time destruction will come to them quickly."*

Be prepared for Jesus to come again. Follow and serve Him every day.

Prayer: *Dear God, I don't want to be surprised when Jesus comes again. Thank You for salvation through Jesus. In His name. Amen.*

My Favorite Toys (6) by Jo Krueger

Today's Reading: 1 John 1:5-10

When I was a child, I spent hours and hours playing with my Etch-a-Sketch. An Etch-a-Sketch looks like a small slate with two dials. When I turned the dials, I could draw pictures on the screen. I was an average drawer, but some people can become very skilled with an Etch-a-Sketch and draw very intricate designs.

But there's one problem with an Etch-a-Sketch. When you tip it up or shake it, the picture that you drew disappears – forever! I was often disappointed when I drew a picture and ran to show it to my mother. But along the way, I bumped the screen, and the picture was gone.

The Etch-a-Sketch shows us how God removes our sins. When we repent of our sins, accept Jesus as our Savior and are baptized, God removes all our sins. Our sins disappear - just like the picture on the Etch-a-Sketch. And Jesus' blood continues to remove the sins that we commit after we become a Christian. John talked about this in verse 7 of our Bible verses for today. *"We should live in the light, where God is. If we live in the light, we have fellowship with each other, and the blood sacrifice of Jesus, God's Son, washes away every sin and makes us clean."*

If you are one of God's children, you don't need to worry about your sins. They have been erased forever by Jesus' blood. Thank God for His forgiveness today!

Prayer: *Heavenly Father, thank You for forgiving me and removing my sins. In Jesus' name. Amen.*

My Favorite Toys (7) by Jo Krueger   **Today's Reading:** Hebrews 10:19-25

The game of jacks was very popular when I was in grade school. Jacks are made of metal and have six prongs. To play the game you need a small rubber ball and a set of 10 jacks. You play the game by scattering the jacks and bouncing the ball. While the ball is in the air, you grab as many jacks as you can and catch the ball before it bounces again.

When I first started playing jacks, I was terrible, but I wanted to become a good player. So every evening I would sit on the concrete stoop in front of our house and practice. My playing hand became calloused from scraping against the concrete, and often I wanted to quit. But I kept on practicing, and I became a skilled player.

Sometimes it is hard to follow Jesus every day. In Hebrews, chapter 10, the writer gives us some instructions on how we can keep on serving God. Verse 25 tells us, *"We must no quit meeting together as some are doing. No, we need to keep on encouraging each other. This becomes more and more important as you see the Day getting closer."* Even though we may become tired and want to quit following Jesus, we need to keep on fellowshipping with other Christians and encouraging them.

Don't give up following Jesus! Keep on spending time with other Christians and encouraging them in their Christian walk.

Prayer: *Dear Lord, sometimes it is hard to keep following You. Please help me to not give up. In Jesus' name. Amen.*

My Favorite Toys (8) by Jo Krueger   **Today's Reading:** Psalm 148:1-14

When I was in junior high, I got a chemistry set. I guess that it might not be considered a toy, but it was fun to play with. I spent many hours mixing the chemicals and doing experiments. I can still remember the smell of the chemicals. I was fascinated by the way the chemicals changed when mixed together. I would often tell my parents about the experiments that I did. They helped me understand that the rules and processes of chemistry were part of God's creation and that I should thank Him for everything that He made.

Psalm 148 is a song of praise to God for all He has created. *"Everything on earth, praise him! Great sea animals and all the oceans, praise the Lord! Praise him, fire and hail, snow and clouds, and the storm winds that obey him. Praise him, mountains and hills, fruit trees and cedar trees"* (verses 7-9). Think about all the things God has created, each with its own special purpose – snowflakes, mosquitoes, lightning, frogs and even daffodils.

Many people today are quick to say that they don't believe in God and that everything in the world "just happened by accident." I don't know how a person can watch the birth of a baby or a bright orange sunrise and think that they are accidents. Look around you today and thank God for all He has made for you!

Prayer: *Father, Your world is so beautiful. Thank You for making it all for me! In Jesus' name. Amen.*

A Home for His Name by Bonnie Hall   **Today's Reading:** Deuteronomy 12:1-14

God was leading the Israelites through the wilderness toward the new home He had promised to them. As they traveled, they set up a tent where they worshiped God. But nothing was permanent – everything was temporary. In our Bible verses for today, God told the Israelites that after they crossed the Jordan River, He would set up a permanent place where they could worship Him. Verse 11 describes that place. *"Then the Lord your God will choose a place that will be the home for his name. You must bring everything I command you to that place. Bring your burnt offerings, your sacrifices, one-tenth of your crops and animals, your special gifts, and any gifts that you promised to give to the Lord."*

God gave the Israelites a place to worship that would be a home for His name. Then other people could hear about the miracles God had done and know that the Israelites were His special people. As the Israelites came to that place and offered their gifts and sacrifices, they showed God that He was truly their Father.

Today we can worship God anywhere – in a church building, in someone's home or out in nature. Offer God your praise and adoration today and thank Him for the many ways that He takes care of you every day. Make your life to be a home for His name!

Prayer: *Dear God, I love You and worship You. Thank You for giving me salvation through Jesus. In His name. Amen.*

God's Punishment by Gayle Thorn   **Today's Reading:** Proverbs 11:19-21

Some of the punishments that God gave to people in the Old Testament seem horrible to us. For example, God sent a flood, snakes, fire and burning sulfur and plagues as punishments. God didn't give these people punishments quickly or without thought. God patiently gave the people many years to ask for His forgiveness and change their ways. Sadly, they refused to change. They chose to keep living in the wickedness that separated them from God. They brought the punishment that they received on themselves.

Our Bible verse for today says, *"The truth is, evil people will be punished, and good people will be set free."* This verse points out that God will punish ALL sin and ALL wrongdoing!

Thanks to Jesus' death and resurrection, we don't have to suffer eternal punishment for our sin. We can go to God, tell Him we're sorry, and ask for His forgiveness. We can do that because Jesus already took the punishment for our sin.

When we ask God to forgive us, and obey Him, God will give us His Holy Spirit to help us start living in ways that please Him. Have you asked God to forgive your sin and accepted Jesus' punishment and salvation as your own?

Prayer: *Heavenly Father, I know that I have done things that have angered You. Please forgive me. In Jesus' name. Amen.*

Encourage One Another by Bob La Forge   Today's Reading: Hebrews 10:24-25

Last night I had a fire blazing in the fireplace. When I went upstairs there were three logs burning brightly. Thirty minutes later I came back and saw that one of the logs had rolled off the grating and was by itself. The other two logs were still together and flames were dancing joyfully over them. But that one log had turned dark and provided no warmth or light.

Sometimes when we are struggling with problems or going through a trial, we become discouraged and want to be left alone. Often the first thing we give up is going to church. That is a big mistake. The times in my life when I least felt like going to church, I forced myself and found them to be the best services ever.

Our Bible verses for today talk about being with other Christians and encouraging one another. *"We should think about each other to see how we can encourage each other to show love and do good works. We must not quit meeting together, as some are doing. No, we need to keep on encouraging each other. This becomes more and more important as you see the Day getting closer."*

God uses other people to warm us, give us light and to support us. When we go off by ourselves, we become cold and dark and lonely. Stay close to the warmth and light of Jesus!

Prayer: *Father, when I am tempted to be alone, please draw me back into the warmth of Your fellowship. In Jesus' name. Amen.*

Encouraging Letters by Pam Davis   Today's Reading: 2 Timothy 1:2-8

I miss corresponding with my mother and one of my closest friends. Both are now with the Lord. When they were living, they took time to write to me often. I was always excited to find their letters in my mailbox. They wrote about things in their lives that almost made me feel like we were together. We had a lot in common. Most of all, we loved the Lord and loved each other.

Paul wrote letters to his friends, Christian workers and churches. Many of his letters are in the New Testament of the Bible. Some letters Paul wrote were passed around from church to church. That way, many people could read his letters. Other New Testament books, like Philemon and 1 and 2 Timothy, were written as personal letters to his friends.

Timothy was like a son to Paul. Paul wrote two letters to him that gave him fatherly advice and encouragement. Paul wrote words of strength and encouragement to Timothy in verses 7-8 of our Bible reading for today. *"The Spirit God gave us does not make us afraid. His Spirit is a source of power and love and self-control. So don't be ashamed to tell people about our Lord Jesus. And don't be ashamed of me — I am in prison for the Lord. But suffer with me for the Good News. God gives us the strength to do that."*

Paul's words can encourage us, too. Rely on God's strength to help you each day.

Prayer: *Dear God, thank You for encouraging me and for Your presence and power in my life. In Jesus' name. Amen.*

Hair (1) by Jennifer Forrester

It has been estimated that people around the world spend over $75 billion on hair care products each year. This shows us that people think their hair is very important to them. Today and for the next few days we will look at Bible verses that talk about hair.

The word "Nazarite" means to be consecrated or separated. When a Hebrew man took a Nazarite vow, he promised not to drink wine or anything made from grapes, to not cut his hair, and to keep his body pure by not touching a dead body.

In our Bible reading for today, we learn that Hannah did not have any children. One time when she was worshiping, she prayed to God. *"She made a special promise to God and said, 'Lord, All-Powerful, you can see how sad I am. Remember me. Don't forget me. If you will give me a son, I will give him to you. He will be yours his whole life, and as a Nazarite, he will not drink wine or strong drink and no one will cut his hair'"* (verse 11). Hannah was willing to offer her son to live a special life for God. God blessed Hannah with a son, Samuel, who became one of God's prophets.

When we become a Christian, we are making a vow to God. We don't have to stop cutting our hair, but we do need to promise to live and serve Him all of our life. I hope you are serving God today.

Prayer: *Heavenly Father, I promise that I will faithfully love and serve You all my life. In Jesus' name. Amen.*

Hair (2) by Jennifer Forrester

Judges, chapter 13, tells us about another woman who did not have any children. An angel came to her and told her that she would have a son who would be a Nazarite and would save the Israelites from the Philistines. She had a son and named him Samson. God blessed Samson, and he served as a judge over Israel for many years. And God also blessed Samson with great strength.

The Philistines were enemies of the Israelites. So when Samson fell in love with Delilah, the Philistines asked her to find the source of Samson's great strength. Delilah asked Samson many times to tell her why he was so strong. *"Finally Samson told Delilah everything. He said, 'I have never had my hair cut. I was dedicated to God before I was born. If someone shaved my head, I would lose my strength. I would become as weak as any other man'"* (verse 17). While Samson was asleep, Delilah called someone to come and cut off Samson's hair. Samson's strength left him, and he was captured by the Philistines. While Samson was a prisoner, he prayed and God gave him his strength back one more time. Then Samson killed more Philistines than he had killed all his life.

This story is a great reminder that we need to follow and obey God in every part of our lives. God has a plan for each of us, and we need to stay close to Him.

Prayer: *Father, I want to stay close to You every day. Help me to study Your Word and obey it. In Jesus' name. Amen.*

Hair (3) by Jennifer Forrester

Today's Reading: Matthew 10:28-30

Since we are talking about hair, here are some interesting facts I learned. The average person has between 90,000 and 150,000 hairs on their head, depending on the color of their hair. Each year a person's hair grows about 6 inches. And, we lose between 50 and 100 hairs each day. These facts were found after many research studies were done through the years. But one thing no person can know is exactly how many hairs are on a person's head at a given time. It is impossible for a human to know that.

In our Bible verses for today, Jesus reminded His followers about God's protection. He told them that they should not be afraid because God knew them and would protect them. In verse 30, Jesus said, *"God even knows how many hairs are on your head."* This shows me two things: 1) If God can know this, He surely is all-powerful and all-knowing, and 2) If God cares about the number of hairs on my head, then I know that I can depend on Him to take care of me each day.

Are you facing something today that is scary? A child custody battle? A diagnosis from your doctor? A new job? The funeral of a loved one? You can face all these things because God will be with you to encourage and strengthen you. Depend on Him and His Word today!

Prayer: *God, thank You for loving me and knowing all about me. I will trust You to take care of me today. In Jesus' name. Amen.*

Hair (4) by Jennifer Forrester

Today's Reading: Ezra 9:1-4

To punish the Israelites for their refusal to follow Him, God allowed some of them to be taken captive by foreign countries. Years later, many of the Israelites were allowed to go back to Israel. Ezra led a group of people back home. When Ezra arrived, he was told that many of the Israelites who had stayed in Israel had not been obeying God. They had inter-married with people who were not Israelites. This was strictly forbidden by God.

When an Israelite was mourning the death of a loved one, he might put ashes on his head, pull out some of his hair or tear his clothes as a sign of mourning. Ezra was so upset and shocked to learn about the Israelites' disobedience that he went into a time of mourning. Verse 3 of our Bible reading tells us what he did. *"When I heard about this, I tore my robe and my coat to show I was upset. I pulled hair from my head and beard. I sat down, shocked and upset."*

We should be sad and upset about the all the terrible sin that is around us in the world today. This should lead us to pray for sinful people and to show them how they can change their lives and follow God. Do you know someone who is struggling with sin? Pray for them and encourage them to obey God and His Word today.

Prayer: *Dear Father there is so much sin in the world. But I know Jesus is the answer. Help me to share the Good News about Jesus with someone today. In His name. Amen.*

Hair (5) by Jennifer Forrester   **Today's Reading:** Luke 7:36-50

Today our Bible verses tell us about something unusual that happened to Jesus. One day Jesus was eating in the home of Simon who as a Jewish Pharisee. A sinful woman came to Simon's home with a jar of expensive perfume. *"She stood at Jesus' feet, crying. Then she began to wash his feet with her tears. She dried his feet with her hair. She kissed his feet many times and rubbed them with the perfume"* (verse 38).

Simon was upset that this sinful woman would come into his home and do this. Maybe he was embarrassed that this would happen in front of his guests. But Jesus knew that the woman was showing her sorrow and repentance. Jesus said that this woman showed great love and that her sins were forgiven. Simon judged the woman by what he had heard about her, but Jesus knew what was in the woman's heart. He knew that she wanted to change her life and start obeying God.

How many times have you looked at someone and judged them by their appearance or by the rumors you have heard about them? It is easy to judge someone by the way they look, but it is much harder to be patient with them and to show God's love to them. We cannot know another person's true thoughts and feelings like Jesus does. But we can be like Jesus and have compassion on them. Will you do that today?

Prayer: *Lord, please forgive me for judging people by the way they look. Help me to be patient and to be like Jesus. In His name. Amen.*

Hair (6) by Jennifer Forrester   **Today's Reading:** 1 Peter 3:1-4

This is the last devotion in our series about hair. In our first devotion, we talked about the millions of dollars that people spend on hair care products alone. It is also estimated that men and women spend more than $352 billion annually for all kinds of products to make their hair, face and body look more beautiful. It is great if a person can be beautiful and maybe win a beauty contest. But it is even more important that their true beauty comes from a heart filled with love and desire to serve God.

In our Bible verses, Peter was talking about a woman's relationship to her husband. But I think that we can apply his advice to all people. In verses 3 and 4 Peter said, *"It is not fancy hair, gold jewelry, or fine clothes that should make you beautiful. No, your beauty should come from inside you – the beauty of a gentle and quiet spirit. That beauty will never disappear. It is worth very much to God."* This is the kind of beauty that is important to God.

You don't need to look into a mirror every day to see if you are beautiful or not. Instead, look into God's Word, the Bible. Are you applying God's words to your life? Are you trying to be like Jesus? If you are serving and obeying God every day, then you are truly beautiful!

Prayer: *Dear Loving God, I want to be truly beautiful for You. Help me to obey Your Word and to do what You want me to do every day. In Jesus' name. Amen.*

Clean Water by Rachel Burkum
Today's Reading: John 4:5-14

You may live in the United States, or you may be from another country. I'm in the US, and there are a lot of things I take for granted. One of those things is clean water. For the last few years, my church has been collecting money to send to a large mission that uses the money to dig new, clean water wells for people in India. The villages that receive these wells usually have no other source of clean water. Women and children must sometimes walk miles just to bring home a bucket of dirty water from a pond or stream where animals live. This creates a lot of sickness and even death. These people need clean water in order to survive.

The verses we read for today talk about Jesus meeting a woman at a well, and they discussed water. Jesus wasn't talking about literal water, though. He was talking about spiritual water. Jesus said, *"But anyone who drinks the water I give will never be thirsty again. The water I give people will be like a spring flowing inside them. It will bring them eternal life"* (verse 14). The woman was confused. But because we have the rest of the Bible, we can understand. We know that Jesus was talking about Himself and the salvation that He offers. His "water" is eternal life. By drinking it, this means we accept Him as our Lord and follow Him.

I take actual water for granted. But we should never take Jesus' "water" for granted.

Prayer: *Father, thank You for Your spiritual water — salvation through Your Son, Jesus. In His name. Amen.*

Run to the Name of the Lord by Gayle Thorn
Today's Reading: Proverbs 18:10

Throughout history, people have built buildings like towers, castles and forts to protect them from danger. Our Bible verse for today tells us, *"The name of the Lord is like a strong tower. Those who do what is right can run to him for protection."* God's very name is the tower or safe place for Christians. When Christians feel afraid, threatened or alone, we don't run to a building to feel safe. We run to the name of the Lord.

How can we do this? There are four ways we can run to the name of the Lord. First, we can run through our faith. That means we remind ourselves that God will always be there when we need Him. Second, we run through prayer. That means that we tell God our troubles and fears and ask Him for His help and protection. Third, we run through devotion. That means we commit our lives to God and obey Him, even in the middle of our fear. Fourth, we run through dependence. That means we trust only God to help and protect us. We know that no one else can do for us what God can do.

I hope that when you are afraid or struggling with problems that you will run to the name of the Lord for your help and protection. You can depend on God – He will never let you down.

Prayer: *Heavenly Father, forgive all the wrong things that I have done. Save me and become my "strong tower" today. In Jesus' name. Amen.*

Love Wins by Norma Mezoe   **Today's Reading:** Luke 6:27-36

Greg was a private in the army. He was ridiculed by his fellow soldiers because of his Christian witness. One sergeant in particular tried to break Greg's gentle spirit. One night Greg came in from guard duty. He was soaking wet and tired. But before he went to bed, Greg knelt to pray. As Greg was praying, the sergeant came into Greg's barracks. His boots were covered in mud, and he started kicking Greg, first on one side of the head, then on the other side. Greg didn't say a word but silently went on praying.

The next morning when the sergeant awoke, he found his boots beside his bed. All the mud was gone, and they were polished to a high gloss. That was how Greg responded to being kicked. That act of love and kindness melted the sergeant's heart, and that same day he gave his life to God and became a Christian.

Verses 27-28 of our Bible reading say, *"But I say to you people who are listening to me, love your enemies. Do good to those who hate you. Ask God to bless the people who ask for bad things to happen to you. Pray for the people who are mean to you."* Greg truly obeyed Jesus' words.

Even in the darkest times we can know that God's love will win. Treat others with God's love today!

Prayer: *Loving God, help me to be like Greg and be the right kind of witness for You. In Jesus' name. Amen.*

May 13

God's True Peace by Donna Howard   **Today's Reading:** Isaiah 26:1-6

In the weeks following my husband's unexpected death, I became overwhelmed with trying to do things that he normally took care of. I knew nothing about things such as changing a burned out light in the freezer, taking care of the bills, questions about our tax return or a driveway full of snow. I didn't know what to do. I walked around the kitchen, banging pots and pans to relieve my stress. I cried out, "Lord, please help me!"

Shortly after this, a neighbor called to see if I needed anything. He came over, flipped a small switch and restored the light in the freezer. A few minutes later, my son came and plowed the driveway. That afternoon, my daughter, who has owned a tax business for many years, called and assured me that she would help me with my finances. Then I truly had God's peace.

Later I scolded myself for having forgotten that God knows all my troubles and is always with me. And I remembered verses 3-4 of our Bible reading. *"God, you give true peace to people who depend on you, to those who trust in you. So trust the Lord always, because in the Lord Yah you have a place of safety forever."*

Are you overwhelmed with troubles today? Think about God's true peace and depend on Him.

Prayer: *Lord, thank You for Your true peace that. In Jesus' name. Amen.*

God's Time by Bonnie Hall   **Today's Reading:** Deuteronomy 9:1-21

In our Bible verses for today Moses continues giving instructions to the Israelites before they enter the new land that God had given to them. He explains that the people there are tall and strong. But in verse 3 Moses encourages them by telling them what God will do for them. *"But you can be sure that it is the Lord your God who goes across the river before you – and God is like a fire that destroys! He will destroy those nations and make them fall before you. You will force those nations out and quickly destroy them. The Lord has promised you that this will happen."*

Moses told the Israelites that God wasn't helping them because they were righteous people. In fact, they were very stubborn people. Moses reminded them of what they had done in the past when they became impatient while waiting for Moses to come back from meeting with God. Their impatience led them to rebel against God, build a golden calf and worship it. After that Moses was afraid for the people, so he prayed and fasted and asked God to keep the Israelites safe. God listened to Moses and did not destroy the people.

God's time is always right, and we need to learn to be patient and wait for God's answers. He always knows what is best for us, and He will give us just what we need at the right time.

Prayer: *Father, help me to be patient as I wait for You to answer my prayers according to Your will. In Jesus' name. Amen.*

Bible Missionaries (1) by Jo Krueger   **Today's Reading:** Luke 4:40-44

The word "mission" means a special job. So a missionary is a person who does a special job. Today, missionary usually means a person who does a special job for God. The Bible tells us about many people who were missionaries. These people told others the Good News about Jesus. Often these people were mistreated or even killed, but they kept talking about Jesus. Today and for the next few days, we will read about some of these missionaries.

The first missionary we will talk about is Jesus. Jesus used His whole life to share the Good News with other people. This Good News was that He came to earth to die for sinners and then rise again.

Jesus shared the Good News in several ways. First, Jesus did many miracles that showed He was powerful and that He was truly God's Son. Second, Jesus taught about God's plan for His life on earth. Jesus told His followers that His job was to come to earth and accept the punishment for their sins. In verse 43b of our Bible reading for today, Jesus said, *"I must tell the Good News about God's kingdom to other towns too. That is why I was sent."*

Jesus wants you to know the Good News, too. Study the Bible, read about Jesus' life and sacrifice and decide to follow Him every day.

Prayer: *Dear God, thank You so much for Your Son, Jesus, who told people about Your plan of salvation. In His name. Amen.*

Bible Missionaries (2) by Jo Krueger   **Today's Reading:** Acts 8:26-40

Acts 6:5 tells us about seven men who were chosen to help the people in the early church in Jerusalem. One of those men was Philip.

In our Bible reading for today, we learn that an angel told Philip to got to a road that led to Jerusalem. There Philip met a man from Ethiopia. This man was reading from the Old Testament book of Isaiah, but he did not understand what he was reading. So Philip explained that the verses were talking about Jesus.

Philip told the man more about Jesus and about His plan of salvation. Then the man said, *"Look, here is water! What is stopping me from being baptized?"* (verse 36b). They went down into the water and Philip baptized the man. Verse 39 tells us that the man was very happy. He returned to Ethiopia and hopefully he shared about Jesus with his family and friends.

Philip was a missionary. He shared the Good News about Jesus with many people. Wherever Philip went, he talked about salvation through Jesus. We should be like Philip. We should share Jesus with people we will meet today – the cashier at the grocery store, the person who delivers our mail and the neighbors who live next door to us. Ask God to help you be bold as you share His message with other people today.

Prayer: *God, I want to be like Philip and tell other people about Your Son, Jesus. In His name. Amen.*

Bible Missionaries (3) by Jo Krueger   **Today's Reading:** Acts 9:32-43

Peter, one of Jesus' twelve special disciples, was a missionary, too. Our Bible reading for today tells us that he traveled to the cities of Lydda and Joppa to see the Christians who lived there. While Peter was in those cities, he told people about Jesus.

When Peter was in Lydda, he met a man who was paralyzed. His name was Aeneas. Verse 33b tells us that Aeneas *"had not been able to get out of bed for the past eight years."* Peter healed Aeneas, and immediately he was able to walk again. This was something that could only happen with God's power. Many people heard about this miracle and believed in Jesus.

Our Bible verses also tell us about Tabitha. She was a woman who did kind things for other people and gave her money to people in need. But Tabitha became sick and died. Jesus' followers there asked Peter to come and help. Peter made Tabitha alive again. *"People everywhere in Joppa learned about this, and many believed in the Lord"* (verse 42).

God gave Peter the ability to do miracles, but his message was the same as our message – that Jesus died and rose again so we can have our sins forgiven. You can be like Peter and tell someone this wonderful news today!

Prayer: *Dear Heavenly Father, show me people that I can tell about Jesus today. In Jesus name. Amen.*

Bible Missionaries (4) by Jo Krueger   **Today's Reading:** Acts 10:34-48

At first, God's plan of salvation was only for His people, the Jews. But after Jesus died and arose from the dead, God wanted His gift of salvation to be offered to both Jews and non-Jews. God spoke to Peter in a dream and told him it was okay to share the Good News with non-Jews, too. This was probably something that was hard for Peter to do, but he obeyed God.

God led Peter to go to a non-Jew named Cornelius, a Roman army officer who worshiped God. Peter told Cornelius about Jesus and all He had done. Peter said he was an eye witness – he had seen Jesus' miracles and His resurrection from the dead. Then God sent His Holy Spirit on Cornelius and the people who were listening to Peter.

In verses 47-48a Peter said, *"How can anyone object to these people being baptized in water? They have received the Holy Spirit the same as we did!' So Peter told them to baptize Cornelius and his relatives and friends in the name of Jesus Christ."*

Before that time, Peter had only preached to Jews. Now he preached to non-Jews, too. Peter was able to share the Good News about Jesus with every person that he met. Maybe you have a friend who needs to know about Jesus. Tell that person about Jesus today and show them how they can live forever with God!

Prayer: *God, thank You for giving me the courage to share about Jesus with my friends. In Jesus' name. Amen.*

Bible Missionaries (5) by Jo Krueger   **Today's Reading:** Acts 12:1-17

It is not easy to be a missionary. Sometimes people do bad thing to missionaries. Why? Because these people want the missionaries to stop teaching about Jesus. Our Bible verses today tell us that King Herod did bad things to some Christians. He arrested Peter and put him in jail. Then he had a group of 16 soldiers guard Peter there.

An angel from God came to Peter while he was in jail. Then the angel helped Peter escape. In verse 11b Peter said, *"Now I know that the Lord really sent his angel to me. He rescued me from Herod and from everything those Jews thought would happen to me."* God took care of Peter and kept him safe.

The Bible is full of stories about how God took care of people who loved and obeyed Him. Sometimes it can be difficult to do what God wants you to do. But when you are a missionary, you need to remember that God will always take care of you.

Is there someone you know who needs to know about Jesus today? Don't be afraid. Depend on God's strength and protection to give you the right words to say and to keep you safe.

Prayer: *Father, I know that You will give me strength and protect me as I share the Good News about Jesus with others. In His name. Amen.*

Bible Missionaries (6) by Jo Krueger   **Today's Reading:** Acts 16:16-40

The next missionary we will talk about is Paul. Paul traveled to many cities throughout the Roman Empire to tell people about Jesus. The book of Acts tells us about some of Paul's travels.

One time Paul was traveling with Silas. They removed a demon from a young girl. The men who owned this girl became upset. They had Paul and Silas put in jail. While Paul and Silas were in jail, they prayed and sang praises to God. *"Suddenly there was an earthquake so strong that it shook the foundation of the jail. All the doors of the jail opened, and the chains on all the prisoners fell off"* (verse 26). Paul and Silas were freed from their chains.

The jailer was scared that Paul and Silas had escaped. But then he saw that they were still in the jail. He took Paul and Silas to his home, washed their wounds and gave them some food. Paul and Silas told the jailer and his family about Jesus. Verse 33b says that *"the jailer and all his people were baptized."* All the people were happy because they now believed in Jesus and followed Him.

Paul and Silas praised God, even though they were in jail. I hope that you will use every situation – good and bad – to tell people about Jesus. God will be with you and bless you as your share about His Son.

Prayer: *Dear Loving God, I praise You and thank You for all You have done for me. In Jesus' name. Amen.*

Bible Missionaries (7) by Jo Krueger   **Today's Reading:** Acts 20:7-12

Many wonderful things happened while Paul was a missionary. Our Bible reading today tells us about the time he was in the city of Troas. Paul preached to a group of Christians there. These people met together to share the Lord's Supper and to remember Jesus' sacrifice.

Verse 9 tells us what happened during the meeting. *"There was a young man named Eutychus sitting in the window. Paul continued talking, and Eutychus became very, very sleepy. Finally, he went to sleep and fell out of the window. He fell to the ground from the third floor. When the people went down and lifted him up, he was dead."* That was a terrible thing that happened! But the next verse tells us that Paul raised Eutychus from the dead. The people who witnessed this miracle must have been very happy and amazed.

God gave Paul the ability to do wonderful miracles. These miracles helped people believe the message Paul preached. Today we can read about these miracles in the Bible. This helps us to believe that God is powerful and that Jesus is His Son.

God was always with Paul, and He will be with you, too, as you share the Good News about Jesus with people that you meet every day. Ask God to help you be bold like Paul and to never stop telling people about Jesus.

Prayer: *Heavenly Father, I know that You are powerful. Thank You for the miracles that show us how awesome You are. In Jesus' name. Amen.*

Bible Missionaries (8) by Jo Krueger   Today's Reading: Acts 27:13-44

Paul had many interesting experiences as he traveled and told people about Jesus. Sometimes he would only stay in one place for a few days. Other times he would stay in a city for many months. To support himself, Paul made tents.

Our Bible verses for today tell us about one time that Paul was on a ship going to Rome. *"For many days we could not see the sun or the stars. The storm was very bad. We lost all hope of staying alive — we thought we would die"* (verse 20).

An angel told Paul that no one on the ship would die. Finally the ship *"hit a sandbank. The front of the ship stuck there and could not move. The big waves began to break the back of the ship to pieces"* (verse 41b). The ship was destroyed, but Paul and the other passengers were safe.

Paul faced many other bad things while he was traveling as a missionary. Everywhere he went, people wanted to stop him from telling about Jesus. He was beaten and put in jail several times. But Paul trusted God to take care of him. And God gave Paul the courage to be strong.

You can be a missionary today – tell someone you meet about Jesus. And remember that God will always be with you and help you to be strong.

Prayer: *Dear God, I know You will be with me today as I share Jesus with others. In Jesus' name. Amen.*

Bible Missionaries (9) by Jo Krueger   Today's Reading: Acts 28:16-31

Finally Paul reached the city of Rome, but he was a Roman prisoner. Our Bible reading tells us that in Rome *"Paul was allowed to live alone. But a soldier stayed with him to guard him"* (verse 16b). What a blessing that must have been that Paul could stay in a house instead a prison!

It was God's plan for Paul to be in Rome. Even though Paul was a prisoner, he continued to share about Jesus with the people he met. Paul did not let his circumstances keep him from talking about Jesus. Verses 30 and 31 say, *"Paul stayed two full years in his own rented house. He welcomed all the people who came and visited him. He told them about God's kingdom and taught about the Lord Jesus Christ. He was very bold, and no one tried to stop him from speaking."*

Maybe you are facing bad circumstances in your life. Maybe you are sick or having family or financial problems. You can still be a missionary for Jesus. In fact, through your bad circumstances, God may help you meet people who need to know about His Son.

Ask God to help you be a bold missionary among your friends and family members today.

Prayer: *Dear God, no matter what happens today, please help me to share with someone about Jesus. In His name. Amen.*

Bible Missionaries (10) by Jo Krueger   **Today's Reading:** Matthew 28:16-20

Today is the last devotion in the series about Bible missionaries. The last missionary we will talk about is YOU! If you are a Christian, then you need to be a missionary for Jesus.

The verses in our Bible reading today are some of the last words Jesus spoke on earth. Jesus' words are repeated in Mark 16:14-20. Mark 16:19 tells us, *"After the Lord Jesus said these things to his followers, he was carried up into heaven. There, Jesus sat at the right side of God."*

Jesus was speaking to His followers who were with Him, but I believe those words are for us, too. Jesus does not simply suggest that we should talk to people about Him if we feels like it or if we have the time. Jesus *commands* us to do this in verses 19-20a. *"So go and make followers of all people in the world. Baptize them in the name of the Father, and the Son and the Holy Spirit. Teach them to obey everything that I have told you to do."*

We should obey Jesus' command to teach and baptize people. These new Christians will teach other people. Then God's church will grow and grow. Why? Because we are missionaries who share the Good News about Jesus and His wonderful plan of salvation!

Prayer: *Father, I want to be Your missionary today. Show me how I can reach out to others with Your life-saving message. In Jesus' name. Amen.*

Share with Others by Bonnie Hall   **Today's Reading:** Deuteronomy 15:1-18

In our Bible verses for today, Moses gave the Israelites God's specific instructions about debts and helping poor people. In verses 4 and 5 he said, *"There should not be any poor people in your country, because the Lord your God is giving you this land. And the Lord will greatly bless you. But this will happen only if you obey the Lord your God. You must be careful to obey every command that I have told you today."*

Then in verses 7 and 8, Moses added more of God's instructions, *"When you are living in the land the Lord your God is giving you, there might be some poor people living among you. You must not be selfish. You must not refuse to give help to them. You must be willing to share with them. You must lend them whatever they need."* God's instructions were very clear. He expected the Israelites to obey, and if they obeyed, He would bless and protect them. But if they rebelled and did not obey, God would punish them with terrible things.

Just like the Israelites, we have opportunities to share with people in need. We can give a homeless person a place to live, help a disabled person around their house or share a meal with someone who is hungry. If we do these kinds of things, God will bless us.

Look around you today. What can you do to help someone in need?

Prayer: *Dear Lord, thank You for blessing and taking care of me. Show me how I can share with someone in need today. In Jesus' name. Amen.*

Son of Man by Gayle Thorn
Today's Reading: Mark 10:35-45

Mark 10:45 says, *"Follow my example: Even the Son of Man did not come for people to serve him. He came to serve others and to give his life to save many people."* The "Son of Man" mentioned in this verse is Jesus. God sent Jesus to earth to live the life of a human. Jesus was sent by God to be someone who felt and experienced everything that we feel and experience. But Jesus was to do it perfectly, without sinning. Disobeying God was something Jesus was unable to do if He was to be our Savior.

For about 33 years, Jesus lived on earth in a human body. Jesus willingly chose to set aside all the power and privileges of being God to put on a human body of flesh and bones. Why was He willing to do this? Jesus did that to give us the opportunity to become free from sin.

Because Jesus was able to live His human life in perfect obedience to God, we can have life that lasts forever. We can't earn eternal life. We do not obey God perfectly, but God still gives us life that lasts forever because of Jesus. He is God's Son, and He lived a perfectly obedient life on earth as the Son of Man.

Thank God today that Jesus was willing to come to earth and die for you. You can show your thankfulness by depending on the Holy Spirit to help you obey Him every day.

Prayer: *Heavenly Father, thank You for sending Jesus to die for me Help me to rely on the Holy Spirit to help me obey You. In Jesus' name. Amen.*

Only Follow God by Bonnie Hall
Today's Reading: Deuteronomy 13:1-11

There are many people in the world today who want to draw us away from serving God. People show us things that look good like wealth and fame. Or they show us how we can avoid responsibility and always take the easy way out. But we need to remember what Moses told the Israelites in verse 4 of our Bible reading. *"You must follow the Lord your God. Respect him. Obey his commands and do what he tells you. Serve the Lord your God, and never leave him."*

Just like today, the Israelites met people who told them false prophecies or tried to persuade them to follow other gods. Moses told them to refuse to listen to these people, even if they were friends or family members. In fact, Moses instructed them to get rid of the people who were worshiping false gods. Then the Israelites would not be influenced to fall away from God.

Often we are not able to control the people in the world who want to pull us away from God. But we can control what we read in books and on the Internet, what we watch on TV and the people who are our friends. We need to keep ourselves pure and continue to stay close to God. Then we will become stronger and it will be easier to trust and obey Him.

Remember to only follow God. Ask God to help you stand strong on His Word!

Prayer: *God, I want to make choices in life that bring me closer to You, not draw me away from You. In Jesus' name. Amen.*

Test Your Motives by Gayle Thorn **Today's Reading:** Proverbs 16:1-3

When was the last time you asked yourself why you do the things you do? If it's been a while, now is a good time to test your motives.

Proverbs 16:2 says *"People think that whatever they do is right, but the Lord judges their reason for doing it."* We need to be careful that everything we do is done for the right reasons. Everything we do should be done to please and honor God. We need to regularly examine our motives and adjust our actions to align with that goal.

How can you do that? Here is a way to examine your motives. Make a list of all the things you do. Include daily devotions, prayer, volunteer work, helping people and any other activities that you do. Next, ask yourself these questions about each activity: 1) Am I doing this to impress people? 2) Am I doing this to impress God? 3) Am I doing this to attract attention to myself? 4) Am I doing this to bring honor and attention to Christ?

Look at your answers. If you answered "Yes" to questions 1, 2 or 3, stop doing those things. If you sincerely answered "Yes" to question 4, then keep doing those activities.

You may be able to fool people into believing that you are serving God with pure motives, but you can't fool God. He knows the truth!

Prayer: *Dear Heavenly Father, search me and know my heart. Forgive and cleanse me. In Jesus' name. Amen.*

Hanging in There by Donna Howard **Today's Reading:** Luke 6:20-23

I am normally a joyful person, but over the last two months, my heart and life have been filled with gloom and sadness. For three weeks my life was filled with unexpected trips to the hospital to visit my sick husband, Lynn, and then, the love of my life was gone. Lynn and I were married for more than 67 wonderful years. We raised a family of three beautiful children, laughed together and shared many great times together. Now sadness has filled my heart and life. When family and friends ask me how I am doing, I reply, "I'm hanging in there!"

Last week I saw a man who had known my husband for many years. He had seen my husband's obituary in the newspaper, so he asked me, "How are you doing?" When I replied, "I'm hanging in there," he smiled. He told me that he had lost his wife a few months earlier. He, too, was overwhelmed by her death, but as a Christian he had decided to change his outlook. He said, "Now when people ask me how I'm doing," I tell them "I'm hanging in there with Jesus!"

Verse 21b of our Bible reading says, *"Great blessings belong to you who are crying now. You will be happy and laughing."* I know there will come a day when I will happy and laughing when I see my Savior in heaven. But for now, I am hanging in there with Jesus!

Prayer: *Father, thank You for being with me during my times of sorrow and for giving me the hope of eternal life with You. In Jesus' name. Amen.*

Son of God by Gayle Thorn   Today's Reading: John 20:31

The best person to describe a father to someone is that father's child. John 20:31 says, *"But these are written so that you can believe that Jesus is the Messiah, the Son of God. Then, by believing, you can have life through his name."* Jesus is the Son of God. As God's Son, Jesus is in the unique position of being best qualified to describe and reveal to us just what kind of father God is.

That is just what Jesus did while He was on earth. Jesus used His words and actions to describe His Father. Jesus wanted His disciples to know His Father.

Jesus is still showing us what His Father is like today. Jesus uses His Holy Spirit and His Word to teach about His Father and what His Father did for us. God sent Jesus to die because He loves us. Jesus said in John 3:16 that His Father loved us *"so much that he gave his only Son, so that everyone who believes in him would not be lost but have eternal life."*

Jesus wants you to believe that His Father loves you and sent Jesus to die for you so that you, too, can be a child of God.

Are you a part of God's family? If not, you can join God's family by accepting Jesus as Your Lord and Savior and obeying Him.

Prayer: *Heavenly Father, I believe that You sent Jesus to die for me. Thank You for making a way for me to become Your child. In Jesus' name. Amen.*

No Gimmicks by Jennifer Forrester   Today's Reading: Acts 2:22-39

Recently my husband and I were taken in by a gimmick. A gimmick is a scheme or a plan to get your attention. We started watching three years of a 1990s TV show on a free streaming service. Several times a week we would watch new episodes. Last week we were nearing the end of the 3rd season. We watched an episode that had two parts. The first part ended with us not knowing what was going to happen next, so we were anxious to see the last episode. But when we turned it on, the screen said that we had to sign up for a paid subscription to watch that last episode. We were very disappointed.

It is so wonderful that God does not use gimmicks to draw us to Him. God is exactly who He says He is and His Word, the Bible, is true – it has no tricks or schemes. God doesn't promise us one thing and then turn around and give us something else. That's what Peter talked about in verses 23b-24 of our Bible reading he said, *"God knew all this would happen. It was his plan – a plan he made long ago. Jesus suffered the pain of death, but God made him free. He raised him from death. There was no way for death to hold him."*

You can depend on God and His Word. Follow Him and obey His Word today!

Prayer: *God, thank You for always being truthful with me. And thank You that I can depend on Your Word. In Jesus' name. Amen.*

Three Faithful Men (1) by Rachel Burkum   **Today's Reading:** Daniel 3:1-30

Daniel, chapter 3, is a long chapter to read, but I want you to know the whole story about three faithful men. The king of Babylon ordered that a very large, golden idol be made, and a new law was announced – everyone who heard the special music must immediately bow down and worship the statue. The king had created a false god, and he was forcing all the people to worship it.

Shadrach, Meshach and Abednego were Israelites who had been taken to Babylon. They had faith in the one true God, so they refused to bow down and worship the statue. When the king learned about these three men, he gave them one more chance. He explained the new law to them again. But in verse 18 the three men said, *"we refuse to serve your gods."*

The king became very angry and ordered his soldiers to throw Shadrach, Mechach and Abednego into a blazing hot furnace. It was obvious that anyone who went into the furnace would surely die. But did the three men change their minds? No! Even though they faced death, they refused to worship anything other than the one true God. They would not compromise their faith for any reason.

These three faithful men are a wonderful example for us today. How strong is your faith? Would you face death for God?

Prayer: *Father, I want to be faithful only to You. Please help me to have a strong faith like these three men. In Jesus' name. Amen.*

Three Faithful Men (2) by Rachel Burkum   **Today's Reading:** Daniel 3:1-30

Today we will continue learning about Shadrach, Meshach and Abednego. If you have read chapter 3 of Daniel, you know how the story ends. But I want to focus especially on verses 17 and 18. The three men said, *"If you throw us into the hot furnace, the God we serve can save us. And if he wants to, he can save us from your power. But even if God does not save us, we want you to know, King, that we refuse the serve your gods. We will not worship the gold idol you have set up."*

The three men had great faith. They knew God was powerful enough to save them, even from a furnace full of extremely hot fire. No physical body could survive, and they knew that. But they also knew God has control over everything and could save them if He wanted. The most interesting thing about these verses though, is when they said, *"But even if God does not save us . . ."*

Shadrach, Meshach and Abednego understood that what God wants is not always the same as what we want. I am sure these men didn't want to die! But they knew it was in God's hands, not theirs. And even if God decided not to save their lives, they would not give in to the king's demands. What a wonderful lesson for us today. God may not do things exactly the way we want, but we must always continue to have faith in His perfect plans.

Prayer: *Dear God, I know You are in control. I know Your plans are perfect. Help me to trust You no matter what. In Jesus' name. Amen.*

Three Faithful Men (3) by Rachel Burkum   Today's Reading: Daniel 3:1-30

In this last devotion from Daniel, chapter 3, I would like to take us to the end of this story. Did you read the entire chapter? If you did, you know that the king of Babylon tried to force Shadrach, Meshach and Abednego to worship a golden idol. They refused because they were faithful only to God.

As punishment, these three men were thrown into a furnace that was so hot, the soldiers who forced them inside died themselves! But Shadrach, Meshach and Abednego lived. And when the king called them back out of the furnace, they didn't even smell like smoke! Nothing on them was burned at all. It was an amazing miracle!

It would have been easy to praise these three men. Witnesses might have thought it was their own power that saved them. Or maybe the men had magic or special abilities. But the king recognized who the powerful One was. *"No other god can save his people like this"* (verse 29b). Shadrach, Meshach and Abednego showed extremely strong faith. But it was God who was glorified.

When wonderful things happen in our lives, it's important to remember nothing happens without God's power. We should always work on strengthening our faith. But God is the One who deserves all the praise!

Prayer: *God, You are all-powerful. Please help me to learn from these three faithful men. I want to always give You praise. In Jesus' name. Amen.*

Paul's Travels (1) by Jo Krueger   Today's Reading: Mark 16:14-18

On the Day of Pentecost, Peter preached to a large group of people about Jesus. Over 3000 people were baptized and became Christians that day. That was the start of God's church in Jerusalem. Soon the church spread to other areas beyond Jerusalem and many more people started following Jesus. This growth happened because Paul and other Christians traveled and shared the Good News about Jesus. Paul also wrote letters to churches to encourage them and help them be strong Christians.

When Paul went on a missionary journey, he took other Christians with him. For the next seven days we will look at some of the people who traveled with Paul to help him spread the Gospel.

As Paul told people about Jesus, he was obeying the command that Jesus gave His followers in our Bible reading for today. *"He said to them, 'Go everywhere in the world. Tell the Good News to everyone. Whoever believes and is baptized will be saved. But those who do not believe will be judged guilty'"* (verses 15-16). That command was for Jesus' followers at that time as well as for us today.

You can be a missionary like Paul, too. Find someone who doesn't know about Jesus today and tell them about God's love and gift of salvation.

Prayer: *Dear God, I want to share the Good News about Jesus with someone today. Help me to be bold like Paul. In Jesus' name. Amen.*

Paul's Travels (2) by Jo Krueger   **Today's Reading:** 2 Timothy 4:11-18

One man who is mentioned several times as Paul's traveling companion is Luke. Colossians 4:14 tells us that Luke was a doctor. He also wrote the New Testament books of Luke and Acts. The book of Luke tells us about Jesus' birth, ministry, death and resurrection, and the book of Acts tells about the start and growth of the church.

There are several sections in the book of Acts where Luke uses the pronoun "we." This shows us that at those times, Luke was traveling with Paul. Acts 16:10 says, *"After Paul had seen the vision, we immediately prepared to leave for Macedonia. We understood that God had called us to tell the Good News to those people."*

In our Bible reading for today, Paul wrote to Timothy. Paul wanted Timothy to come help him. In verse 11a Paul says, *"Luke is the only one still with me."* This shows us that Luke was Paul's good friend. Luke faithfully obeyed God and helped Paul tell people about Jesus. Luke may have been with Paul to also help him with any physical problems that he had.

Do you want to be like Luke and help other Christians? If so, you can support and encourage your Christian friends to grow closer to Jesus. And don't forget to pray for them, too!

Prayer: *Father, thank You for my Christian friends. Show me how I can encourage them in their Christians lives. In Jesus' name. Amen.*

June 6

Paul's Travels (3) by Jo Krueger   **Today's Reading:** Acts 9:26-28

Barnabas was a man from the island of Cyprus in the Mediterranean Sea. Acts 4:36-37 tells us that Barnabas' name means *"one who encourages others."* These verses also tell us that Barnabas sold some land and gave the money to the apostles so they could help Christians in need. And Acts, chapters 13 and 14, tell us that Barnabas traveled with Paul on one of his missionary journeys.

Barnabas was truly a person who encouraged other Christians. In our Bible verses for today, we learn how Barnabas encouraged Paul (also called Saul). Paul was a person who had done many bad things to Christians. Then Paul learned about Jesus and became a Christian. But some Christians did not trust Paul. They thought that he would do bad things to them, too. *"But Barnabas accepted Saul and took him to the apostles. He told them how Saul had seen the Lord on the road and how the Lord had spoken to Saul. Then he told them how boldly Saul had spoken for the Lord in Damascus"* (verse 27). Barnabas helped Paul be accepted as a person who loved Jesus and told others about Him.

Barnabas truly encouraged Paul as he grew in his Christian faith. Look for ways today that you can serve and encourage your Christian brothers and sisters like Barnabas did.

Prayer: *Dear God, thank You for the example of Barnabas. I want to be like him and encourage others. In Jesus' name. Amen.*

Paul's Travels (4) by Jo Krueger   Today's Reading: Galatians 2:1-3

Our Bible reading for today tells us about a man named Titus. He was a Greek man who learned about Jesus and became a Christian. Verse 1 tells us that Titus traveled with Paul and Barnabas when they went to Jerusalem. In Titus 1:4 Paul called Titus *"a true son to me in the faith we share together."*

Later Paul traveled with Titus to the island of Crete. When Paul moved on, he left Titus on Crete to *"finish doing what still needed to be done"* and to *"choose men to be elders in every town"* (Titus 1:5). Paul trusted Titus to carry on his church work. Later Paul wrote a letter to Titus to help him do his work. This letter is the book of Titus in the New Testament.

Titus grew from a new Christian into a man who was able to carry on the work Paul had started in the churches on Crete. Titus became a strong leader with the help of Paul and other Christians.

We need to be like Titus and continue to grow in Christ every day. Reading the Bible, worshiping, praying and fellowshipping with our brothers and sisters in Christ are ways that we can become stronger Christians. Be sure that you are doing those things so that you can have a close relationship with Jesus and grow like Titus did.

Prayer: *Dear God, thank You for Christian friends who help me grow every day. In Jesus' name. Amen.*

Paul's Travels (5) by Jo Krueger   Today's Reading: 2 Timothy 1:1-8

Timothy was another young man who traveled with Paul. Like Titus, Paul called Timothy *"a dear son to me"* (1 Timothy 1:2). In verse 3a of our Bible reading for today, Paul told Timothy, *"I always remember you in my prayers day and night. And in these prayers I thank God for you."* Paul truly loved Timothy and helped him to grow in Jesus.

Our Bible verses today also tell us about Timothy's background. His father was Greek, and his mother was a Jew. Timothy's mother, Eunice, and grandmother, Lois, taught him how to have faith in God.

In 1 Thessalonians 3:1b-2, Paul tells us more about Timothy. *"Timothy is our brother. He works with us for God to tell people the Good News about Christ. We sent Timothy to strengthen and encourage you in your faith."* Timothy became a strong Christian because of his faith in God. That faith was taught to him by his mother and grandmother.

Reading about Timothy should be a reminder to us that we need to teach our children, our grandchildren and the children in our neighborhood about God. Show them God's love and share His Word with them. Then they can become strong Christians like Timothy.

Prayer: *God, thank You for the children in my life. Be with me as I teach them about You. In Jesus' name. Amen.*

Paul's Travels (6) by Jo Krueger   **Today's Reading: Acts 16:16-34**

Another Christian who traveled with Paul was Silas. Acts 15:22 tells us that Silas was a man *"respected by the believers."*

Our Bible reading for today talks about a time when Paul and Silas were in the city of Philippi. While they were there, they met a servant girl. She had a spirit from the devil that helped her *"tell what would happen in the future"* (verse 16). Paul commanded the evil spirit to leave the girl. The men who owned the girl were upset *"because they could no longer use her to make money"* (verse 19). So Paul and Silas were thrown into jail.

What did Paul and Silas do in jail? Did they complain about their situation? No! *"About midnight Paul and Silas were praying and singing songs to God"* (verse 25a). God sent an earthquake to shake the building and free Paul and Silas from their chains. Then they were able to tell the jailer and his family about Jesus. The jailer took Paul and Silas to his home, and he and all the people in his household were baptized.

Maybe you will face family, job or financial problems today. Will you complain about your problems and feel sorry for yourself? Or will you sing and praise God like Paul and Silas did?

Prayer: *Dear Father, help me to praise You when I am facing difficult situations. In Jesus' name. Amen.*

Paul's Travels (7) by Jo Krueger   **Today's Reading: Romans 16:3-4**

In Acts, chapter 18, we learn about a Christian husband and wife named Aquila and Priscilla. *"They were tentmakers, the same as Paul, so he stayed with them and worked with them"* (Acts 18:3). Aquila and Priscilla traveled to the city of Ephesus and helped Paul spread the Good News about Jesus to the people who lived in that city.

We do not know a lot about Aquila and Priscilla, but our Bible reading for today tells us some important things about them. First, Paul says that they worked with him for Christ Jesus (verse 3). Second, Paul says in verse 4a, *"They risked their own lives to save mine."*

Aquila and Priscilla were willing to die so that Paul's life could be saved. They were strong Christians, and they knew that God would take care of them in every situation they had to face. They were willing to suffer persecution and even death so that people could hear and receive the message about Jesus' salvation and eternal life.

No matter what circumstances you will face in the future, you can know that God is your protection and source of strength. Be like Aquila and Priscilla and depend on Him!

Prayer: *Dear God, thank You for protecting me and giving me strength. Help me to be like Aquila and Priscilla. In Jesus' name. Amen.*

Paul's Travels (8) by Jo Krueger

Today's Reading: 2 Timothy 4:9-10

The last few days we have talked about some strong Christians who traveled and worked with Paul. The final person we will talk about who traveled with Paul was Demas. He is mentioned in Philemon 24 as someone who worked together with Paul. Demas was working with Paul when he wrote his letter to the Christians in the city of Colossae (Colossians 4:14).

But the story about Demas is not a happy story. In verse 10a of our Bible reading Paul says, *"Demas loved this world too much. That is why he left me."* We don't know for sure what happened, but it seems that Demas wanted to serve the world more than he wanted to serve God. Paul was probably very sad that Demas chose to stop following Jesus.

Serving God is not always easy. Sometimes we may look at exciting things in the world and think that it would be easier to stop following God. But we need to remember that serving God is the very most important thing we can do as we live on earth.

Today you may need to make some choices about serving God or serving the world. Don't be like Demas. Don't stop serving God. Serve Him with all your heart, your soul and your strength.

Prayer: *Lord, I want to serve You today. Help me keep my life focused on You. In Jesus' name. Amen.*

The Master's Hand by Donna Howard

Today's Reading: John 14:27-29

Our dog, Max, is afraid of thunderstorms. He is terrified of loud booms and lightning strikes, especially at night. Max sleeps on a large pillow in one corner of our bedroom. When the thunder rolls, he wakes up, jumps up and runs to his master's bedside. Standing on his hind legs, Max reaches for his master's hand and touches it with his cold nose. This awakens my husband, and he reaches down and pets Max and tells him it will be okay. Content to know that his master is near, Max returns to his bed and goes back to sleep.

When I am facing problems and struggles in life, I think I understand how Max feels during a thunderstorm. And I think that's how Jesus' disciples were feeling in our Bible verses for today. Jesus had told them he was going away, and they were scared. But in verse 27 Jesus said, *"I leave you peace. It is my own peace I give you. I give you peace in a different way than the world does. So don't be troubled. Don't be afraid."*

How can I touch the Master's hand and receive His peace? By reading the Bible! When I read Jesus' words in the Bible, I am assured that He loves me and that He is always with me. So if you are afraid today, open your Bible and receive Jesus' words of comfort. Then you will feel at peace.

Prayer: *God, thank You for always being near me. Help me to receive Jesus' peace and comfort through Your Word. In Jesus' name. Amen.*

Celebrate! by Bonnie Hall
Today's Reading: Deuteronomy 16:1-17

Do you like to celebrate special occasions with your family and friends? The festivals of the Israelites helped them to celebrate God and to remember all the good things He had done for them. In our Bible reading for today, Moses explained about three festivals they were to celebrate every year.

The first festival the Israelites were to celebrate was the Passover. This was to honor the time when God brought them out of slavery in Egypt. The second festival was the Festival of Harvest which started at the beginning of the harvest season. In verse 10 Moses said, *"Then celebrate the Festival of Harvest for the Lord your God. Do this by bringing him some special gift you want to bring. Decide how much to give by thinking about how much the Lord your God has blessed you."*

The third time of celebration was the Festival of Shelters. This festival was celebrated for seven days after the harvest was completed. Moses said, *"Do this to honor the Lord your God. The Lord your God blessed your harvest and all the work you did, so be very happy!"* (verse 15b).

These verses remind us that we need to stop and praise and honor God for all He has done in our lives. Take some time today to celebrate and give thanks to God!

Prayer: *Thank You, Father, for Your goodness and the many ways You have blessed me through my life. In Jesus' name. Amen.*

Learning by Example by Bob La Forge
Today's Reading: John 13:5-15

One winter a friend said he wanted to take me skiing. I had never skied, so I bought a book about it. I envisioned each technique until I thought I understood the fundamentals of the sport. I told my friend, "I know how to do this!" Needless to say, I went down the slope on my side, my skis and poles trailing behind me. I learned the lesson that the best way to learn to ski was to watch my friend and follow his example.

When we read the New Testament, we can learn from Jesus' words. But Jesus also showed us what we should do by His example. In our Bible reading today, Jesus taught a lesson on humility when He washed His disciples' feet. *"I am your Lord and Teacher. But I washed your feet. So you also should wash each other's feet. I did this as an example for you. So you should serve each other just as I served you"* (verse 14-15).

Jesus experienced life just like we experience it today. He was tempted just like we are, but He set the example of resisting the devil and turning away from sin. Jesus was treated unfairly and even killed, but He gave us His example of love and forgiveness.

Think about what Jesus did for you today. Then follow His example and live a life that is filled with His goodness and love!

Prayer: *Father, thank You for sending Jesus to die for me and for His example of living for You. In Jesus' name. Amen.*

The Door (1) by Jody Bethards

Today's Reading: Genesis 4:1-8

For today and the next few days, we will talk about "doors" that are mentioned in the Bible and how they can apply to our Christian lives.

Today we will learn about two brothers that were born to Adam and Eve. Abel was a shepherd, and Cain was a farmer. At harvest time, Cain brought some of the food he had grown as an offering to God. But Abel brought the best lamb from his flock. God accepted Abel's offering, but He did not accept Cain's offering. Cain became very angry. Verse 7 of our Bible reading says, *"You know that if you do what is right, I will accept you. But if you don't, sin is ready to attack you. That sin will want to control you, but you must control it."* Some Bible translations say, "sin is crouching at the door." When Cain became angry, the temptation to sin was waiting for him to do something wrong. Eventually Cain gave in to that sin, and he killed Abel.

There are times in our lives when we become angry or disappointed when things aren't going our way. We may think negative thoughts on how to get even with the person who hurt us. We must control our negative thoughts, pray for forgiveness and forgive the people who have hurt us.

Is sin crouching at the door of your heart? If so, then don't open the door! Instead, follow God's example of love and forgiveness.

Prayer: *Heavenly Father, help me to stay true to You and to turn away from the temptation to sin. In Jesus' name. Amen.*

The Door (2) by Jody Bethards

Today's Reading: Genesis 6:1-7:24

Chapters 6-8 of Genesis tell the story about Noah and his family. Genesis 6:5-6 tell us, *"The Lord saw that the people on the earth were very evil. He saw that they thought only about evil things all the time. The Lord was sorry that he had made people on the earth. It made him very sad in his heart. But Noah pleased God. God told Noah to build a large boat according to His instructions."* Noah obeyed God's instructions, and after the boat was completed, God sent pairs of animals to go into the boat. After the animals were in the boat, *"the Lord closed the door behind Noah"* (Genesis 7:16b).

It took Noah many years to build the large boat. During those years Noah warned the people that they needed to repent and follow God. But no one listened to him. Probably some people laughed at Noah and made fun of him. Then it must have been an amazing sight to see the long line of animals entering the boat. When all this was done, God's hand shut the one and only door of the boat.

That door of the ark is a picture of the way we can receive salvation. The people and animals who entered the boat through the door were saved. Jesus said that He is "the door" and that the only way to God is through Him. If we reject Jesus, a time will come when God will shut that door and it will be too late! Be sure that you are following Jesus today and that you have accepted His gift of salvation.

Prayer: *Dear Lord, thank You for Jesus — the open door through whom I can receive Your mercy and grace. In Jesus' name. Amen.*

The Door (3) by Jody Bethards   **Today's Reading:** Exodus 12:21-27

The Israelites were slaves in Egypt for more than 400 years. God chose Moses to lead the Israelites to freedom. But Pharaoh's heart was hardened, and he refused to let the Israelites go. So God sent 10 terrible plagues to show His power and to convince Pharaoh to change his mind. But Pharaoh's heart remained hardened until the tenth plague. Moses said that this last plague would be one of death for the firstborn of Egypt.

In order to save the Israelites from this plague, Moses told them what they should do. They were to kill a lamb, take the blood and spread it on the door frames of their houses. *"At the time the Lord goes through Egypt to kill the firstborn, he will see the blood on the sides and top of each door frame. Then he will protect that house and not let the Destroyer come into any of your houses and hurt you"* (verse 23). It happened just as God said it would, and the Israelites were protected by the blood on the doors.

Just as the Israelites had to kill a lamb, Jesus had to die on the cross. Through Jesus' blood, we receive God's forgiveness and we are cleansed of our sins. When we accept Jesus as our Lord and Savior, our sins are forgiven and we will live forever with Him.

Thank God today for Jesus' sacrifice on the cross for you!

Prayer: *Thank You, Lord, that Jesus' blood covers my sins and that I can live forever with You. In Jesus' name. Amen.*

The Door (4) by Jody Bethards   **Today's Reading:** John 10:1-10

In the Gospel books of Matthew, Mark, Luke and John, Jesus used the phrase "I Am" to explain who He was. In verse 9 of today's Bible reading, Jesus said, *"I am the gate. Whoever enters through me will be saved. They will be able to come in and go out. They will find everything they need."* Some Bible translations use the word "door" instead of gate.

There is only one way to go in and out of the sheep pen. In the same way, there is only one way that we can be saved. In John 14:6 Jesus said, *"I am the way, the truth, and the life. The only way to the Father is through me."* The only way for us to receive salvation is through God's Son, Jesus.

The world is full of people who talk about different ways to be saved. Some people say that "all roads lead to God." That is not true. The only way to God is through Jesus. He came to work as a humble servant and shared His Gospel message of love. Then Jesus offered Himself as the sacrificial lamb. He suffered and died an excruciating death so that we can be saved through His blood. When we accept His sacrifice, we enter through the door and find peace and comfort.

Be sure that you are paying attention to God's Word, the Bible, and following it so you can enter through the door of Jesus.

Prayer: *Dear Lord, thank You for the door through which we can enter and be saved from our sins. In Jesus' name. Amen.*

The Door (5) by Jody Bethards   **Today's Reading:** Revelation 3:14-20

Today is the last devotion about doors mentioned in the Bible. In Revelation, chapter 3, Jesus gave a message and a warning to the Christians in the city of Laodicea. He said that these people were not for Him or against Him – that they were lukewarm. And Jesus said was ready to spit them out of His mouth!

Jesus was not happy with these people. They called themselves Christians but were not truly following Him. So in verses 19 and 20, He offered a solution. *"I correct and punish the people I love. So show that nothing is more important to you than living right. Change your hearts and lives. Here I am! I stand at the door and knock. If you hear my voice and open the door, I will come in and eat with you. And you will eat with me."* Jesus said that He was standing at the door of their hearts, knocking and asking them to follow and obey Him again.

If you have turned away from following God, Jesus stands at the door of your heart and knocks. But it is up to you to respond and open your life to Him. You can do that by asking for forgiveness and living for Him every day. Remember Jesus' words in Matthew 11:28-29. *"Come to me all of you who are tired from the heavy burden you have been forced to carry. I will give you rest. Accept my teaching. Learn from me. I am gentle and humble in spirit. And you will be able to get some rest."*

Prayer: *Heavenly Father, I have opened the door of my heart to You. Help me to be close to You each day. In Jesus' name. Amen.*

Study God's Word by Bonnie Hall   **Today's Reading:** Deuteronomy 17:14-20

In Deuteronomy, chapter 17, Moses continued to give the Israelites instructions on how they should live in the new land that God was giving to them. In our Bible verses, Moses talked about choosing a king to rule over them. He reminded them that they must choose the king that God wanted them to have. Then in verses 18 and 19 he said, *"When the king begins to rule, he must write a copy of the law for himself in a book. He must make that copy from the books that the priests from the tribe of Levi keep. He must keep that book with him and read from it all his life, because he must learn to respect the Lord his God. He must learn to completely obey everything the law commands."*

Wow! That's sounds like a lot of work for the king to do – copy all God's laws, read those laws every day and obey all of them. But God knew that the king needed to set an example for the Israelites. If the king knew God's law and obeyed it, then the people would be willing to follow his example. When the whole nation was following God, then He would bless them and give them a time of peace.

If it was important for the king to study God's Word, then it is equally important for us to do the same. Think about the time you spend each day in God's Word. Maybe you need to be more diligent in reading the Bible every day. Then ask God to show you how you can apply His words to your life.

Prayer: *Lord, I know it is very important for me to study Your Word. Please bless me as I read and study today. In Jesus' name. Amen.*

Not Playing Fair by Pam Davis

My earliest playmates were my older sister and the children in our neighborhood. Our parents always taught us to be kind and play fair. When I was in gym class in school, the coaches taught me the basic rules of basketball and volleyball. They also taught that our behavior was important – we needed to play fair by following the rules. As an adult, I watch high school football. I don't know all the rules, but I do know that the players are encouraged to always play fair.

Maybe you have heard someone say, "Life's not fair!" That is certainly true in our world today. Good people are often punished while those who commit crimes are free to do more bad things. But there's one thing I know for sure – the devil doesn't play fair. He knows that he is losing and that Jesus will come again soon to take His followers to live with Him forever. So the devil will use all his tricks to try and get us to turn away from God. Verse 12 of our Bible reading says, *"So rejoice, you heavens and all who live there! But it will be terrible for the earth and sea, because the devil has gone down to you. He is filled with anger. He knows he doesn't have much time."*

The devil is busy in the world today trying to convince people to follow him instead of God. Don't be fooled by him and his schemes. Stand strong on God's Word and stay close to Him as you wait for Jesus' return.

Prayer: *Father, I know Jesus will be coming soon to take me to live with Him forever. Help me to stay close to You every day. In Jesus' name. Amen.*

Snakes (1) by Jo Krueger

If you know me well, you are probably surprised that I am writing a series of devotions about snakes. Why? Because snakes are probably the first thing on a list of things I am scared of. But I believe that God knows about my fear of snakes and has protected me in life. One time when we were living out in the country, my daughter asked me if I had just seen a snake out in the yard. When I answered, "No," she said, "I don't know how you missed it. You just stepped over a six-foot bull snake!"

The first time we read about a snake in the Bible is in the Garden of Eden when the devil appeared to Eve in the form of a snake. The devil wanted Eve to disobey God, so he told her a lie – that it was okay to eat the fruit from the tree in the middle of the garden. *"The woman could see that the tree was beautiful and the fruit looked so good to eat. She also liked the idea that it would make her wise. So she took some of the fruit from the tree and ate it. Her husband was with her, so she gave him some of the fruit, and he ate it"* (verse 6). This was the beginning of sin on the earth.

The devil is still very active in our world today, and he wants you to disobey God and sin. Be very careful and watch out for His temptations. Use God's Word, the Bible, to help you stand strong!

Prayer: *Heavenly Father, help me to obey You and to stand strong for You every day. In Jesus' name. Amen.*

Snakes (2) by Jo Krueger   **Today's Reading:** Exodus 4:1-5

Moses became one of God's greatest leaders, but in the beginning he lacked self-confidence. In our Bible verses today, God called Moses to lead the Israelites out of slavery in Egypt. But Moses was afraid that the Israelites would not believe God had really called him. So God responded with a solution. Verses 3 and 4 tell us, *"Then God said, 'Throw your walking stick on the ground.' So Moses threw his walking stick on the ground, and it became a snake. Moses ran from it, but the Lord said to him, 'Reach out and grab the snake by its tail.' When Moses reached out and caught the snake's tail, the snake became a walking stick again."* God gave Moses this sign to show to the Israelites as proof that he was truly God's leader. Moses posed a problem, and God provided a solution.

In the same chapter, Moses gave God another excuse. He said that he was not a good speaker. So God told Moses that his brother, Aaron, would speak for him. Again Moses posed a problem, but God provided a solution. When God calls us to do something for Him, He will make a way so that we can succeed. We can make all kinds of excuses, but God will always prevail.

What has God called you to do? Are you doing it or are you giving God excuses as to why you think you can't do it? Stop making up excuses and depend on God to help you today.

Prayer: *Dear Father, I know that I can always depend on Your strength. Be with me and help me to serve You today. In Jesus' name. Amen.*

Snakes (3) by Jo Krueger   **Today's Reading:** Numbers 21:4-9

As the Israelites were traveling to their new home, they became impatient. Our Bible reading for today tells us that they started complaining to God and Moses that they were thirsty and hungry. So God sent poisonous snakes to bite the disobedient people. Then Moses prayed and asked God to forgive the people. *"The Lord said to Moses, 'Make a bronze snake and put it on a pole. If anyone is bitten by a snake, that person should look at the bronze snake on the pole. Then that person will not die.' So Moses made a bronze snake and put it on a pole. Then when a snake bit anyone, that person looked at the bronze snake on the pole and lived"* (verses 8-9).

God listened to Moses' prayer and provided a way for the people to live, even though they had been bitten by a poisonous snake. In the same way, God has made a way so that we can be forgiven of our sins. John talked about this in John 3:14-15. *"Moses lifted up the snake in the desert. It is the same with the Son of Man. He must be lifted up too. Then everyone who believes in him can have eternal life."*

Just as the Israelites looked at the bronze snake on the pole and lived, we can live forever if we look to Jesus as our Lord and Savior. Through His death on the cross, Jesus provided a way that our sins can be forgiven. Thank Him today for His wonderful gift of salvation!

Prayer: *Dear Loving God, thank You for sending Jesus to die for my sins so that I can live forever with Him. In His name. Amen.*

Snakes (4) by Jo Krueger
Today's Reading: Deuteronomy 8:11-20

In our Bible verses for today, Moses reminded the Israelites about how God had blessed them as they traveled to the new land He had given to them. Here are some of the ways Moses said that God had blessed them: 1) He gave them food and water, 2) Their clothes did not wear out, and 3) Their feet did not swell as they walked through the desert. Moses said, *"He led you through the great and terrible desert where there were poisonous snakes and scorpions. The ground was dry, and there was no water anywhere. But he gave you water out of a solid rock."* (verse 15). As the Israelites traveled, they encountered dangers like snakes and scorpions, but God kept them safe.

God told the Israelites that if they would obey His commands, He would take care of them. God kept that promise, and the Israelites finally came into the new land He had promised to them. God has promised that if we keep our lives focused on Him, He will take care of us. That is a promise that we can depend on. Things may not always work out the way we think they should, but God will make sure that we are taken care of.

You may not see any snakes or scorpions today, but you may face problems and struggles. Keep trusting in God. He will always be with you.

Prayer: *Lord, no matter what happens today, I know that You will help me be strong. In Jesus' name. Amen.*

Snakes (5) by Jo Krueger
Today's Reading: Matthew 23:23-33

Some people like snakes and keep them as pets. Sometimes I see pictures of people playing with their pet snakes. But many people (like me!) are scared of snakes and hate them. So when someone today calls another person a "snake," they are saying that person is bad and to be avoided.

The Jewish religious leaders in Jesus' time had become very evil. They made many picky laws that required the people to do things that God did not require. These leaders were greedy and proud, and they were constantly trying to find ways to get rid of Jesus. In Matthew, chapter 23, Jesus condemned these leaders several times. In verse 33 Jesus said, *"You are snakes! You are from a family of poisonous snakes! You will not escape God. You will all be judged guilty and go to hell!"*

Jesus' words here serve as a reminder to me when I am teaching a person about Him. I should not burden that person with man-made rules that will cause them to take their focus off of Jesus. That's what the Jewish religious leaders were doing. Instead, I need to share Bible verses that show how they can obey God and accept His gift of salvation.

Are you trying to lead a friend to Jesus? Simply stick with God's Word. Then it will be easy for them to learn about Jesus and obey Him.

Prayer: *Thank You, God, for Your Word which is sufficient to lead people to salvation through Jesus. In His name. Amen.*

Snakes (6) by Jo Krueger

Today's Reading: Acts 28:1-6

Paul was God's missionary to the Gentiles. He told non-Jewish people that God loved them and wanted them to share in salvation through Jesus. Paul traveled many, many miles all over the Roman Empire to teach people about Jesus. Many times, bad things happened to Paul, but God was always with him, protecting him and keeping him safe.

Our Bible verses today tell us about the time Paul was on his way to Rome. A storm came up, and the ship that Paul was sailing on was destroyed. All the people survived, and they ended up on a beach on the island of Malta. Verse 3 tells us, *"Paul gathered a pile of sticks for the fire. He was putting the sticks on the fire, and a poisonous snake came out because of the heat and bit him on the hand."* But the snake's bite did not harm Paul. The people were sure that he would die, but he didn't. Then they thought that Paul was a god. But of course, Paul was not a god. He was just being protected by the true God!

Earlier in this devotional series, we talked about how God provided for Moses when He called him to lead the Israelites. In the same way, God took care of Paul and other people who became missionaries for Him. You can look to God for encouragement and strength as you serve Him today.

Prayer: *Dear Father, thank You for always being with me. I'm so glad I can depend on You! In Jesus' name. Amen.*

Obey God by Bonnie Hall

Today's Reading: Deuteronomy 18:1-22

In our Bible reading for today, Moses is giving the Israelites instructions on how they should live when they would enter the new land that God was giving to them. Moses knew that the people often strayed away from God and stopped focusing on following and obeying Him.

In verses 9 and 12-13 Moses told the people what they should not do. *"When you come into the land that the Lord your God is giving you, don't learn to do the terrible things the people of the other nations there do. The Lord hates anyone who does these things. And because these other nations do these terrible things, the Lord your God will force them out of the land as you enter it. You must be faithful to the Lord your God, never doing anything he considers wrong."*

Sometimes we may move to a new city, relocate to a new neighborhood or get a different job. Then we are the "new person" there, and we may want to impress the people we meet. But we should be careful not to do anything that goes against God's rules in the Bible. We may want to fit in and be accepted by our new friends, but we must remember to always obey God.

God wants us to always be careful to follow Him and make Him most important in our lives.

Prayer: *Dear Heavenly Father, help me each day to focus on You and to obey Your Word. In Jesus' name. Amen.*

Telling the World by Rachel Burkum   **Today's Reading:** Matthew 28:16-20

When you think about telling the world about Jesus, what do you envision? Maybe you think about missionaries who travel to Africa. Or maybe you envision far-off countries where people have never heard English spoken before. You might think about very poor villages where there is little food or water. Today's Bible reading is often called "The Great Commission." It is Jesus' final words to His followers before returning to heaven after He had died and risen again. Here He tells them, *"So go and make followers of all people in the world"* (verse 19a). Jesus said, "all" people in the world! But what if we are not able to travel? Of what if we can't afford it?

I don't know about you, but I like staying close to home. God has never given me a desire to travel long distances or become a foreign missionary. But that doesn't mean I can't share the Good News about Jesus with people in my small town or at my job. On Sunday mornings I volunteer at my church to help with their live-streaming service. This means that I am helping broadcast my pastor's sermon – virtually to the whole world! Not "all" people watch it, but many do, and anyone with Internet can access these videos, even if they are in a different country.

I am helping to share God's Word, even from behind a computer at my church. How will you share Jesus today?

Prayer: *Dear God, help me see the opportunities I have to tell others about Jesus every day. In His name. Amen.*

God's Help by Jennifer Forrester   **Today's Reading:** Psalm 62:1-12

My friend developed an infection in her foot and had a hard time walking. I offered her my grandfather's walker that had been hanging up in our garage since he passed away. But she said no. Later her husband called and asked if they could borrow the walker. When my friend finally gave in and tried walking with the walker, she was amazed how much it helped her. She has since recovered, and the walker is hanging in the garage again.

In Psalm 62, the writer talks about depending on God. In verses 1 and 2 and then again in verses 5 and 6 he says, *"I must calm down and turn to God; only he can rescue me. He is my rock, the only one who can save me. He is my high place of safety, where no army can defeat me."* Just as my friend needed to give in and accept the walker, we need to become humble and accept God's help. When we do, He will bless us beyond our imagination.

God offers us His help every day, but often we are too stubborn to accept it. His help may come in the form of a Christian friend, a new opportunity or an encouraging Bible verse. But we want to do things on our own, so we refuse His help and go on struggling. Don't be like that. Depend on God and allow Him to work in your life today.

Prayer: *Father, You know what is best for me. Help me to depend on You every day. In Jesus' name. Amen.*

Recipe by Jo Krueger   Today's Reading: Psalm 119:9-16

This morning I made some pasta salad that will be part of our evening meal. I have made it so many times, that I don't follow a recipe anymore. I just throw all the ingredients together and it tastes great! But I can't do that with all foods that I make. Many times I need to follow a recipe in order to make sure that the food turns out okay. I have learned that after having several bad cooking experiences.

It's the same with being a Christian. We need to follow God's recipe! And where is this? We can find God's recipe for being a Christian in the Bible. There is only one way to God and that is through Jesus. So we need to carefully follow the instructions He gave us while He was on earth. If not, we will not be saved with the promise of eternal life.

In our Bible verses for today, the psalmist talked about the importance of reading and obeying God's Word. Verses 10 and 11 say, *"I try with all my heart to serve you. Help me obey your commands. I study your teachings very carefully so that I will not sin against you."* The only way we can know how to obey God and not sin is to read and follow the Bible.

How important is God's Word to you? I hope you will spend time today searching the Bible and learning how to be close to God.

Prayer: *Dear Lord, thank You for Your Word which shows us how to live for You. In Jesus' name. Amen.*

Honey Guide by Gayle Thorn   Today's Reading: 1 Corinthians 1:22-25

The honey guide is a small bird. He loves to eat the waxy comb of a beehive, but he isn't strong enough to crush the beehive himself. If he tried, he would never survive the attack of the angry bees. So, when a honey guide finds a beehive, he calls his strong friend, the honey badger. The honey badger crushes the beehive and eats the bees and the honey. The honey guide can then eat the comb. This little bird knows when to ask someone stronger for help and protection.

Do you try to do everything by yourself? Do you always think that you can handle everything alone? Sooner or later, you will come across a situation in your life that will be too much for you to handle. When that happens, remember what Paul said in verse 25 of today's Bible reading. *"Even the foolishness of God is wiser than human wisdom. Even the weakness of God is stronger than human strength."* Like the honey guide, we aren't strong enough to handle everything in life by ourselves. We need help. We need to go to someone stronger than we are to help and protect us. We need Jesus!

Don't try to live life on your own and do everything by yourself. Jesus wants to live life with you. He wants to be the wisdom and strength you need to face all of life's challenges.

Prayer: *Heavenly Father, I'm not strong enough to handle many of the things that come my way. I need Your strength to help and protect me. In Jesus' name. Amen.*

True Hero by Jennifer Forrester   **Today's Reading:** 1 Peter 2:18-25

When I was young, my hero was a major league baseball player. I watched his games on TV, and I clipped newspaper articles about him and put them in a scrapbook. I even got to see him play in person when my dad took me to a ballgame one summer. Then his career ended, and I grew up. One day I read a magazine article about him and learned that while he was playing baseball, his personal life was a mess. He had a problem with alcohol, and his marriage was not good. I was very disappointed to read this about my hero. Then several years later, I heard that he had changed his way of living and given his life to Jesus!

Our heroes are human, and therefore they are not perfect. But there is one true hero that we can look up to who *is* perfect. That is Jesus! Jesus faced every kind of temptation while He was on earth, but He never sinned. That's what Peter was talking about in verses 21 and 22 of our Bible reading for today. *"This is what you were chosen to do. Christ gave you an example to follow. He suffered for you. So you should do the same as he did: 'He never sinned, and he never told a lie.'"*

Don't try to be like famous athletes or movie stars. Make Jesus your hero! Try to be like Him every day. You can do that by being kind, forgiving, showing mercy and being a servant to others.

Prayer: *Dear Lord, thank You for Jesus' example. Help me to be like Him every day. In Jesus' name. Amen.*

God's Purpose by Donna Howard   **Today's Reading:** Romans 8:26-28

Near my home is a very old tree. Years of strong winds have twisted the limbs into grotesque shapes. On one side there is a shallow, hollowed-out place where the bark has fallen off. With a little bit of imagination, I can see the face of an old man. My husband once said that the old tree would be perfect in a scary movie. But, the way the tree is now, we would say that it has no purpose. Yet, the tree does have a purpose. Looking at the tree brings delight to my husband and me and perhaps to others who pass by. Maybe that is God's purpose for the old tree.

I am 84 years old, nearly deaf, and I suffer from arthritis. So I am limited in what I can do. Sometimes I feel useless. But I know that God has an important purpose for me. Verse 28 of our Bible reading for today says, *"We know that in everything God works for the good of those who love him. These are the people God chose, because that was his plan."* God has a purpose for each person, and He works in our lives to help us fulfill that purpose.

I may be old and not feel well, but I can still pray for people who are sick, struggling or facing family problems. And I can tell people what God has done for me and encourage them to accept Jesus as their Savior. If you ever feel useless, remember that God has a wonderful purpose for you!

Prayer: *Thank You, Father, for showing me that You have a purpose for my life. In Jesus' name. Amen.*

Follow Jesus by Bonnie Hall

Today's Reading: Luke 5:1-11

Our Bible reading tells us that many people came to see Jesus. In order for everyone to be able to hear Him, Jesus asked Simon (also called Peter) to bring over his boat. Then Jesus got into the boat and taught the people. *"When Jesus finished speaking,* "He said to Simon, `Take the boat into the deep water. If all of you will put your nets into the water, you will catch some fish'"* (verse 4).

Simon told Jesus that the night before they had been out fishing and had not caught any fish. But they obeyed Jesus and put out their nets. Soon the nets were so full of fish that they began to break. They called their friends from another boat to help them. Then both boats were filled so full that they were almost sinking.

All the men were amazed! Then Simon bowed before Jesus and admitted that he was a sinner. Jesus said to him, *"Don't be afraid. From now on your work will be to bring in people, not fish!"* (verse 10b). Then the men brought their boats to shore and left everything to follow Jesus.

Jesus wants us to follow Him, too. But we need to be like those fishermen and give up our pride and our earthly goals to follow Him. We may not know how we will follow Jesus, but we can know for sure that He will always be with us to lead us, comfort us and bless us.

Prayer: *Dear God, I want to follow You every day. Show me what You want me to do for You. In Jesus' name. Amen.*

Hot Weather by Jo Krueger

Today's Reading: Daniel 3:1-30

It is summertime here in Iowa. Today and for the next few days we will look at some things that Iowans experience during the summer. One thing that we have for sure every summer is hot weather. This year we have had unusually high temperatures. But we normally have several weeks during July and August when the temperature is 90 degrees and higher. Some people love the hot weather, and others hate it!

In our Bible reading today, we learn about three men who experienced some very hot temperatures! Shadrach, Meshach and Abednego were Israelites who loved and obeyed God. The king of Babylon made a golden idol and commanded that everyone bow down to the idol. But Shadrach, Meshach and Abednego refused to worship the idol. *"The king was very angry when he gave the command, so the soldiers quickly made the furnace very hot. The fire was so hot that the flames killed the strong soldiers. They were killed when they went close to the fire to throw in Shadrach, Meshach, and Abednego"* (verse 22).

God protected Shadrach, Meshach and Abednego, even in the fire. Why? Because they loved Him and refused to worship the idol. God will protect you, too, no matter what you face today. Be sure to obey His Word and worship only Him.

Prayer: *God, thank You for always protecting me. Help me to stay close to You. In His name. Amen.*

Picnics by Jo Krueger   **Today's Reading:** Luke 9:10-17

Many people in Iowa enjoy summer picnics. It is fun to pack a lunch and eat it in the backyard, at a park or by a lake. Our Bible verses today tell us about a time when Jesus, His disciples and a group of more than 5000 people ate a lunch together outside.

One day many people followed Jesus and listened to His teaching. It became late, and the people were hungry. Jesus' disciples did not know how they could find enough food to feed that many people. They searched and only found five loaves of bread and two fish.

Jesus took the food that they found and thanked God for it. Then He gave the food to the people. *"They all ate until they were full. And there was a lot of food left. Twelve baskets were filled with the pieces of food that were not eaten."* (verse 17a). How did Jesus feed all those people? It was a miracle – something amazing done with God's power. Jesus fed the people, but He also showed them that He was truly God's Son.

The Bible tells us about many wonderful things that God has done for His people. God is still very powerful today. Thank Him and praise Him for His power and strength.

Prayer: *Father, I am very weak, but You are all-powerful. Thank You for taking care of us every day. In Jesus' name. Amen.*

Flies by Jo Krueger   **Today's Reading:** Exodus 8:20-32

For many years, my husband and I lived in the country. Every summer we would have lots of flies. Most of the time the flies didn't bother me – a few of them would get into the house. But they often bothered our animals. And sometimes they would bite us and become a nuisance.

God's people, the Israelites, were slaves in Egypt. Moses told the king to free the Israelites, but he refused to let them leave Egypt. In our Bible verses we learn about one of the terrible ways that God punished the Egyptians. *"So the Lord did just what he said. Millions of flies came into Egypt. The flies were in Pharaoh's house, and they were in all his officials' houses. They were all over Egypt. The flies were ruining the country"* (verse 24). I don't like putting up with a few flies in the summer, but that must have been terrible in Egypt!

Yesterday we talked about the miracle that happened when Jesus fed more than 5000 people. Sending the flies to punish the Egyptians was a miracle, too. Only God could do something like this. God wanted to show the Egyptians that He was powerful and that He was the one true God.

God does wonderful things for us today, too. But the most wonderful thing He has done for us was sending Jesus to die for our sins. Isn't God awesome?

Prayer: *Lord, You are so awesome! Thank You for sending Jesus to accept the punishment for my sins. In His name. Amen.*

Fresh Vegetables by Jo Krueger

Today's Reading: Matthew 13:1-9

Every summer for many years, my husband planted a vegetable garden. He spent a lot of time planting, watering, weeding and harvesting the food. Some years our garden produced lots of vegetables, and we had enough that we could share with our family and neighbors. But during a dry, cool summer our garden would not grow well.

In our Bible reading for today, Jesus told a story about a farmer who planted some seeds. Just like our garden, sometimes the seeds grew well and other times they didn't. But in Jesus' story, the seeds that grew well did so because they were planted in good ground.

Later in chapter 13, Jesus explained to His followers about the good ground. *"But what about the seed that fell on the good ground? That is like the people who hear the teaching and understand it"* (Matthew 13:23a). We should be like the good ground in Jesus' story. We need to read the Bible every day and apply God's teachings to our lives. Then we will grow in our faith and share the Good News about Jesus with more people.

I hope you are like the good ground. Pay attention to God's Word and share it with others today.

Prayer: *Father, I want to pay attention to Your Word, obey it and share it with others. In Jesus' name. Amen.*

Tornadoes by Jo Krueger

Today's Reading: 2 Kings 2:1-11

If you live in Iowa, you will experience many nice things during the summer. We are talking about some of those nice things in this devotional series. But one bad thing that can happen in Iowa during the summer is a tornado! Many people have witnessed the terrible destruction of tornadoes and strong winds. Tornadoes truly show us how powerful God is.

In our Bible verses for today, we read about God's prophet, Elijah. He loved God and served Him faithfully for many years. Then God did something very special for Elijah. When it was time for Elijah to leave the earth, he did not die like other people. Instead God took Elijah to heaven. Verse 11 tells us, *"Elijah and Elisha were walking and talking together. Suddenly, some horses and a chariot came and separated Elijah from Elisha. The horses and the chariot were like fire. Then Elijah was carried up into heaven in a whirlwind."* This whirlwind may have been something like a tornado. God showed His great power when He made the whirlwind that took Elijah to heaven.

God is powerful, and we can depend on Him to control the universe. If God can make the world and take care of it, He can take care of you, too. Thank Him today for His amazing power!

Prayer: *Heavenly Father, thank You for taking care of me and for helping me to see how powerful You are. In Jesus' name. Amen.*

Rainbows by Jo Krueger   **Today's Reading:** Genesis 9:1-17

We usually get quite a bit of rain in Iowa during the summer months, although the past few years have been drier than usual. But when it does rain, some storms can be very severe with lots of high winds and hail. Often, though, these storms are followed by a beautiful rainbow in the sky. And a very special treat is to see a double rainbow after a storm!

Long ago, God sent a terrible flood to destroy all the wicked people on earth. But He saved Noah, his family and many animals from the flood. Our Bible verses tell us about when Noah and his family finally came out of the boat onto dry land. God told Noah, *"I will give you something to prove that I made this promise to you. It will continue forever to show that I have made an agreement with you and every living thing on earth. I am putting a rainbow in the clouds as proof of the agreement between me and the earth"* (verses 12-13). God's agreement was that He would never again destroy all life on earth with a flood.

When we see a rainbow in the sky, we can remember that God always keeps His promises. He has promised that Jesus will come again someday to take His followers to live with Him forever. And we can know for sure that will happen!

Praise God today and thank Him for His promises.

Prayer: *Dear God, thank You for Jesus and for the promise that He will come again. In Jesus' name. Amen.*

RAGBRAI by Jo Krueger   **Today's Reading:** Hebrews 12:1-3

Every summer, Iowa is the host to a very special bicycle event called RAGBRAI. The letters of the name stand for Register's Annual Great Bicycle Ride Across Iowa. This ride began in 1973. Each year the event begins at a point on the Missouri Rivers and ends at the Mississippi River, close to 500 miles across the state. As many as 60,000 people have participated in a portion of this ride. Each night on the route, the riders stop and camp in an Iowa city.

If a person wants to ride in RAGBRAI, they need to train for a long time before the event. They also need to focus on the goal of completing the ride and not let other things distract them. In our Bible Reading today, the writer of Hebrews talks about running a race. But it is not a physical race. This is the race to receive the prize of eternal life with God.

These verses tell us several things we should do in order to receive the prize. First, we should try to remove all sin from our lives. Second, we should *"never stop looking to Jesus"* (verse 2a). And third, we should think about Jesus so that we will not become discouraged and give up.

I hope that you will always remember how much God loves you. Keep following Him every day, and never give!

Prayer: *God, thank You for loving me. Help me to want to be near You and to love and obey You. In Jesus' name. Amen.*

Parades by Jo Krueger

Today's Reading: John 12:12-16

There are many parades across Iowa during the summer, especially around the Fourth of July. Small towns often have parades to honor military heroes, to celebrate the culture of their community or to remember an event from the town's history. Floats, marching bands, horses and tractors are often important elements of the parades in Iowa. People from all over gather in the town to watch the parade and to honor the event.

Our Bible verses today tell us about something that happened in Jerusalem that was like a parade. People knew that Jesus was coming into Jerusalem to celebrate the Passover festival. Verse 13 says, *"They took branches of palm trees and went out to meet Jesus. They shouted, 'Praise Him! Welcome! God bless the one who comes in the name of the Lord! God bless the King of Israel!'"*

The people welcomed Jesus like they would welcome an earthly king. But they did not understand that it was not God's plan for Jesus to rule as a king on earth. Jesus came to die for our sins and then be raised from death. Now He rules in heaven with God. Someday Jesus will return to take His followers to live forever with Him.

Praise God for His forgiveness and promise of eternal life!

Prayer: *Father, thank You for Your plan of salvation and that Jesus was willing to die for me. In Jesus' name. Amen.*

Flowers by Jo Krueger

Today's Reading: Matthew 6:25-34

Flowers that bloom in the summertime are so beautiful! I enjoy seeing fields of wildflowers that grow in Iowa. My favorite wildflower is the wild rose, which is the official state flower of Iowa. Wild roses are usually pink with a little red, and they grow best near streams or on wooded hillsides.

When I look at wildflowers, I remember that God made them and that He makes them bloom year after year. In our Bible verses for today, Jesus talked about wildflowers. He said, *"And why do you worry about clothes? Look at the wildflowers in the field. See how they grow. They don't work or make clothes for themselves. But I tell you that even Solomon, the great and rich king, was not dressed as beautifully as one of these flowers. If God makes what grows in the field so beautiful, what do you think he will do for you?"* (verses 28-30a).

Jesus goes on to explain that God takes care of the wildflowers, and therefore He will take care of us, too. We do not need to worry about having enough food or clothes to wear today. God knows what we need and has promised that He will take care of us.

Focus on following God and obeying His Word today. Then He will take care of you and all your needs.

Prayer: *God, sometimes it is hard to depend on You. I want to trust You to take care of me every day. In Jesus' name. Amen.*

Lemonade by Jo Krueger

Today's Reading: John 4:5-30

When the weather is hot in Iowa, it is good to drink a cold, refreshing glass of homemade lemonade. When I am driving through our town, I often see children who have put up a stand to sell lemonade. During the summer, I make many pitchers of lemonade for my husband when he is working outside in the hot sun.

In our Bible verses for today, John tells us about a time when Jesus met a woman who was from the area of Samaria. They met at a well, and Jesus asked the woman for a drink of water. Jesus continued talking with the woman, and in verse 10 He said, *"You don't know what God can give you. And you don't know who I am, the one who asked you for a drink. If you knew, you would have asked me, and I would have given you living water."*

The "living water" that Jesus was talking about is Himself. If we follow and obey Him, He will bless us and give us eternal life. *"But anyone who drinks the water I give will never be thirsty again. The water I give people will be like a spring flowing inside them. It will bring them eternal life"* (verse 14).

Are you thirsty for God's love and forgiveness? Do you want Him to satisfy your need for love and acceptance? Turn to Him today. Read His Word and accept Jesus as your Lord and Savior.

Prayer: *Father, I love You and want to follow You today. Please give me the "living water" that only comes from Jesus. In His name. Amen.*

Cotton Candy by Bob La Forge

Today's Reading: Isaiah 55:1-6

Whenever I go to a fair or a carnival, I always buy some cotton candy. I enjoy watching the candy swirl around in the vat and gather on the stick. Cotton candy is colorful and tastes sweet, but it is quickly gone and provides no real nourishment. Sin is a lot like that. It seems pleasing at first, but ultimately it will never satisfy. And what is worse, sin keeps us from God's blessings.

In verse 2 of our Bible reading, Isaiah explained that only God can give us spiritual food that will satisfy. *"Why waste your money on something that is not real food? Why should you work for something that does not really satisfy you? Listen closely to me and you will eat what is good. You will enjoy the food that satisfies your soul."*

Imagine that God has placed before you a huge table full of the best and most nourishing foods. But behind you is a small table. On that table is the most tempting cotton candy you have ever seen. You can choose to eat from only one table, not from both. When you sin, you do not experience God's blessings because you have turned your back on His table to eat the cotton candy that the world has to offer.

God's feast is still there waiting for us. All we have to do is repent, turn from our sin and accept God's goodness and blessings.

Prayer: *Lord, I want to please You and to receive Your goodness and blessings. Thank You. In Jesus' name. Amen.*

Names for Jesus (1) by Jennifer Forrester   **Today's Reading:** Matthew 1:18-21

God's Son, Jesus, is called many names throughout the Old and New Testaments. Today we will begin a series of devotions about some of those names. Sometimes these names describe a part of Jesus' character. And some names tell us about Jesus' work.

Of course, the first and best-known name for God's Son is Jesus. Verse 21a of our Bible reading today tells us that an angel spoke to Joseph in a dream. This is what the angel said about Mary. *"She will give birth to a son. You will name him Jesus."* The angel Gabriel also used this name when he told Mary that she would have a son in Luke 1:31. The name Jesus is the Greek form of the Hebrew name Joshua. Joshua means "Jehovah (God) is salvation."

When the angel was speaking to Joseph, he explained that the baby's name would be Jesus because *"he will save his people from their sins"* (verse 21b). Whenever we use Jesus' name, we are acknowledging that He has the power to forgive our sins and give us eternal salvation. We are saved in the name of Jesus.

Think about Jesus today and that God sent His Son to be born to Mary and live a perfect life on earth. Then thank Him for your salvation and eternal life that you have because of Jesus.

Prayer: *Heavenly Father, thank You that Jesus' name still has the power to save us. In His name. Amen.*

Names for Jesus (2) by Jennifer Forrester   **Today's Reading:** Matthew 16:13-20

We have already said that the best-known name for God's Son is Jesus. The next most commonly used name for Him is Christ.

"Christ" is the Greek translation of the Hebrew word "Messiah." This name means the anointed one. In the Old Testament we read that the priests and kings were anointed with oil. This anointing showed that a person was chosen to serve God in a very special way.

In our Bible verses today, Jesus asked His disciples who people said He was. They responded that some people thought He was Elijah or John the Baptizer. Then Jesus asked Peter who *he* thought He was. We can read Peter's answer in verse 16b. *"You are the Messiah, the Son of the living God."* In the next verse, Jesus accepted Peter's answer and said, *"You are blessed, Simon son of Jonah."*

Peter was saying that he believed Jesus was the person that the prophets had talked about in the Old Testament. This name, Messiah, also meant that Peter was acknowledging Jesus was the one God chose to be the Lord and Savior for all people in the world.

When we talk about Jesus and call Him Christ, we are telling people that we believe Jesus is our Lord and Savior. Share that with someone today!

Prayer: *Dear Father, show me someone that I can tell about Your Son, Jesus, today. In His name. Amen.*

Names for Jesus (3) by Jennifer Forrester   **Today's Reading:** Mark 10:35-45

It seems that Jesus' favorite name for Himself was Son of Man. He used it 78 times in the New Testament books of Matthew, Mark, Luke and John.

"Son of Man" is also used many times in the Old Testament. In many of these verses, son of man means a human being. But in Daniel 7:13-14 there words describe the Messiah (Jesus). *"The one who looked like a human being was given authority, glory, and complete ruling power. People from every nation and language group will serve him. His rule will last forever. His kingdom will continue forever. It will never be destroyed"* (verse 14). Jesus quoted this prophecy from Daniel in some of His teachings.

Why did Jesus call Himself Son of Man? Maybe He was showing people that He was their representative before God. As our Bible reading shows us today, Jesus may have used this title so that people would know that He came to earth to be a servant and to die for them. *"Follow my example: Even the Son of Man did not come for people to serve him. He came to serve others and to give his life to save many people."* (verse 45).

We may not understand why Jesus used this title, but this name helps us remember that Jesus came to earth and lived as a man so He could bring people to the right relationship with God.

Prayer: *Lord, thank You for Jesus and that He was willing to come to earth as a man. Help me to love and serve Him. In His name. Amen.*

Names for Jesus (4) by Jennifer Forrester   **Today's Reading:** Matthew 22:41-46

So far we have looked at the names Jesus, Messiah and Son of Man when referring to God's Son. In the very first verse of the New Testament (Matthew 1:1), Jesus is called the Son of David. *"This is the family history of Jesus the Messiah. He came from the family of David, who was from the family of Abraham."*

However, the title "Son of David" was used by Jewish people to mean the Messiah. In our Bible Reading, the Jewish religious leaders answered Jesus' question about Christ by saying, *"The Messiah is the Son of David"* (verse 42b). This is the same name the people shouted when Jesus rode into Jerusalem a few days before He was crucified. *"Praise to the Son of David! Welcome! God bless the One that comes in the name of the Lord! Praise to God in heaven"* (Matthew 21:9b).

David was the greatest king of Israel. So the name Son of David shows that Jesus is a king. But His kingdom does not have a fancy palace, and it is not built on powerful armies and wealth. Jesus' kingdom is built on love and faith and His teachings that can be found in the New Testament.

Jesus' kingdom will last forever and ever. If we follow and obey Him, we can be part of that wonderful kingdom and live with Him without sickness, pain, sorrow and sin.

Prayer: *Dear Heavenly Father, thank You for making a place for me in Jesus' kingdom. In His name. Amen.*

Names for Jesus (5) by Jennifer Forrester   **Today's Reading:** Job 19:23-27

Today we will look at another name for Jesus. The name Redeemer is often used to describe God's Son. However, this name is not used in the New Testament. But it is used many time in the Old Testament to refer to Jesus as the one who would bring salvation to all people.

In our Bible reading today, Job is talking with his friends who came to comfort him about the loss of his family and possessions. In verse 25 Job said, *"I know that there is someone to defend me and that he lives! And in the end, he will stand here on earth and defend me."* The words "someone to defend me" are translated as "redeemer" in many Bible versions.

The word "redeem" explains what Jesus has done for us. Two different Greek words are translated as redeem in the New Testament. The first one means to buy out. That word was used when a slave was bought and set free. The other word means to release by paying a price.

Jesus is truly our Redeemer. He paid the price for our sins through His death to buy us out of our slavery to sin. Now we are free in Christ and have the gift of eternal life. Thank God today for sending Jesus to be your Redeemer and for freeing you from sin.

Prayer: *Dear Loving God, thank You for sending Your Son, Jesus, to be our Redeemer. In Jesus' name. Amen.*

Names for Jesus (6) by Jennifer Forrester   **Today's Reading:** Isaiah 59:16-21

So far we have looked at five names for God's Son – Jesus, Christ, Son of Man, Son of David and Redeemer. Another name that people sometimes call Jesus is Intercessor. This name, like the name Redeemer, is not found in the New Testament. But it is found one time in the Old Testament.

Verse 16 of our Bible reading for today says, *"He did not see anyone speak up for the people. He was shocked to see that no one stood up for them. So with his own power he saved them. His desire to do what is right gave him strength."* In some Bible versions, the words "one stood up for them" are translated as "intercessor."

The word intercession is used in the New Testament to describe what Jesus does for us. The word means to pray for or to speak for someone else. That is what Jesus does for us before God. He speaks for us. Jesus is our Intercessor. Jesus can do this because He knows our needs, our weaknesses and our sins. He also knows God, the Father. Hebrews 7:25 also talks about how Jesus speaks for us. *"So Christ can save those who come to God through him. Christ can do this forever, because he always lives and is ready to help people when they come before God."*

It is so wonderful to know that Jesus is always ready to speak for us before God, our heavenly Father!

Prayer: *Dear God, I need an Intercessor who understand me and knows You. In Jesus' name. Amen.*

Names for Jesus (7) by Jennifer Forrester   Today's Reading: Hebrews 4:14-5:10

In the book of Hebrews, we learn that Jesus is our High Priest. To understand this, we must know something about Jewish priests under the Law of Moses. The writer of Hebrews discusses the priesthood. He explains that Jesus, our High Priest, is greater than all the Jewish priests.

A Jewish high priest represented God to His people, the Israelites, and represented the people to God. Jesus is a perfect High Priest. Why? Because He is God's Son and lives with God in heaven. Verse 14 of our Bible reading today says, *"We have a great high priest who has gone to live with God in heaven. He is Jesus the Son of God. So let us continue to express our faith in him."* Only Jesus can represent God to people in a perfect way.

And Jesus perfectly represents people to God. Hebrews 2:14-18 tells us that Jesus lived as a person in this world. Jesus experienced the same temptations, sorrows and weaknesses that every person on earth experiences. So Jesus is the only one who can represent people to God in a perfect way. *"He became like people so that he could be their merciful and faithful high priest in service to God. Then he could bring forgiveness for the people's sins"* (verse 17b).

If you are a Christian, then Jesus is your High Priest. Thank God for Jesus!

Prayer: *Dear God, thank You for giving us Your Son to be our perfect High Priest. In His name. Amen.*

I Never Imagined by Jo Krueger   Today's Reading: Revelation 21:11-27

I love to watch Antiques Roadshow! Every Monday night you can be sure that I will turn on our local PBS station and watch one or two episodes. I don't really know why I like the show so much, because I am not really interested in antiques. But I do love to watch people's reactions when their items are appraised. Sometimes the people are so happy with the appraisal that they start to cry. Other times people are so shocked that they don't know what to say. But I love to hear someone say, "I never imagined that it was worth so much!"

I think that is maybe how we will be in heaven. Although our Bible verses for today give us a description of what heaven will be like, I am not sure that we can fully imagine its beauty and magnificence. John describes the Holy City as being built with precious stones and jewels, with the streets made of pure gold.

Verse 23 tells us something that is hard to imagine. *"The city did not need the sun or the moon to shine on it. The glory of God gave the city light. The Lamb was the city's lamp."* Won't that be wonderful to live in the presence of God, a place where there is no sickness, no sadness and no sin?

I am so looking forward to saying, "I never imagined heaven would be this wonderful!"

Prayer: *Dear God, thank You for preparing a place where I can live with You forever. In Jesus' name. Amen.*

All-Seeing by Rachel Burkum   Today's Reading: Hebrews 4:12-13

I recently installed a camera on my front porch. Whenever it senses movement, I'm notified on my smart phone. When I receive a notification, I can open the app and view my front porch to see what caused the alert. Usually it's the mailman. Sometimes it's a cat or even an opossum! No matter what is on my porch, I feel safer knowing I can look to see what's happening. If someone delivers a package, no matter how sneaky they are, I can see it.

Today's Bible reading tells us very clearly that God sees everything. Verse 13 says, *"Nothing in all the world can be hidden from God. He can clearly see all things. Everything is open before him. And to him we must explain the way we have lived."* Not some things. Not one or two little things. Nothing. God is all-knowing and all-seeing. Isaiah 40:28b say, *"He created all the faraway places on earth."* God made everything! There is nothing we do or say that is hidden from God – the good things we do, and also the bad. He knows when we are following Him, or when we are sinning.

It's great that I can see what's going on at my house, even when I'm far away. But that's nothing compared to God's power. We need to remember no matter where we are or what we're doing, God is there, too. He sees us, and He loves us. Are you making Him proud of you today?

Prayer: *Father, thank You for watching me every moment of every day. I ask for forgiveness for my sins. Help me do what pleases You. In Jesus' name. Amen.*

My Dad (1) by Jo Krueger   Today's Reading: Proverbs 17:22

My dad was a wonderful Christian man, and he was a great father to me. I was an only child, so I got all of his attention as I was growing up. And I had the privilege of taking care of my dad and mom when they were older. For the next several days I want to share some special things with you about my dad and apply them to our Christian lives.

My dad had a wonderful sense of humor! He loved to tell jokes, and we would often sit down together and read all the jokes in the *Reader's Digest* magazine. Dad smiled a lot, and he would often use his sense of humor to diffuse tense family situations. He especially enjoyed making jokes and laughing with his grandson and granddaughter.

Our Bible verse for today says, *"Happiness is a good medicine, but sorrow is a disease."* Dad died just a few weeks before his 95th birthday. I really believe that his positive outlook and sense of humor contributed to his long life span. I don't think that means we have to go around telling jokes all the time, but I do think it means that happiness and laughter are good for us mentally, physically and spiritually.

Look for ways today that you can bless and encourage others with your sense of humor. And don't forget to smile!

Prayer: *God, thank You for blessing me with happiness and laughter. Help me to share that with others today. In Jesus' name. Amen.*

My Dad (2) by Jo Krueger

Today's Reading: Colossians 3:22-25

I wouldn't say that my dad was a workaholic, but I rarely saw him just sitting around and doing nothing. For most of his life, Dad was an accountant for an animal feed company, and he loved his job. Fall was his busiest time, and I remember going to his office with him when he occasionally had to work in the evenings. Those were special times that we had together. Dad also loved doing things for the people in our church and helping his family members or others in the community.

In our Bible verses for today, Paul is talking about slaves and their masters. But I think we can still apply these verses to the jobs we have today. In verse 23 Paul says, *"In all the work you are given, do the best you can. Work as though you are working for the Lord, not an earthly master."* I really believe that my dad obeyed that verse. He worked hard, not only to take care of his family, but to also please God.

What about your job? Maybe you love your job, or maybe you dread going to work every day. But no matter how we feel about our jobs, we should still do our very best – not to please our boss, but to please God.

Thank God for the work He has given you to do and ask Him to help you do your very best!

Prayer: *Heavenly Father, thank You for my job. Help me to do my best and to bless others today. In Jesus' name. Amen.*

My Dad (3) by Jo Krueger

Today's Reading: Philippians 2:1-4

My dad was a humble man, and he was always thinking about other people. One way he did this was to always be on time. Dad felt that being late caused problems for other people, so he always made sure that he arrived early for his job, appointments or events. In fact, my dad earned such a reputation for being early that we started his funeral service 10 minutes early!

It is very important that we think about other people and show them kindness. In verses 3-4 of our Bible reading, Paul said, *"In whatever you do, don't let selfishness or pride be your guide. Be humble, and honor others more than yourselves. Don't be interested only in your own life, but care about the lives of others too."* I think that is a description of my dad and the way he lived.

It is sad, but I rarely see acts of kindness in public today. As Christians, I think we need to purposefully show kindness to others – letting someone go ahead of you in the grocery line, opening a door for a handicapped person or a struggling mother, or being patient when the driver in front of you doesn't start moving immediately when the light turns green. When we do these things, we are showing God's love to other people.

I challenge you to be humble and show kindness to the people you meet today.

Prayer: *Lord, help me to think about other people and show kindness to them today. In Jesus' name. Amen.*

My Dad (4) by Jo Krueger   **Today's Reading:** Proverbs 12:5

My dad loved to play golf. When he was younger, he belonged to two golfing clubs and would play every weekend and sometimes in the evening after work. When he was too old to golf, he watched golf tournaments on TV. As a teenager, I learned to golf, and we played together a lot. Dad taught me about golf etiquette, but I think the greatest lesson I learned from Dad while golfing was to be honest.

When Dad and I were playing golf, it would have been easy for him to cheat on his score. He could have written down a lower score, and if I was concentrating on the game, I might not have known that he cheated. But Dad taught me to be honest – in golf and in all aspects of my life. Our Bible verse for today talks about that. *"Good people are honest and fair in all they do, but those who are evil lie and cannot be trusted."*

The world today is full of people who cheat on their taxes, lie to their spouses, or steal supplies from their workplace, and they get away with it. But that doesn't mean that we should be like the world. We need to be like Jesus, and that includes being honest and trustworthy.

You may be tempted today to be dishonest. Remember our verse from Proverbs and choose to be honest.

Prayer: *Dear Loving Father, I want to always be honest and fair and to please You. In Jesus' name. Amen.*

My Dad (5) by Jo Krueger   **Today's Reading:** James 4:7-9

If you knew my dad, you probably knew that there was one thing he truly hated – onions! I remember one time when we ate in a restaurant and he ordered a hamburger without onions. When he got it, he took one bite and realized there were onions on the hamburger. He reminded the waitress that he didn't want any onions, and sent the hamburger back to the kitchen. But when he got it again, the taste of the onions was still on the meat and the bun. So dad sent the hamburger back again and asked them to make him a new hamburger. That was a real hatred of onions!

My dad's reaction to onions may seem a little dramatic, but that is exactly how we should feel about sin. God hates sin, and we need to feel the same way. Verse 7 of our Bible reading for today shows us how we can hate sin. *"So give yourselves to God. Stand against the devil, and he will run away from you."*

If we truly hate sin, then we will give our lives to God and show that we are against the devil. But that is not always easy to do. When we show that we hate sin, we may offend some people or we may lose some friends. But we need to stand strong and say, "No!" to the devil and his temptations.

Ask God to help you stay away from sin today!

Prayer: *Father, I know that I will be tempted to sin today. Help me to be strong and to obey You. In Jesus' name. Amen.*

My Dad (6) by Jo Krueger   **Today's Reading:** Ephesians 5:19-20

This is the last in our series of devotions about my dad. I have really enjoyed sharing some things about him with you. Today I will talk about my dad's love of music. My dad had a wonderful tenor voice, and he sang all the time. He sang as we were driving down the road, and he sang along with singers on TV. He also sang with groups in our community. But Dad's favorite singing was done at church. He sang in the church choir for more than 60 years and loved joining in congregational singing. My dad has been gone for more than 12 years, but even now someone in church may say to me, "I think I could hear your dad singing along with that hymn!"

In our Bible verses for today Paul said, *"Encourage each other with psalms, hymns, and spiritual songs. Sing and make music in your hearts to the Lord. Always give thanks to God the Father for everything in the name of our Lord Jesus Christ."* Dad truly encouraged other people through his singing. And he also taught me how to worship God through music.

Maybe you think that you can't sing or you don't like to sing. That's okay, but you can still worship God by listening to others sing or by concentrating on the words of the song. That's how you can *"make music in your hearts to the Lord."*

Prayer: *Thank You, God, for music. Show me how I can worship and praise You today. In Jesus' name. Amen.*

Surrender All by Norma Mezoe   **Today's Reading:** Mark 10:17-22

A minister visited the home and estate of a very wealthy man. After they had toured his fancy house, the host took the minister outside to look at his property. He pointed in one direction to his oil wells and then to the many acres of golden grain. Next, the two men inspected a large herd of cattle.

Finally, the rich man pointed to a beautiful forest in the distance. After he had showed off all of his possessions, the man proclaimed, "It's all mine!" The minister had been quiet throughout the tour. At last, he pointed to heaven and quietly asked, "How much do you have in that direction?"

The rich man in our Bible verses for today was curious about eternal life. He told Jesus that he had obeyed God's commands, and then he asked what more he needed to do. Verse 21 says, *"Jesus looked at the man in a way that showed how much he cared for him. He said, 'There is still one thing you need to do. Go and sell everything you have. Give the money to those who are poor, and you will have riches in heaven. Then come and follow me.'"* The rich man turned away from Jesus because he was not willing to surrender his wealth to God.

Is there something standing between you and God? Are you willing to surrender your entire life and possessions in order to follow Him?

Prayer: *Father God, help us to surrender our possessions to You so that we can have Jesus. In His name. Amen.*

Hair Salon (1) by Rachel Burkum   **Today's Reading:** Romans 8:27-30

A few years ago, I lost my job. It was a very hard time for me because I didn't know what I was going to do. I was worried about paying my bills, taking care of my pets, and paying for gas to go find another job. I admit I was more worried than I should have been. God knew all along how He was going to take care of me! I just needed to trust Him.

It took a while, but eventually I found work again. Now I actually have several part-time jobs, and I'm very happy. One of my jobs is cleaning a local hair salon once a week. I feel very blessed to have this job. God knew just when I was going to need it, and He provided for me. It wasn't what I expected, but looking back, I can now see how He worked everything out. It makes me think of the Bible verses for today. Verses 28-29a say, *"We know that in everything God works for the good of those who love him. These are the people God chose, because that was his plan. God knew them before he made the world."* God works in my life for my good. That means He takes care of me. And He knew about me before He even made the world! He blesses me because I love and follow Him.

I have been blessed through the jobs God has given me. I've learned many lessons, and I'm going to share some of them over the next few days.

Prayer: *Dear Heavenly Father, thank You so much for loving and blessing me. In Jesus' name. Amen.*

Hair Salon (2) by Rachel Burkum   **Today's Reading:** 2 Corinthians 5:16-19

Many people go to hair salons on a regular basis. Where I have my cleaning job, they offer haircuts, manicures, pedicures and waxing. A lot of women go there because they want to get a "new look." The hair stylists are very skilled, and they work hard to make sure their customers are happy. Some women want a quick, simple haircut. Others want to look entirely different. They may want their hair cut, dyed and styled. Maybe they have a manicure, too. When they step out of the salon, they might look like a whole new person! If their hair is very different, other people might not even recognize them.

In today's Bible reading, Paul talks about what happens when we decide to follow Jesus. *"When anyone is in Christ, it is a whole new world. The old things are gone; suddenly, everything is new!"* (verse 17). When we make the decision to give our lives to Christ, it is as if the world around us changes. We see and experience things differently. We make different decisions, act differently, and hopefully we are a new and better example for people around us. The "old" us is gone.

A new hairstyle means looking fresh and new on the outside. Following God means being fresh and new on the inside. We can all enjoy looking our best, and it's okay to go to a hair salon. It can be a lot of fun! But we also need to remember that what's inside our hearts is most important. Have you been made new?

Prayer: *Dear God, I want to be made new through You every day. In Jesus' name. Amen.*

Hair Salon (3) by Rachel Burkum
Today's Reading: Luke 12:1-3

Have you ever dyed your hair? Maybe you have gone to a hair salon to have it dyed professionally, or maybe you have done it yourself at home. I've experienced both. Actually, as I write this devotion, my hair is purple! I like to be different and have fun with colors. A lot of people dye their hair. Sometimes no one else even knows their true color because they may keep it dyed for a very long time. If they go to their hair salon faithfully, it's easy to hide what's underneath.

Today in our Bible reading, Jesus is speaking to a large crowd of people. In verse 2, He warns, "*Everything that is hidden will be shown, and everything that is secret will be made known.*" He was advising people not to be hypocrites. That means saying one thing but doing another. It means hiding your true intentions and making people think something about you that isn't true. People like to make others believe they are good, while maybe they are hiding the bad things they do. But in the end, everything is always exposed. Proverbs 5:21a says, "*The Lord clearly sees everything you do.*" Nothing is ever hidden from God no matter how hard we try.

It's easy to cover our true hair color, and it's okay to dye it! Some people don't like their natural color, or maybe they want to hide what is gray. Just remember that our actions are always known. So let us live for Christ today.

Prayer: *Heavenly Father, You see everything! I praise You for this. Please help me do what is right. In Jesus' name. Amen.*

Hair Salon (4) by Rachel Burkum
Today's Reading: Romans 6:1-7

Every week when I clean my local hair salon, most of my tasks are the same. I take out the trash, sweep and mop the floor, and dust the shelves. One thing that never changes is the amount of hair. It gets everywhere! Each week I sweep up a lot of hair. It falls on the floor and on the chairs. It hides under the shelves, and gets stuck under the front desk. There is always hair! Obviously a lot of people have their hair cut every week, so it's understandable. But sometimes it can feel a little frustrating. Sometimes I wonder... should I just stop cleaning because the hair will be back next week anyway? No!

Just as it would be silly to stop cleaning up the hair, it would be silly to continue sinning just because we know God forgives us. In verses 1 and 2 of our reading today, Paul says, "*So do you think we should continue sinning so that God will give us more and more grace? Of course not! Our old sinful life ended. It's dead. So how can we continue living in sin?*" We all sin. Even after we accept Jesus as our Savior and follow Him, we still fail. Everyone does, and it is a daily struggle. But that doesn't mean we should just give up. That doesn't mean we should simply give in and continue sinning because we know we will fail anyway. Yes, we sin. But we all should work towards a better relationship with Jesus, and that means avoiding sin the best we can. Don't give up. Keep trying!

Prayer: *Dear God, please help me avoid sin so I can be closer to You. In Jesus' name. Amen.*

Hair Salon (5) by Rachel Burkum   **Today's Reading:** Psalm 23:1-6

One reason many people go to a hair salon is because it can be very relaxing. Having someone else wash your hair can feel good. A pedicure can be very enjoyable and make a person feel pampered or special. It can be a nice treat just to have someone else do things for you and make you feel pretty or handsome.

The verses I chose for today are very well-known. A lot of people have memorized Psalm 23, and it is often used in sermons or for special occasions. It's not surprising, because these verses can be very comforting. *"I will not be afraid of any danger, because you are with me. Your rod and staff comfort me"* (verse 4b). King David wrote this Psalm, and he's comparing God to a shepherd. Shepherds work very hard at keeping their sheep safe. They look out for danger, make sure the sheep have plenty of good grass and water, and lead them around danger. If the shepherd does a good job, his sheep will feel content, relaxed and safe. This is how we can feel with God. He is always caring for us, making sure our needs are met, and keeping us from harm.

There's nothing wrong with finding physical relaxation, like enjoying a trip to the hair salon. But what feels even better is when our spirit can find comfort and peace in God.

Prayer: *Father, You make me feel loved and safe. Thank You! Help me to always come to You for peace. In Jesus' name. Amen.*

Hair Salon (6) by Rachel Burkum   **Today's Reading:** James 1:19-25

One thing I must do when I clean the hair salon each week is make sure all the mirrors are clean. There is a large mirror at each hair cutting station, cleaning station, and in the bathroom, too. Hair stylists use a lot of different products that can cause streaks or smudges on the mirrors, so I try to make sure all of that is removed. Then, when the next person comes in for a haircut, they can see themselves clearly. A lot of people want their hair to look exactly one way, so they will study their style closely in the mirror before leaving.

Today's Bible reading mentions a mirror. In verses 23 and 24, James says, *"Hearing God's teaching and doing nothing is like looking at your face in the mirror and doing nothing about what you saw. You go away and immediately forget how bad you looked."* If you look in a mirror and see dirt on your face, do you ignore it? Hopefully not! If I see dirt on my face, I want to fix it immediately. I don't want to be embarrassed by other people seeing me that way. That's James' point. If we read the Bible, understand it, agree with it, but then we don't change our behavior, what good is it? We need to apply God's Word, not just read and forget it.

Just as we improve our appearance after looking in a mirror, we need to improve our lives after learning what God wants.

Prayer: *Heavenly Father, help me to not just read Your Word, but also to apply it to my life. In Jesus' name. Amen.*

Hair Salon (7) by Rachel Burkum
Today's Reading: Proverbs 3:5-8

In this final devotion about my local hair salon, I want to talk about trust. It takes a lot of trust for someone to allow another person to cut their hair. I've seen some bad haircuts, and it can be embarrassing! That's why people are willing to pay for a professional haircut. Even so, if you need to visit a hair salon where you've never been before, it can be a risk. You have to trust that the stylist knows what they are doing and won't ruin your hair.

Today's Bible reading is another one that is well-known. When I think about trusting God, these verses always come to mind first. "*Trust the Lord completely, and don't depend on your own knowledge*" (verse 5). We are told to not only trust God, but also not depend on our own knowledge. Both of these need to happen if we are to have complete faith in God.

When someone else cuts my hair, I need to trust they know what they're doing. Their methods might not make sense to me. Maybe halfway through the haircut, it looks strange, or I don't understand why they use certain scissors or combs. But I have to trust the stylist. In the same way, I don't always understand God's methods. I can't see the end result like He can. But that doesn't mean I should doubt Him. It means I need to trust Him even more. The whole world's knowledge all together can't compare to God's knowledge. Let's remember that today.

Prayer: *Father, I recognize that You are wise and know all things. In Jesus' name. Amen.*

God's Point of View by Jim Godsey
Today's Reading: Colossians 3:12-15

Justice, mercy, grace and forgiveness are four ideas that we should think about. Justice, from our point of view, involves making sure other people get exactly what they deserve. Mercy means not giving to people something they deserve. Grace involves giving to people something they don't deserve. And with forgiveness we try to "forgive and forget" when other people have done something to us that we don't deserve.

Now, let's look from God's point of view. God's justice involves His patience. We get what He has told us we will get if we disobey, but only after leaving God no other choice. Mercy, with God's love, keeps us out of situations He knows we can't handle on our own. God's grace involves His generosity. We receive favors and gifts that we haven't earned. And His forgiveness involves the sacrifice of His only Son, Jesus, who died on the cross for us.

In our Bible verses Paul encouraged the Colossian Christians to think about things from God's point of view. "*Show mercy to others. Be kind, humble, gentle, and patient. Don't be angry with each other, but forgive each other. If you feel someone has wronged you, forgive them. Forgive others because the Lord forgave you*" (verses 12b-13). I like the way God thinks better than the way we humans do. Don't you?

Prayer: *Dear Lord, help me to show your justice, mercy, grace and forgiveness to other people. In Jesus' name. Amen.*

I Will Never Leave You by Donna Howard   **Today's Reading:** Hebrews 13:1-5

Last spring, a robin chose to build her nest in one of my flower boxes on our front porch. Soon three eggs appeared. When the eggs hatched, there were three fuzzy babies in the nest. The babies grew and eventually left the nest. However, one baby bird seemed fearful of venturing very far from the nest. For several days it sat on the porch steps, chirping for its mother.

Then one day the baby bird hopped onto the lawn. As the bird moved about, the mother bird hovered nearby, ready to fly into action should her baby bird be threatened by a cat or other animal. Finally the little bird gathered enough courage to fly off on its own.

This reminds me of a verse from our Bible reading for today. In verse 5b, the writer of Hebrews reminds us that God said, *"I will never leave you; I will never run away from you."* We can be comforted in knowing that God watches us, just as a mother bird watches her babies. And God is always ready to spring into action to help us, comfort us and encourage us. When we know that God is always watching us, we can feel at peace.

Remember that whatever happens today, God will be with you!

Prayer: *Dear Lord, thank You for the comfort of knowing You are watching over me and that You will never leave me. In Jesus' name. Amen.*

Sharing our Story by Jo Krueger   **Today's Reading:** Acts 9:1-22

Today I had the honor of speaking for a ladies' brunch at the church where I grew up. There were about 70 ladies there. Some I did not know, but some I have known all my life. It was good to look over the crowd and see the faces of people who have impacted my life.

The theme of the brunch was "Sharing the Heart of Jesus." I talked about different ways that we can do this using our possessions, our food, our money and our time. I also talked about sharing our story as we reach out and help other people. We all have a story about how God has worked in our lives and shaped us into being His faithful servants.

In our Bible reading for today, Saul shared the story of how he met Jesus and how Jesus changed His life. Saul went into the city of Damascus, and a man named Ananias taught him about Jesus. Saul was baptized and immediately started telling people what God had done for him. Verses 19b-20 tell us, *"Saul stayed with the followers of Jesus in Damascus for a few days. Soon he began to go to the synagogues and tell people about Jesus. He told the people, 'Jesus is the Son of God!'"*

How has God worked in your life? How has He changed you and helped you become like Jesus? Be sure to share your story with someone today.

Prayer: *Dear God, thank You coming into my life, forgiving me and saving me. In Jesus' name. Amen.*

Be Like Jesus (1) by Jo Krueger

Today's Reading: John 20:30-31, 21:25

A few years ago many Christians wore bracelets or shirts or carried Bible covers with the letters "WWJD." Those letters stood for "<u>W</u>hat <u>W</u>ould <u>J</u>esus <u>D</u>o?" These items were a way for Christians to remember that they should always try to be like Jesus – to do what He did, to say what He said, to forgive like He forgave and to love like He loved.

Today and for the next few days, we will talk about ways that we should be like Jesus. We will learn about some things that Jesus did when He lived here on earth. And we will be encouraged to follow Jesus' example of obedience and love every day of our lives.

The New Testament Gospel books of Matthew, Mark, Luke and John tell us many things that Jesus did when He was on earth. In our Bible reading for today, John tells us why he wrote about Jesus' life. *"But these are written so that you can believe that Jesus is the Messiah, the Son of God. Then, by believing, you can have life through his name"* (verse 31).

I hope that you are excited to try to be like Jesus. He wants you to love and follow Him every day. It won't be easy, but with the help of the Holy Spirit, you can grow and live closer to God every day.

Prayer: *God, thank You that we can read about Jesus in the Bible and follow His example. In Jesus' name. Amen.*

Be Like Jesus (2) by Jo Krueger

Today's Reading: Matthew 4:1-11

Our Bible reading today tells us about the time right before Jesus began His ministry on earth. *"Then the Spirit led Jesus into the desert. He was taken there to be tempted by the devil. Jesus ate nothing for 40 days and nights. After this, he was very hungry"* (verses 1-2).

While Jesus was in the desert, the devil came to Him and tempted Him. The devil wanted Jesus to disobey God, and sin. Three times the devil suggested that Jesus do something. Jesus knew that doing those things would be wrong. What did Jesus do? Each time Jesus was tempted, He answered the devil by repeating a verse from the Bible. Those verses encouraged Jesus and helped Him say, "No!" to the devil.

Every day the devil tempts us to do wrong things. Sometimes we are weak and we choose to do the wrong thing. The Bible can help us to be strong and stand against the devil. If the devil tempts us to steal, we can remember Exodus 20:15. *"You must not steal anything."* If we are tempted to tell a lie, we can think about Ephesians 4:25 which tells us to stop telling lies.

Study the Bible every day. Remember the verses that you read. Then you can be like Jesus and say, "No!" to the devil.

Prayer: *Dear Father, I want to be like Jesus and stand strong against the devil. In Jesus' name. Amen.*

Be Like Jesus (3) by Jo Krueger   **Today's Reading:** Matthew 9:35-38

Jesus was often surrounded by crowds of people. Some people wanted to see Jesus because they were curious. Others wanted to learn from Him. And some people wanted Jesus to heal them.

Our Bible reading today tells us how Jesus responded to these people. Verse 36 says, *"Jesus saw the many people and felt sorry for them because they were worried and helpless – like sheep without a shepherd to lead them."*

What did Jesus do? He loved these people. Jesus felt sorry for them and helped them. Jesus healed some people, but He encouraged and taught all the people. Jesus wanted everyone to know about God's love.

You can be like Jesus today by serving other people like He did. Encourage them to read God's Word. And most of all, tell them about God's wonderful gift of salvation through His Son, Jesus. Paul talked about this in 2 Timothy 4:2. *"Tell everyone God's message. Be ready at all times to do whatever is needed. Tell people what they need to do, tell them when they are doing wrong, and encourage them. Do this with great patience and careful teaching."*

Do you want to be like Jesus? Then love and encourage people you will meet today.

Prayer: *Dear God, thank You for Jesus' example of service and love. I love You. In Jesus' name. Amen.*

Be Like Jesus (4) by Jo Krueger   **Today's Reading:** Luke 8:4-15

Jesus was a very special teacher. He taught simple lessons. People were drawn to Him and wanted to learn more. When Jesus talked with people, He taught in two ways. First, Jesus taught be telling people about God and how they should follow and obey Him. Second, Jesus taught by His example. Jesus obeyed and served God and encouraged people to be like Him.

Our Bible verses today talk about a time when Jesus taught a large group of people. As Jesus often did, He told the people a story about everyday things they could understand. In this story Jesus talked about a farmer planting seeds. The seeds were planted in different kinds of ground – by the side of the road, on rocks, among the weeds and on good ground. Some seeds grew, some withered after growing, and some seeds didn't grow at all.

Jesus explained that the seeds represent God's teaching. Some people will not accept or obey what God says. Others will accept it for a short time but then fall away. But some people *"hear God's teaching with a good, honest heart. They obey it and patiently produce a good crop"* (verse 15b).

God wants us to teach other people about Him by sharing God's message with them. We can also teach them by our example of being like Jesus every day.

Prayer: *Dear God, I want to teach other people about You. Help me to follow Jesus' example. In His name. Amen.*

Be Like Jesus (5) by Jo Krueger
Today's Reading: Mark 11:15-19

Our Bible reading today is about a time when Jesus and His followers went to the Temple in Jerusalem. Jesus was very upset when He saw that some people were buying and selling things in the Temple, which was a holy place for the Jews. He said, *"It is written in the Scriptures, 'My Temple will be called a house of prayer for all nations.' But you have changed it into a 'hiding place for thieves'"* (verse 17b). Jesus quoted this verse so the people would know that He knew God's laws and was obeying them.

Often when Jesus was speaking, He quoted verses from the Scriptures. The Scriptures were the books of the Old Testament that the Jews studied. Jesus knew what God's Word said, and He was able to share it with people.

We need to follow Jesus' example and know God's Word. Knowing the Bible happens when we study it every day. Then we can be ready to share Bible verses with people who want to know about God. It is good if we can memorize some verses, but it is also good to know where to look in the Bible to find verses that talk about salvation and obeying God.

Study God's Word, the Bible, today. Be like Jesus. Ask God to help you keep His Word in your heart.

Prayer: *Dear Heavenly Father, I want to study Your Word, know it and share it with others. In Jesus' name. Amen.*

Be Like Jesus (6) by Jo Krueger
Today's Reading: John 13:1-5

Jesus was a very humble person. He was always thinking about other people and how He could help them. Jesus looked for opportunities to show His love to the people that He met.

At the time Jesus lived on earth, many people wore sandals on their feet. They walked on dusty roads all the time, so their feet became very dirty. It was their custom to wash people's feet when they came into a house. Usually a slave or servant had the job of washing people's feet.

Our Bible verses for today tell us that Jesus and His followers were at an evening meal. Evidently no one had offered to wash the feet of Jesus and His followers. *"So while they were eating, Jesus stood up and took off his robe. He got a towel and wrapped it around his waist. Then he poured water into a bowl and began to wash the followers' feet. He dried their feet with the towel that was wrapped around his waist"* (verses 4-5).

Jesus was a humble servant. He was willing to wash people's dirty, smelly feet! This is a good example of how we should serve other people. When we see that someone needs help or encouragement, we should be humble and serve them.

Be like Jesus today. Look for ways to be humble and serve God.

Prayer: *God, I want to be like Jesus and be Your humble servant. Show me how I can serve others. In Jesus' name. Amen.*

Be Like Jesus (7) by Jo Krueger   **Today's Reading:** John 17:1-26

John, chapter 17, is a prayer that Jesus prayed on the night before He was crucified. First, Jesus prayed that God would give Him the glory that He had with God before the world was made. Then, Jesus prayed for His followers and for all the people who would follow Him in the future. Verse 21 says, *"Father, I pray that all who believe in me can be one. You are in me and I am in you. I pray that they can also be one in us. Then the world will believe that you sent me."*

The books of Matthew, Mark Luke and John tell us that Jesus prayed many times. Jesus always prayed before He made important decisions, like choosing His twelve disciples. Sometime He prayed all night. Often He went to a quiet place to pray where He could be alone.

If we want to be like Jesus, we need to pray, too. It is always good to say a short prayer at mealtime and bedtime. But it is also important to spend time sharing our thoughts and needs with God. The more we pray, the more we know about God and what He wants us to do.

If prayer is not an important part of your life, you can change that today. Spend some time talking to God, and let Him speak to you through His Word, the Bible. God will pay attention to your prayers and bless you!

Prayer: *Father, I want to make prayer an important part of my life. Thank You that I can communicate with You and that You will listen to me. In Jesus' name. Amen.*

Be Like Jesus (8) by Jo Krueger   **Today's Reading:** Matthew 26:36-46

Yesterday we talked about Jesus' prayer in John, chapter 17, for His followers and for people who would follow Him in the future. After Jesus prayed that prayer, He and His disciples went to a garden outside of Jerusalem. While they were there, Jesus prayed again to God.

Jesus was very upset and sad. In verse 38b He said, *"My heart is so heavy with grief, I feel as if I am dying."* He knew that very soon He would die. Jesus knew that people would beat Him, make fun of Him and then hang Him on a cross to die. Jesus did not want to face the terrible pain and separation from God. He prayed to God, *"My Father, if I must do this and it is not possible for me to escape it, then I pray that what you want will be done"* (verse 42b). Jesus knew that He should obey God and do what God wanted Him to do.

Sometimes it is easy to obey God. But other times we may not want to obey God because we don't want to suffer pain or do something that is difficult for us to do. But we need to be like Jesus and be willing to surrender to God's will and do what He wants.

No matter what happens to you today, remember to always obey God and do what He wants you to do. Then you will be like Jesus!

Prayer: *God, I thank You for Jesus' example of obedience. Help me to always accept Your will for my life. In Jesus' name. Amen.*

Be Like Jesus (9) by Jo Krueger   **Today's Reading:** Luke 23:26-43

Sometimes we may feel that we cannot forgive people who have hurt us. We may want to hurt them and make them pay for what they did to us. When Jesus was dying on the cross, He gave us a wonderful example of how we should forgive other people.

As Jesus and His followers were in the garden, soldiers came and arrested Him. They subjected Him to false trials and told lies about Him. Then they did terrible things to Him. They hit Him, spit on Him, mocked Him and put a crown of thorns on His head. If people did those things to you, how would you feel? What would you do?

Our Bible reading today tells us what Jesus did. He didn't shout at the people or ask God to destroy them. Jesus didn't say bad things about the people or try to hit them back. Instead, Jesus forgave them! Verse 34a says, *"Jesus said, 'Father, forgive them. They don't know what they are doing.'"*

Jesus was in terrible pain. He was ready to die. Because Jesus accepted our sins, He was separated from God. But Jesus still forgave the people who were hurting Him. Maybe someone will lie about you today or say bad things to you. Will you get mad and say bad things back to them? Or will you be like Jesus and forgive?

Prayer: *Dear God, thank You for Jesus' example of forgiveness. Help me to be forgiving like Him. In His name. Amen.*

Be Like Jesus (10) by Jo Krueger   **Today's Reading:** Philippians 2:5-11

For the past few days we have talked about things that Jesus did while He was on earth. Today I want to talk about *why* Jesus did those things.

Our Bible verses for today begin with these words in verse 5: *"In your life together, think the way Christ Jesus thought."* Then these verses tell us some of the things Jesus did. He gave up His place with God and became a lowly servant on earth. Jesus was always humble and obedient. He was even willing to die on a cross. Why did Jesus do these things? Because He loves us so much!

1 John 3:16a says, *"This is how we know what real love is: Jesus gave his life for us."* Jesus loves us so much that He was willing to die so we can have forgiveness and eternal life with Him. Jesus doesn't just love rich or beautiful or successful people. He loves everyone! Maybe it is hard for you to understand that Jesus loves you, but He does, and He wants you to live forever with Him. And He wants you to give Him honor and praise. *"God did this so that every person will bow down to honor the name of Jesus. Everyone in heaven, on earth, and under the earth will bow"* (verse 10).

I hope that you have learned more about Jesus through this devotional series, and I challenge you to be like Him today. Be humble and serve and forgive other people. Obey God and love other people the way that Jesus loved.

Prayer: *Heavenly Father, help me to be loving, humble and obedient like Jesus was. In His name. Amen.*

Simple Obedience by Bob La Forge   **Today's Reading:** 2 Kings 5:1-15

Our Bible reading for today tells us about Naaman. He was the captain of a foreign army. He also had leprosy, a terrible skin disease. Naaman heard that a prophet in Israel was able to cure leprosy, so he came in all his splendor to see Elisha.

Elisha told Naaman to simply wash in the Jordan River seven times and he would be healed. *"Naaman became angry and left. He said, 'I thought Elisha would at least come out and stand in front of me and call on the name of the Lord his God. I thought he would wave his hand over my body and heal the leprosy'"* (verse 11). Perhaps Naaman thought that marvelous signs would appear in the sky and the ground would tremble. But instead, the solution was very simple. Fortunately, Naaman's servants encouraged him to obey Elisha and go wash in the Jordan River. After he had dipped himself in the river seven times, he was healed.

How often are we like that? We want God to guide us and we look for a sign. But God says, "Read my Word." We are hurting and are expecting a magical touch but God says, "Pray and go to church." And, we are unsaved and wanting salvation but God says, "Believe and obey."

God does not need to do tricks to prove anything. We should obey Him simply because He is God.

Prayer: *Heavenly Father, help me today to simply follow and obey You and Your Word. In Jesus' name. Amen.*

They are Your Life! by Bonnie Hall   **Today's Reading:** Deuteronomy 32:1-47

Most of Deuteronomy, chapter 32, is a song that Moses and Joshua sang to the Israelites. It was a way to teach them and to remind them of what God had done for them. The song begins by talking about God. *"The Lord is the Rock, and his work is perfect! Yes, all his ways are right! God is true and faithful. He is good and honest"* (verse 4).

Next, the song reminds the people of all the ways God took care of them as they traveled from Egypt to the new land. And finally, Moses and Joshua talk about the importance of God's teachings. *"When Moses finished giving these teachings to the people, he said to them, 'You must be sure to pay attention to all the commands I tell you today. And you must tell your children to obey completely the commands in this Law. Don't think these teachings are not important. They are your life! Through these teachings you will live a long time in the land across the Jordan River that you are ready to take"* (verses 45-47). Moses said that God's teachings were so important that they were the Israelites' life.

God's teachings are still important to us today. If we follow His teachings, then we will be blessed in our life on earth. And, we will have the promise of life forever with Him.

Prayer: *Lord, thank You for Your teachings that show me how to live and be with You forever. In Jesus' name. Amen.*

Ezekiel's Visions (1) by Gayle Thorn

In this series we will talk about Ezekiel, God's prophet, and the visions that he saw. A vision is an appearance or manifestation of God. A vision can be dreamlike or it can be an actual, physical appearance of God or beings or objects that God is working through. God gives visions in order to either give someone direction or to reveal some truth to them.

In Ezekiel, chapter 10, Ezekiel begins to describe what he saw in his vision. *"Then I looked up at the bowl over the heads of the Cherub angels. The bowl looked clear blue like sapphire, and there was something that looked like a throne over it"* (verse 1). Ezekiel goes on to describe the four cherubim – angelical beings with wings and wheels. These cherubim appeared in the clouds. Fire came from their wheels. It seems that this fire was a form of God's wrath directed at judging the city of Jerusalem because of her sin.

I don't fully understand Ezekiel's vision in this chapter. But I do know that God used this vision to reveal His plan to Ezekiel. Ezekiel then wrote down what he saw so we can read it, and even if we don't understand it all, we can certainly learn from Ezekiel's vision. Tomorrow we will look at some of the things we can learn from this first vision of Ezekiel.

Prayer: *Heavenly Father, thank You for my salvation through faith in Jesus. Speak to me and teach me how to please and honor You. In Jesus' name. Amen.*

Ezekiel's Visions (2) by Gayle Thorn

Yesterday we started talking about Ezekiel's vision from God. *"Then the cloud filled the Temple, and the bright light from the Glory of the Lord filled the whole courtyard"* (verse 4b). What can we learn from Ezekiel's vision? First, we can learn that God created all things. He can use those creations to accomplish all of His plans because He controls everything. Second, we can learn that God is powerful. He can do anything. Nothing is too hard for Him.

Third, we can learn that it isn't wise to make God angry. To avoid God's anger and judgment, we must confess and repent of our sins and believe that Jesus died as the punishment for our sins. We must allow God's Holy Spirit to control our lives. Fourth, we can learn that God wants us to know about His plans. If we sincerely pray and ask Him to teach us and show us His plans, He will do that.

If you have never experienced a dream or vision from God, don't worry. Most of us haven't. What is important is that we want to know God and understand His plan by spending time with Him every day. We can do that by reading our Bible and praying and by listening to the teachings of pastors and other wise Christians. God is waiting for your heart to be willing, your mind to be open to His teaching and your ears to be ready to hear His voice.

Prayer: *Heavenly Father, thank You for Your teachings. Show me how to apply Your Word to my life. In Jesus' name. Amen.*

Ezekiel's Visions (3) by Gayle Thorn   **Today's Reading:** Ezekiel 23:1-49

In Ezekiel, chapter 23, God tells Ezekiel about two wicked sisters – Oholah and Oholibah. In verses 36-39, the Lord describes their evil, saying, *"Son of man, will you judge Oholah and Oholibah? Then tell them about the terrible things they have done. They committed the sin of adultery. They are guilty of murder. They acted like prostitutes – they left me to be with their filthy idols. They had my children, but they forced them to pass through fire. They did this to give food to their filthy idols. They also treated my special days of rest and my holy place as though they were not important. They killed their children for their idols, and then they went into my holy place and made it filthy too! They did this inside my Temple!"*

Oholah and Oholibah weren't real people. These two sisters symbolized the region of Samaria and the kingdom of Israel, God's own people!

God had chosen the people of Israel to be His special people. Samaritans were people from Israel who had intermarried with foreigners. Therefore, their roots were in being part of God's chosen people, too. Tomorrow we will talk more about these two sisters.

For now, I hope you will take a few moments and ask God to show you any sin in your life so you can ask His forgiveness and turn away from it.

Prayer: *Father, please show me my sin. Forgive me and help me to turn away from it. In Jesus' name. Amen.*

Ezekiel's Visions (4) by Gayle Thorn   **Today's Reading:** Ezekiel 23:1-49

Let's continue talking about the two sisters in Ezekiel's vision. Sadly, the Israelites and the Samaritans had rejected God and defiled His holy place. Verse 5a of our Bible reading says, *"Then Oholah became unfaithful to me – she began to live like a prostitute. She began to want her lovers."* Then verse 11 adds, *"Her younger sister Oholibah saw all these things happen. But Oholibah sinned more than her sister did! She was more unfaithful than Oholah."*

We must be careful to not be like these two symbolic sisters. We must watch that we don't slip or turn away from God. If God's chosen people could turn away from Him, like this vision describes, we could turn away from Jesus and turn our backs on our Heavenly Father, too.

How can we protect ourselves from the judgment of the two sisters? We should read our Bibles every day and memorize Bible verses. That is our weapon against sin. We must use it to protect our hearts. Also, don't forget to worship God with other believers. Times of fellowship with other Christians will strengthen and encourage us.

Pray continually, never – NEVER – stop praying! Ask God to protect you and draw you close to Him. God's presence is the safest place to be.

Prayer: *Heavenly Father, draw me close to You. Guard my heart and don't let me stray or abandon You. In Jesus' name. Amen.*

Ezekiel's Visions (5) by Gayle Thorn   **Today's Reading:** Ezekiel 41:1-26

Ezekiel, chapter 41, records yet another vision given to the prophet Ezekiel by God. In this vision, Ezekiel saw a man. Verse 1 says, *"Then the man led me into the Holy Place. He measured the walls on either side of the room. The side walls were 6 cubits thick on each side."* The rest of chapter 41 describes the parts of God's tabernacle that Ezekiel watched the man measure.

How does this apply to Christians today? I don't have all the answers, and neither does anyone else. Some experts think the vision is about Solomon's Temple. Others think it's about Zerubbabel's Temple. However, most experts agree that this Temple is a real Temple of God. They believe it will be built by God and used to worship God during Christ's 1,000 year reign.

No matter what happens here on earth, God will always exist. God wants us to be with Him and to worship Him. Personally, I agree that this Temple is a Temple yet to come – a Temple that believers in Jesus Christ will see and worship in. I am looking forward to the day when I can worship and praise God in that Temple. Are you?

If you have confessed and repented of your sin, and have been obedient to Jesus, He is preparing you to worship Him in that glorious Temple someday!

Prayer: *Father, thank You for the hope and encouragement that comes from Ezekiel's vision of Your Temple. Prepare me to worship in Your holy Temple. In Jesus' name. Amen.*

Not New and Improved by Pam Davis   **Today's Reading:** Galatians 1:6-9

Advertisers use many different words and ways to draw in new customers. But it's all about money – the companies who make the products want our money. So they often use the words "new and improved" in their commercials and packaging. And it works! Many people buy these products because they think they are better.

We want new things and we want them to be better than what we had before. One example is new cars. Each year customers are excited to see what the new cars look like and what new features they have.

Some Christians are also looking for something that is new and improved. But God's message that was taught by Paul was the same message that was preached by Peter on the Day of Pentecost. False teachers tried to tell people a new message, but the Gospel didn't change. Paul talked about this in verses 8-9 of our Bible reading. *"We told you the true Good News message. So anyone who tells you a different message should be condemned – even if it's one of us or even an angel from heaven! I said this before. Now I say it again: You have already accepted the Good News. Anyone who tells you another way to be saved should be condemned!"*

We don't need a new and improved Gospel! We need to pay attention to God's message of saving people through His love and grace.

Prayer: *Father, thank You for Your message of salvation that was shown to us when Jesus died on the cross. In His name. Amen.*

U-Turn by Rachel Burkum

Today's Reading: Acts 2:36-40

I do a lot of driving every day, to and from my job. That also means I see a lot of different drivers doing a lot of different things! I see good drivers, bad drivers, and drivers that take risks. Some drivers follow the law very well, and others seem to ignore it. Today, I saw someone do a "u-turn" at an intersection of a busy highway. Thankfully, they had a green light, so they did not cause an accident. I rolled my eyes, but it made me stop and think about our Bible reading.

Verse 38 says, "*Change your hearts and lives and be baptized, each one of you, in the name of Jesus Christ. Then God will forgive your sins, and you will receive the gift of the Holy Spirit.*" Some versions of the Bible use the word "repent." Repenting is like a u-turn. If someone sins, tells God they are sorry, then goes right back to that same sin, is that what God wants? No. To change your heart (to repent) is to make a u-turn in life. It means not only stopping the sin, but turning around and heading in the opposite direction.

No one is perfect. Romans 3:23 tells us, "*All have sinned and are not good enough to share God's divine greatness.*" But that doesn't mean we should stop trying to be like Jesus! In order to follow Him completely, we need to change our hearts - repent - and leave behind the sins that hurt our relationship with Him.

Prayer: *Dear God, I am sorry for my sins. Please forgive me and help me avoid those sins from now. In Jesus' name. Amen.*

Hard to Swallow by Pam Davis

Today's Reading: John 6:51-66

Some people believe everything they hear or read. Others take time to think things through and decide whether it is true or false. When a person accepts a lie, we say that they have swallowed it. Just as a fish hooks itself then swallowing a worm, foolish people swallow the lies that people tell. But sometimes we hear something that is true, and we find it hard to believe. Then we say that it is "hard to swallow."

In John, chapter 6, Jesus was teaching the people, and He called Himself the Living Bread. Verse 51 tells us what Jesus said. "*I am the living bread that came down from heaven. Whoever eats this bread will live forever. This bread is my body. I will give my body so that the people in the world can have life.*" This concept was hard for some people to understand. For those people, Jesus' teaching was hard to swallow.

Just as bread keeps us alive physically, accepting and following Jesus keeps us alive spiritually. Jesus explained this in verses 57-58. "*The Father sent me. He lives, and I live because of him. So everyone who eats me will live because of me. I am not like the bread that your ancestors ate. They ate that bread, but they still died. I am the bread that came down from heaven. Whoever eats this bread will live forever.*"

Don't reject God's Word! Accept it and let it guide your life everyday. You can always trust what Jesus says.

Prayer: *Dear Heavenly Father, I trust You and believe that Your Word is true. In Jesus' name. Amen.*

Tackle Your Problems by Gayle Thorn   **Today's Reading:** Ephesians 3:14-20

How do you deal with your problems? Do you try to avoid them and forget them or do you tackle them head on? Jesus' actions show us what He expects us to do about our problems.

Matthew, chapter 4, tells us that the devil attacked Jesus in the desert by tempting Him three times. Jesus tackled each of the devil's temptations head on. He didn't avoid the temptations. Jesus didn't try to push the devil around by using His own human strength. Jesus used God's Word to tackle His problems.

We can't tackle the devil or our earthly problems successfully on our own, using our own strength either. But with the strength of God's Word, we are unbeatable!

How can you be sure that you will have the strength of God's Word available when you need it? Memorize it! The more Bible verses you have memorized, the stronger you will become. You will have the strength of God's Word hidden in your heart and mind, ready to use to tackle any problem that comes your way.

In our Bible verses for today, Paul prayed for the church at Ephesus. In verse 16, he said, *"I ask the Father with his great glory to give you the power to be strong in your spirits. He will give you that strength through his Spirit."* That is my prayer for you as you face the devil and his temptations, and tackle your problems today.

Prayer: *Father, thank You for showing me how to overcome the devil. In Jesus' name. Amen.*

September 2

A Fish Story by Norma Mezoe   **Today's Reading:** Matthew 17:24-27

Jesus' enemies were always trying to trap Him. One time they asked Him if it was right to pay taxes to the Caesar, the ruler of the Roman government. Jesus' answer was, *"Then give to Caesar what belongs to Caesar, and give to God what belongs to God"* (Luke 20:25b).

One day Jesus showed His disciples a unique way of doing that. It involved a fish story, but one that is true and can be found in our Bible verses for today. Every year, a tax was collected for the upkeep of the Temple. This tax was collected from every Jew over the age of 20.

Our Bible reading tells us that Jesus and His disciples arrived in the city of Capernaum. Some tax collectors asked Peter if Jesus paid taxes. Peter said that yes, Jesus did. Then Jesus told Peter, *"Go to the lake and fish. After you catch the first fish, open its mouth. Inside its mouth you will find a four-drachma coin. Take that coin and give it to the tax collectors. That will pay the tax for you and me"* (verse 27b).

That is quite a fish story! But what is the lesson? We can learn from this story that Jesus obeyed the laws of the land where He lived. That is a good example for us to follow. We should honor God by obeying His laws as well as the laws of our government.

Prayer: *Father God, please help us to follow Jesus' example to obey Your laws as well as the laws of our country. In Jesus' name. Amen.*

An Unsteady Boat by Gayle Thorn   Today's Reading: Malachi 3:6a

The world is in turmoil today. Wars are happening. People are confused about what is right and what is wrong. Does it seem like things around you are changing so fast that you can't keep up? Do you feel like you aren't sure who and what you can trust? Does it feel like you are sailing through life in an unsteady boat that is about to tip over?

Thankfully, when we feel like that, we can cling to a promise from God's prophet, Malachi. What is this promise? Malachi 3:6a says, *"I am the Lord, and I don't change."* Yes, it is true. God never changes. God is always the same. He always keeps His promises, and He will always punish sin. God hates sin and always rewards obedience. God always loves sinners (including you and me). God always forgives sinners (including you and me). And God will always be there to help anyone who comes to Him for help.

When you think that you can't handle one more change in your life, you can go to God. He is the same today as He was yesterday. And He will still be the same tomorrow. When you feel like your boat is about to tip over, you can count on God to keep you steady and headed in the right direction. Tell God that you need His help and ask Him to comfort and strengthen you as you face a new day.

Prayer: *Father, my life seems to be unstable. But I know that You never change. I need You to keep me on the path that leads to You. In Jesus' name. Amen.*

Keep Focused on Jesus by Jo Krueger   Today's Reading: Hebrews 12:1-3

As I am typing this devotion, my husband is watching a Sunday night NFL football game. Although I can see the TV screen, I am trying not to be distracted and watch the game. But the noise of the crowd in the football stadium is almost deafening. I can't imagine how noisy it would be to actually sit in the stadium.

I would think that the noise would bother and distract the football players. They need to focus and keep their mind on the game or they won't play well. It would be easy to listen to the crowd, lose focus and drop the football.

Our Bible reading today reminds us to keep our focus in life on Jesus. *"We have all these great people around us as examples. Their lives tell us what faith means. So we, too, should run the race that is before us and never quit. We should remove from our lives anything that would slow us down and the sin that so often makes us fall. We must never stop looking to Jesus. He is the leader of our faith, and he is the one who makes our faith complete"* (verses 1-2a).

Whatever you are doing today, remember to stay focused on Jesus. How can you do that? Think about the things Jesus did while He was on earth. Remember His words of encouragement and help. Take time to think about how Jesus has worked in your life and blessed you today. And don't forget to praise Him!

Prayer: *Dear God, please help me to stay focused on Jesus today and to not pay attention to the world. In Jesus' name. Amen.*

God's Anger by Gayle Thorn

Today's Reading: Psalm 4:1-5

2 Samuel 24:1 says, *"The Lord was angry with Israel again."* God does become angry, and often He was angry when the people of Israel turned away from Him and worshiped false gods.

What things make God angry? God becomes angry when we argue with Him like Moses did (Exodus 4) and think we know better than He does. God becomes angry when we complain and aren't content with what He has provided for us. This happened a lot with the Israelites as they were traveling to the new land God gave them. God becomes angry when we don't honor Jesus or when we reject Him as our Lord and Savior. God becomes angry when we refuse to admit that we are sinners. And God becomes angry when we disobey.

In our Bible verses for today, the psalmist shows us how we can please God, instead of making Him angry. Verses 4-5 tell us, *"Tremble with fear, and stop sinning. Think about this when you go to bed, and calm down. Selah. Give the right sacrifices to the Lord, and put your trust in him!"* We please God when we stop sinning, obey Him and trust Him.

Ask God to help you do things today that will please Him and bring honor to His holy name.

Prayer: *Heavenly Father, I am sorry that I sin and make You angry. Help me to change my behavior and stop sinning. In Jesus' name. Amen.*

Compassion by Bonnie Hall

Today's Reading: Matthew 8:1-5

Our Bible verses today from Matthew tell us about a time when Jesus met a man who was sick, and had compassion for him. *"Then a man sick with leprosy came to him. The man bowed down before Jesus and said, 'Lord, you have the power to heal me if you want.' Jesus touched the man. He said, 'I want to heal you. Be healed!' Immediately the man was healed from his leprosy"* (verses 2-3). Jesus felt sorry for this man. He even touched the man – something that people were afraid to do. And then Jesus healed the man.

God has compassion on sick people today. He gives strength, peace and even healing to whatever sickness we have. I have a dear friend who was diagnosed with ALS. The doctor told her that she had 18 months to live. But my friend prayed in faith and asked God to heal her. My friend was not healed, but she did live for three more years. When times were rough, God gave her peace and helped her face each day and to stay strong.

My friend's family and friends saw her faith and how God worked in her life. Because of that, many of them accepted God's message of salvation and became followers of Jesus. God cares about what happens to you every day. He will always be with you to comfort you and give you peace.

Prayer: *Heavenly Father, thank You for loving us and showing us Your compassion. In Jesus' name. Amen.*

Live God's Way by Gayle Thorn

We all need to come to a point in our lives where we ask Jesus Christ to forgive us and take control of our lives. When we do that, we are asking Him to come live in us. We are saying that we don't want to live the way we lived in the past. We want to start living for Him!

That's what Paul was talking about in verse 20 of our Bible reading for today. *"So I am not the one living now — it is Christ living in me. I still live in my body, but I live by faith in the Son of God. He is the one who loved me and gave himself to save me."* Paul was reminding the Galatian Christians that Jesus was the one making a difference their lives.

When we begin our new lives in Jesus, we begin to make new choices. We want to live God's way. Since we can't live in a way that pleases God by ourselves, He sends His Holy Spirit to live in us. The Holy Spirit gives us comfort, guidance, strength and the ability to live for God and to live God's way. Without the Holy Spirit helping us, we can't live God's way and please Him.

Do you want to live God's way? Then depend on the Holy Spirit every day. Thank God for sending His Holy Spirit to give us help, guidance and strength. We can't live God's way without the Holy Spirit!

Prayer: *Heavenly Father, forgive me and send me Your Spirit to help me live each day for You. In Jesus' name. Amen.*

Don't Be Afraid by Bonnie Hall

Moses was dead, and Joshua was leading the Israelites. God told Joshua that it was time for them to cross the Jordan River and go into the new land. I am sure Joshua must have looked across the Jordan River and wondered what God had in store for him and the Israelites.

I felt like that when I was working in a daytime summer children's program at a city shelter. The first day I was there, I was afraid, and I wondered where God was leading me. As I crossed the parking lot to the city shelter, I remembered God's words to Joshua. *"Always remember what is written in that book of law. Speak about that book and study it day and night. Then you can be sure to obey what is written there. If you do this, you will be wise and successful in everything you do. Remember, I commanded you to be strong and brave. Don't be afraid, because the Lord your God will be with you wherever you go"* (verses 8-9).

Every evening when I left the shelter and went home, I studied my Bible and then I prayed for each of the children by name. I was excited to see how God would use me to help these children grow and learn about Him. Whenever a problem came up and I was afraid, I remembered that God would be with me and help me find a solution. Don't be afraid – God will be with you today!

Prayer: *Lord, thank You for Your promise that You will be with me every day to guide me. In Jesus' name. Amen.*

Stress Becomes Peace by Gayle Thorn   **Today's Reading:** Philippians 4:1-9

One of the main sources of stress in our lives is our own thoughts. If we are filling our minds with negatives ideas, things that make us worry or be anxious, or things that make us feel afraid, we set ourselves up for stress. Those kinds of thoughts are guaranteed to make us feel stressed. What can we do to get rid of those negative thoughts and the stress?

We need to replace those negative ideas, worrying thoughts and fearful feelings with the kind of thoughts that Paul talked about in verse 8 of our Bible reading for today. *"Brothers and sisters, continue to think about what is good and worthy of praise. Think about what is true and honorable and right and pure and beautiful and respected."* These kinds of thoughts change our stress into a peace that can only come from God. This peace is a confidence that even during stressful times, God is in control, and we can trust Him to take care of us and our stressful situation. This peace knows, beyond a doubt, that God works everything – even those things that worry or frighten us – for our best and for His glory.

Think about your life. I pray that you will talk to God and pray about whatever is stressing you. Then allow Him to take care of those situations and change your stress into peace.

Prayer: *Father, help me to replace all my negative thoughts with positive, godly thoughts. Then fill me with Your peace. In Jesus' name. Amen.*

Salt (1) by Jo Krueger   **Today's Reading:** Judges 9:42-45

I love French fries! Last week my daughter and I ate at McDonald's. They were very busy and it took a long time to get our order. Finally they brought us our lunch, and the French fries were the best French fries I have ever eaten! They were hot and had just the right amount of salt on them. They tasted so good!

Salt is a very important mineral for life on earth. During Roman times, salt was so valuable that some soldiers were paid with salt instead of money. And salt is mentioned many times in the Bible. Today and for the next few days we will learn about references to salt in the Bible.

Our Bible verses for today tell us about Abimelech destroying the city of Shechem. In these verses we learn what Abimelech did after he destroyed the city. *"Then Abimelech tore down the city and threw salt over the ruins"* (verse 45b). Why did Abimelech put salt on the ruins of the city? When salt was put on the ground, the land was no longer good for growing any crops. So the city of Shechem could never be rebuilt on that site.

Salt can be used for both good and bad purposes. In the same way, the things you do each day can be used to please God or to make God unhappy. It's your choice. Depend on God to help you do things today that show your love for Him.

Prayer: *Dear Heavenly Father, I love You and want to do things that show You how much I love You. In Jesus' name. Amen.*

Salt (2) by Jo Krueger

Today's Reading: Genesis 19:12-26

If I were to ask a group of people where salt is mentioned in the Bible, I am sure many people would bring up the story about Lot's wife. Lot, his wife and his daughters lived in the wicked city of Sodom. The city was so wicked that God wanted to destroy Sodom and the nearby city of Gomorrah.

God sent two angels to help Lot and his family escape from Sodom. These men gave Lot and his family an important warning. *"So after the two men brought Lot and his family out of the city, one of the men said, 'Now run to save your life! Don't look back at the city, and don't stop anywhere in the valley. Run until you are in the mountains. If you stop, you will be destroyed with the city!"* (verse 17). Then verse 28 tells us what happened as Lot and his family were fleeing from Sodom. *"Lot's wife was following behind him and looked back at the city. When she did, she became a block of salt."* We don't know for sure why Lot's wife disobeyed the warning, but I think that she wanted one last look at the city and the pleasures that she loved.

When we repent and decide to follow God, we need to put our old life behind us. That means we should stop sinning and thinking about the pleasures of our past life. Keep your eyes focused on Jesus and on obeying Him today. God will be with you and help you stay strong.

Prayer: *Dear Lord, thank You for making me a new person. Help me to obey and follow You. In Jesus' name. Amen.*

Salt (3) by Jo Krueger

Today's Reading: 2 Kings 2:19-22

Today we will learn how salt was used to perform a miracle. Elisha became God's prophet. One day some men from the city of Jericho came to Elisha. They explained that their water was not good and that they could not grow any crops. Elisha asked the men to bring him a bowl and to put salt in it. *"Then he went out to the place where the water began flowing from the ground. Elisha threw the salt into the water and said, 'The Lord said, "I am making this water pure! From now on this water will not cause any more death or keep the land from growing crops."' The water became pure and is still good today. It happened just as Elisha had said"* (verses 21-22).

Did the salt in the bowl make the water in Jericho pure? I don't think so. This was a miracle that God allowed Elisha to perform. This was just another example of God's power. When people witnessed this miracle, there were reminded how powerful and mighty God was. That helped them continue to follow and obey God and His laws.

God may not perform miracles like this today, but there are still miracles all around us. Everything in nature reminds us of God's great power and His love for us. Take some time today to notice a flower, a bird soaring overhead or the stars in the nighttime sky, and then thank God for what He has made for you.

Prayer: *Dear God, I can see Your power and Your love in all the things You have made for me. Thank You. In Jesus' name. Amen.*

Salt (4) by Jo Krueger

Today's Reading: Matthew 5:13-16

When Jesus taught the Jewish people about God, He often talked about common everyday things. In our Bible verses for today, Jesus was teaching a large group of people. He wanted them to understand how important it was for them to be good witnesses for Him.

In verse 13 Jesus used the example of salt. *"You are the salt of the earth. But if the salt loses its taste, it cannot be made salty again. Salt is useless if it loses its salty taste. It will be thrown out where people will just walk on it."* The right amount of salt makes our food taste better. A few days ago I talked about how good the salted French fries tasted. But what if the salt had lost its saltiness? Would the French fries have tasted as good? No!

Just as salt makes food taste better, people who follow God make life on earth better. When God's people are doing good things and obeying Him, they show other people that they should follow God, too.

Whatever you do today, God will give you opportunities to be "salt" for other people. Be sure that you show them you obey God and you do things that please Him. *"Live so that they will see the good things you do and praise your Father in heaven"* (verse 16).

Prayer: *Dear Father, help me to live for You today and to truly be "salt" for the world. In Jesus' name. Amen.*

Salt (5) by Jo Krueger

Today's Reading: James 3:10-12

This is our last devotion about salt. The Dead Sea in Israel is sometimes called the Salt Sea in the Bible. Why? Because it has an exceptionally high salt content and is one of the saltiest bodies of water on earth. The Dead Sea is 8.6 times saltier than the oceans. It has so much salt that when people swim in the Dead Sea, they float and cannot sink. There are no fish, plants or other visible life in the sea. And there are no cities or animal life surrounding the Dead Sea. That is how this body of water got its name.

Because of its saltiness, the Dead Sea cannot give water that is pure. James talked about this in our Bible verses for today. Verses 11 and 12 tell us, *"Do good water and bad water flow from the same spring? Of course not. My brothers and sisters, can a fig tree make olives? Or can a grapevine make figs? No, and a well full of salty water cannot give good water."* But what was James talking about? He was saying that if we truly follow God, the things we do and say will be good things. Bad things should not come from a person who is truly obeying God.

People in the world are watching what you do and say today. Be sure that you are showing those people that You love and follow God. Rely on His Holy Spirit to guide and encourage you!

Prayer: *God, I want to show other people that I love You. Help me to do and say things that will please You. In Jesus' name. Amen.*

True Peace by Gayle Thorn

Things like being abandoned, or being falsely accused or natural disasters often cause people to become depressed, angry and bitter. Or they may blame God for the bad things that happen to them. As Christians, we should have a different response to painful events in our lives.

In verse 27 of our Bible reading, Jesus said, *"I leave you peace. It is my own peace I give you. I give you peace in a different way than the world does. So don't be troubled. Don't be afraid."* The true peace that Jesus gives to those who welcome Him into their lives, should be the foundation of a Christian's response to all events – both joyful events and painful events.

True peace is the kind of peace that only Jesus can give. It shows itself during hard times. True peace is being confident that hard times will pass and that God is with us so we don't have to struggle alone.

Does that mean when we experience painful circumstances we shouldn't cry, grieve or feel pain? No! Jesus did all those things while He was here on earth. But it does mean that when we face hard situations, we can trust God. We know that He is in control. We rest in the assurance that His great peace will calm and comfort us until the hard times pass.

Prayer: *Heavenly Father, I want to experience Your peace. Help me to let go and trust that You are in control of all that happens in my life. In Jesus' name. Amen.*

Dry Ground by Bonnie Hall

Our Bible verses tell us that the time had come for the Israelites to cross the Jordan River and go into the land that the Lord had promised to them. So according to God's instructions, the priests got ready to carry the Box of the Agreement (sometimes called the Ark of the Covenant) across the river.

It was the time of year that the Jordan River flooded, so the river was at its fullest. The priests stopped at the edge of the Jordan and immediately the water piled up like a wall. *"The ground at that place became dry, and the priests carried the Box of the Agreement of the Lord to the middle of the river and stopped. They waited there while all the Israelites walked across the Jordan River on dry land"* (verse 17).

It had been a long journey for the Israelites, and they had learned through bad times that they needed to trust God. So they followed God's plan for crossing the Jordan, and He led them across on dry ground.

When we look back over our lives, we can see how God has blessed and guided us through good times and bad times. We need to have the faith that the Israelites had, remembering that God knows more than we do. We should just trust God and follow what He says. Then we can know that He will always be with us in the future.

Prayer: *Dear Father, You took care of the Israelites, and I know that You will take care of me, too. In Jesus' name. Amen.*

A Better Life by Gayle Thorn

Today's Reading: Philippians 1:15-26

In verse 21 of our Bible reading, Paul wrote, *"To me, the only important thing about living is Christ. And even death would be for my benefit."* How can anyone believe that it is good to die?

When a Christian dies, his life doesn't end. Actually, his true life is just beginning. God created us to live with Him forever, but because of sin, there is a barrier between God and us. That barrier is death.

However, Jesus came to earth and died so that we could go around that barrier. When we believe that Jesus died in our place, death becomes the door that opens into an eternal lifetime of freedom from evil and pain. Death is a door that leads from earth to heaven. When we go through that door, we are reunited with loved ones and will live with them and with God forever. With Jesus as our Lord and Savior, death isn't the end – it's the beginning!

While we may not want to die this minute, we need to be ready when death does come. We need to know what will happen to us. When we know that we have Jesus in our lives, we know that our life won't end; it will only get better. We know that, in fact, for us to die is good. Are you ready?

Prayer: *Heavenly Father, forgive me and come live with me now so that when I die, I'll live forever with You. In Jesus' name. Amen.*

Lessons from Isaiah (1) by Norma Mezoe

Today's Reading: Isaiah 40:1-5

In the days of Isaiah, when a king was about to come into an area, workers went before him and prepared the road. Large stones were removed from the road, brush and trees cut away, and where possible, the road was straightened and the low spots filled.

Isaiah wrote in verse 3 of our Bible reading about someone shouting in the desert. This person would come before Jesus and prepare the way for Him. *"Listen, there is someone shouting: 'Prepare a way in the desert for the Lord. Make a straight road there for our God.'"* This person would preach about repentance to those who needed to change their lives.

Who was this prophecy talking about? John the Baptist was the New Testament prophet mentioned in these verses. John told the people that they needed to change their lives and repent of their sins. Then John baptized them in the Jordan River. In doing so, John prepared the people's hearts for the coming of Jesus, who was the Messiah, God's chosen one.

Today we can be like John the Baptist. We can help prepare people to change their lives and be ready to accept Jesus as their Lord and Savior.

Prayer: *Lord, please help me to prepare someone to accept Jesus and follow Him all their life. In Jesus' name. Amen.*

Lessons from Isaiah (2) by Norma Mezoe   **Today's Reading:** Isaiah 61:1-4

Early one wintry morning, the substation that provides electricity to our small town was destroyed. Quickly, homes cooled and then became uncomfortably cold. A few people were fortunate to have gas heaters or wood stoves. The majority of our town's 400 citizens were left without any type of heat. Many of those people were elderly or suffered from illnesses. The cold was especially severe for them. They needed to be in warm surroundings.

But soon help was on the way. Volunteers went to the homes of those who needed help. A school in another town was opened for shelter. Members of a church prepared nourishing warm food. These people were doing what Isaiah was talking about in verses 2b-3a of our Bible reading. *"He has sent me to comfort those who are sad, those in Zion who mourn. I will take away the ashes on their head, and I will give them a crown. I will take away their sadness, and I will give them the oil of happiness. I will take away their sorrow, and I will give them celebration clothes."*

No one in our town argued about what needed to be done. Instead, the people worked together to provide comfort and warmth as soon as possible. In this way, they showed God's kindness to people in need. Look for ways that you can show God's kindness today.

Prayer: *God, help us to be willing to help when there are people in need. Help us to show comfort and kindness. In Jesus' name. Amen.*

Lessons from Isaiah (3) by Norma Mezoe   **Today's Reading:** Isaiah 65:21-24; 66:4

As I was growing up, there was a younger boy who lived across the road from our house. When the boy's mother called him home for dinner, she began by calling, "Jimmy!" But if he didn't come home right away, she would start calling his complete name. Sometimes he would answer and come home, but often he would ignore her call.

Isaiah 65:24 says, *"I will answer them before they call for help. I will help them before they finish asking."* That is talking about God answering the Israelites even before they called for help. Isn't it wonderful that God knows what we need before we express that need to Him?

But in Isaiah 66:4b God said, *"I will punish them using what they are most afraid of. I will do this because I called to them, but they did not answer. I spoke to them, but they did not listen. They did what I said is evil. They chose to do what I did not like."* God called to the Israelites but they refused to respond to Him. So He punished them for their disobedience.

Jimmy missed some meals because he didn't answer his mother's call, and I am sure that we have missed out on some of God's blessings because we have refused to listen to Him. Be sure to pay attention to God today!

Prayer: *Father, thank You for listening to us. Please help us to listen to Your voice and to answer quickly. In Jesus' name. Amen.*

We Will Win by Gayle Thorn

Today's Reading: 1 Corinthians 15:50-58

In January 1992, the Buffalo Bills football team was losing to the Houston Oilers. The Bills were behind 38 to 3 with only minutes left in the game. The Bills could have given up. They could have believed that the Oilers had already won. They could have thought, "What's the use?" The Bills simply could have quit. But they didn't. The Bills came back to win the game 41 to 38. This game has become known as one of the greatest come-from-behind wins in the history of the National Football League.

We may often feel like giving up on sharing our faith in Jesus. We think that no one is listening to us, that no one cares or no one wants to have a relationship with Jesus – or even know *about* Jesus. We think, "What's the use?" We want to quit telling people about Him.

Like the Buffalo Bills, we need to keep forging ahead. Verses 57-58 of our Bible reading say, *"But we thank God who gives us the victory through our Lord Jesus Christ! So, my dear brothers and sisters, stand strong. Don't let anything change you. Always give yourselves fully to the work of the Lord. You know that your work in the Lord is never wasted."* Although it may seem like we are losing to the devil, we need to keep doing what God wants us to do. We will win in the end!

Prayer: *Heavenly Father, I'm glad that I can know I'm on the winning side. I can't wait until we win! In Jesus' name. Amen.*

Small Things by Bob La Forge

Today's Reading: Genesis 11:1-9; Luke 21:1-3

Today we will be looking at two passages from the Bible. The verses in Genesis talk about the Tower of Babel – a great project that required a tremendous amount of planning, resources and hard work. The result would have been a spectacular building. But God Himself stopped the work of building the tower because the people became proud.

In the second passage Jesus is telling us about an anonymous woman who did a very small thing. Verses 2-3 tell us what she did. *"Then he saw a poor widow put two small copper coins into the box. He said, 'This poor widow gave only two small coins. But the truth is, she gave more than all those rich people.'"* Jesus used this small act as a timeless example of faith.

Today the world teaches us to admire the great and the spectacular. But what is a greater display of grace – the baseball player who slugs the game-winning home run or the single parent who takes time to teach her children to follow God? Is it the millionaire who gives thousands of dollars to charity or the person whose health is failing but still manages to go to church each week and bless people?

Small things done with God's grace are always the greatest! Remember that greatness is not measured by the size of the project but by obedience to God.

Prayer: *Dear Heavenly Father, help me to focus on obeying You every day of my life. In Jesus' name. Amen.*

Loopholes by Gayle Thorn

We are always looking for loopholes. Loopholes are ways to avoid doing things that we must do but don't want to do – like paying taxes or obeying the law. Sadly, many people even look for loopholes in God's Word rather than just simply obeying it.

For example, God has commanded us to forgive others and let God punish those who have hurt us. But, when someone has hurt us, we often look for ways to avoid forgiving them. Instead, we try to think of ways to hurt them or make them pay for what they did.

Looking for loopholes when God has given us a specific command to do something is disobedience. God has told us in the Bible what He expects us to do. God's Word gives us instructions for living, and He expects us to obey those instructions in every area of our lives. God doesn't want us looking for loopholes so we can get out of obeying Him. He expects us to simply obey His commands. God wants us to remember the words of James 1:22 and obey them. This verse says, *"Do what God's teaching says; don't just listen and do nothing. When you only sit and listen, you are fooling yourselves."*

Are you obeying God's Word? Or are you too busy looking for loopholes?

Prayer: *Dear Father, I am sorry that I've been looking for loopholes in Your Word. Forgive me and help me to simply obey You. In Jesus' name. Amen.*

Simple Faith by Bonnie Hall

Our Bible reading for today tells us about Joshua sending two spies into Jericho to look around. When these men were in Jericho, they stayed at Rahab's house. She told the spies that people in Jericho had heard how God's power had helped the Israelites as they crossed the Red Sea. So the people in Jericho were afraid of the Israelites. When the king sent a message to Rahab asking about the spies, she hid the men and said that they were not in her house.

Rahab kept the spies safe. Later she said to them, *"So now, I want you to make a promise to me. I was kind to you and helped you. So promise me before the Lord that you will be kind to my family. Please tell me that you will do this. Tell me that you will allow my family to live – my father, mother, brothers, sisters, and all their families. Promise me that you will save us from death"* (verses 12-13). The spies made the promise to save Rahab and her family. Rahab helped the spies safely escape and go back to the Israelite camp.

Rahab's simple faith in God came just by hearing about how He took care of the Israelites. Her belief led her to keep the spies safe. And because of this, she and her family were saved when Jericho was destroyed. Do you have faith like Rahab did? Do you believe that God will take care of you every day?

Prayer: *God, I believe that You are powerful and that You can take care of me every day. In Jesus' name. Amen.*

Where Will You Live? by Gayle Thorn
Today's Reading: Psalm 90:1-17

The psalmist who wrote today's Bible verses says that God has existed since before the beginning of time. These verses tell us that God will live for eternity – long after life as we know it here on earth ends. Here's how he explained this in verses 1-2. *"My Lord, you have been our home forever and ever. You were God before the mountains were born, before the earth and the world were made. You have always been and will always be God!"*

Compared to the length of God's existence, the length of our lifetime here on earth is very short – like one eye blink or one heartbeat. Thankfully, our short life here on earth isn't the end of our existence. God plans for each one of us to live forever with Him.

While we are living here on earth, God expects us to choose where we plan to spend our eternal life. He gives us two choices: heaven or hell. To choose to follow and obey Jesus is to choose heaven. To not choose Jesus or to not choose at all is to choose hell. It's up to us to prepare now for the eternal life that is to come. We will all live forever. The question is, *"Where* will you live forever?"

I hope you will choose to follow Jesus and to choose heaven!

Prayer: *Heavenly Father, I choose to follow and love You every day of my life. In Jesus' name. Amen.*

Waiting in the Silences by Bob La Forge
Today's Reading: John 11:1-16

Martha and Mary were sisters whose brother, Lazarus, was deathly sick. So they did the right thing and sent for Jesus. But Jesus waited. Martha and Mary did everything they should have done. So did Jesus reward their trust and come quickly to Lazarus? No! In fact, Jesus waited until the point that Lazarus was dead and beyond help. Verse 14 says, *"So then Jesus said plainly, 'Lazarus is dead. And I am glad I was not there. I am happy for you because now you will believe in me. We will go to him now.'"* Were Martha and Mary frustrated that Jesus did not come right away? Were they confused by what Jesus did? I am sure they were. But Jesus knew the outcome. He delayed because He was not merely content to heal a sick man. He wanted to raise a dead man.

Sometimes we face difficult times, and we call on God to help us. But then He does not do what we want. Things get worse and we continue praying, but there is no change or answer. God is often silent in our darkest moments. But during these times, God has a greater plan for us.

Do we trust God because of what He has done for us, or because of who He is? Do we love God because of His responses, or because of His promises? We must trust God even in the silences.

Prayer: *Father, teach me not to desire comfort but to always want to obey Your will. In Jesus' name. Amen.*

When Anger Becomes Sin by Gayle Thorn   **Today's Reading:** 1 Samuel 20:1-34

Saul, king of Israel, had stopped obeying God. So God had chosen David to become king in place of Saul. Saul wasn't happy about God's decision. Because David honored and obeyed God, God caused all David did to succeed, including David's friendship with Saul's son, Jonathan. Saul became jealous of David's successes.

Then Saul's jealousy over David's success turned into anger. This anger was directed at his son, Jonathan. Jonathan had done nothing wrong. There was no reason for Saul to be angry with Jonathan, but verse 30 of our Bible reading says, *"Saul was very angry with Jonathan and said to him, 'You son of a twisted, rebellious woman! I know that you have chosen to support that son of Jesse. This will bring shame to you and to your mother.'"*

When anger is directed at an innocent person, it becomes sin. When anger is directed at someone other than the person who has earned it, it becomes sin. When an angry person reacts to his feelings of anger by verbally or physically harming someone, the anger has become sin.

How do you act when you become angry? Do you deal with the source of the problem or do you act like Saul and attack the first person who walks into the room? Think about it!

Prayer: *Heavenly Father, teach me to learn to control my temper and appropriately direct my anger. In Jesus' name. Amen.*

Changed by Jennifer Forrester   **Today's Reading:** Acts 22:1-29

Last night I watched a movie that was based on a true story. It was about a man who had a problem with alcohol and drugs and physically abused his wife and children. Many people thought that he was without hope and that he could never change his life. But through it all, his wife stayed with him and helped him see that he needed to know Jesus as his Lord and Savior. Today that man is a very successful Christian businessman who preaches about Jesus and helps others to know Him.

Many Christians probably thought that Paul was without hope, too. He was a Jew who did not believe in Jesus and persecuted those who did. In verse 4 of our Bible reading for today Paul talked about this. *"I persecuted the people who followed the Way. Some of them were killed because of me. I arrested men and women and put them in jail."* But Jesus appeared to Paul and told him that he was going the wrong way in life. Paul changed his life – he repented, was baptized and became a bold preacher of the Gospel message about Jesus.

Maybe you know someone that you think is so bad that they will never become a Christian. Don't give up on them! Pray for them every day, encourage them and be an example for them to follow! With God's help they, too can change!

Prayer: *Dear Lord, help me to be an example that will show people how they can follow and serve You. In Jesus' name. Amen.*

Why God Hates Lies by Gayle Thorn
Today's Reading: Psalm 119:65-72

Why does God hate lying so much? Let's look at some verses in Psalms and Proverbs to learn what happens when we lie. Lying ruins relationships. People who lie can't be trusted (Psalm 5:9). People who lie are deceitful (Psalm 12:2-3). Liars are self-centered and don't love other people (Psalm 28:3). People who lie are fools (Psalm 36:3), and they are two-faced (Psalm 62:4). Liars hide their hatred of other people (Proverbs 10:16) and they are destructive (Proverbs 11:9).

What does God want us to do when we are tempted to lie? Let's look at some more verses from Psalms and Proverbs to answer this question. God wants us to know when we should keep quiet and not speak (Psalm 39:1). He wants us to speak with gentleness and wisdom (Psalm 49:3). God wants us to let His Spirit control our speech (Psalm 141:3). He wants us to know what we are talking about (Proverbs 15:2). And He wants us to remember that we are accountable for every word we speak (Proverbs 21:3).

What does God want us to do when other people lie about us? He wants us to follow David's example in verse 69 of our Bible reading. *"People full of pride made up lies about me. But I keep obeying your instructions with all my heart."* Be sure that you please God today!

Prayer: *Dear Heavenly Father, please make my words to be pleasing to You today. In Jesus' name. Amen.*

Lines by Rachel Burkum
Today's Reading: Deuteronomy 31:7-8

On my way to work each day, I pass a popular coffee shop. I love the coffee there, and it's always a treat when I spend a little extra money to buy their drinks. But in the mornings, I rarely have time to stop. Almost every day, their drive-thru line is very long. It usually wraps all the way around their parking lot! If I took the time to get in line and wait, then I would surely be late for work. So, I usually decide to drive on by, even though I really want their coffee.

Waiting in lines can be very frustrating, especially when they are that long. Lines can make us late, make us irritated, and test our patience. Thankfully there is one thing we never have to wait in line for – God. He is always available. Always!

The Bible verses today describe Moses handing over leadership of the Israelites to Joshua. As overwhelming as that job probably was, Moses assured Joshua that God would never leave him. We can trust this promise for ourselves, too. The writer of Hebrews tells us in chapter 13, verse 5, *"...God has said, `I will never leave you...'"* There is no waiting for God to be with us. There is no line, no drive-up window, and no cash price. God is always there when we need Him.

It's easy to take God's presence for granted. But let us always remember and be grateful for the ability to come to Him at any place, and any time.

Prayer: *Dear God, help me to remain focused on Jesus always! Please guide me. In Jesus' name. Amen.*

Water by Debbie Klahn

Today's Reading: John 4:1-42

Water is necessary to live. A person needs to eat, but a person can live longer without food than they can live without water. Rich people, poor people, older people and younger people need clean water. People of all skin colors and language groups need water.

When I have traveled overseas, many times I was told, "Do not drink the water." I had to be careful when I brushed my teeth to use clean water. Drinking dirty water makes people sick, and sometimes they die. Millions of dollars are spent every day to dig wells and find clean water. Water is very important and something all people need.

The Bible has many stories that talk about water. The Israelites begged Moses for water in the wilderness (Exodus 17:2). Jesus talked about giving a cup of cold water as an act of kindness (Matthew 10:42). And in our Bible reading for today, Jesus told a woman at a well that she needed living water. *"But anyone who drinks the water I give will never be thirsty again. The water I give people will be like a spring flowing inside them. It will bring them eternal life"* (verse 14).

Jesus invites everyone to drink the living water that brings eternal life. That living water is Jesus! Follow Him today and satisfy your spiritual thirst.

Prayer: *Father, thank You that we can drink of the living water that only Jesus gives. In His name. Amen.*

Rare Jewel by Gayle Thorn

Today's Reading: Proverbs 20:15

Diamonds. Rubies. Emeralds. Sapphires. These precious jewels are rare and beautiful gifts. We love to look at them and admire them as the sunlight causes them to sparkle. People spend thousands of dollars investing in these beautiful rare jewels. And these precious jewels are often given as a sign of a person's love for another person.

The Bible says that we can possess a jewel that is even more beautiful than a diamond – and even more rare. That jewel is found in Proverbs 20:15. *"The right knowledge can bring you gold, pearls, and other expensive things."* What is the rare jewel spoken of in this verse? That jewel is right knowledge. Some Bible translations translate "right knowledge" as "lips that speak knowledge."

Right knowledge means having a mind that is filled with wisdom and a mouth that is able to clearly share that wisdom with other people. We can't buy this rare jewel for any amount of money. We can only possess this priceless jewel by investing our time in God who is the source of all wisdom, by studying His Word and by asking Him to give us this gift.

How much are you investing in this priceless jewel that God is offering you?

Prayer: *Heavenly Father, fill me with Your wisdom so that I can speak with right knowledge. In Jesus' name. Amen.*

Led by the Spirit by Norma Mezoe

Agonizing sobs came from William's throat as he poured out his sin and distress to his minister. William, a married man, had become attracted to his secretary, and he realized that was wrong.

William was a mature Christian who had studied the Bible and attended worship services since childhood. He knew what the Bible said about the holiness and importance of marriage. He realized that his desire for this other woman was not right. What William was feeling was the Holy Spirit convicting him and telling him that what he was doing was wrong. The Holy Spirit reminded him of his need to surrender his wrong desires to God and allow Him to cleanse him. The writer of Psalm 51 talked about that in verses 9 and 10. *"Don't look at my sins. Erase them all. God, create a pure heart in me, and make my spirit strong again."*

Years later, as William looked back on those days when he faced temptation, he could clearly see God's leading. Now he is very thankful. Through counseling with his minister, through Bible study, and through the conviction of the Holy Spirit, William was able to overcome the temptations and win the spiritual battle.

Are you struggling with sin today? Tell God you are sorry, change your heart and ask God to give you a pure heart again.

Prayer: *Loving Father, thank You for convicting and guiding me through Your Holy Spirit. In Jesus' name. Amen.*

How to Pray (1) by Rachel Burkum

Online shopping is so easy today! Technology has advanced so much that all I have to do is pick up my phone, open a shopping app, pick out what I want, and click a couple buttons. Then in a few days, a package shows up at my house. Cool! I don't have to go anywhere at all or talk to anyone. I see what I want, and I order it. It's that simple.

Do your prayers to God ever feel like a shopping list? "God, I want this, and this and this, and..." It is hard to remain humble and also know God can do anything for us. We have many examples in the Bible of people praying, including what some people call "The Lord's Prayer." In our Bible reading today, Jesus was explaining to the people how to pray. For the next few days, I'd like to learn from what Jesus says about prayer.

Verse 7a says, *"And when you pray, don't be like the people who don't know God. They say the same things again and again."* Jesus was explaining that people who did not truly know God would pray anyway, simply talking to no one special. They would pray over and over, but it was pointless because they did not know God. We need to know God. We need to have a relationship with Him so that our prayers will be sincere as we talk directly to Him.

Prayer: *Father, I want to know You! I want to be close to You as I pray each day. Please guide me. In Jesus' name. Amen*

How to Pray (2) by Rachel Burkum   **Today's Reading:** Matthew 6:7-13

Today we are continuing our discussion about "The Lord's Prayer." We will move on to verses 9b-10. Jesus said, *"Our Father in heaven, we pray that your name will always be kept holy. We pray that your kingdom will come – that what you want will be done here on earth, the same as in heaven."* How did His prayer begin? With humble respect, by acknowledging that God is holy.

When we are hurting or in need, it can be easy to overlook God's holiness and jump straight to our requests to Him. This is not a sin! Sometimes our hearts hurt so badly, all we can do is cry out to Him – and this is okay! But in our daily conversations with God, we need to remember to approach Him with respect. Yes, He can give us anything and everything. But praying to Him should not be like our shopping list. It should be a respectful conversation.

Jesus asked that God's name would be kept holy. He prayed that God's will (what God wants) would be done here on earth, the same as in heaven. This means knowing God's plan is greater and more important than anything we ask for. This means surrendering our own desires if what God wants is different than what we want. That isn't always easy, but we can trust that God will do what is best for us. Let's remember to be humble as we pray today.

Prayer: *God, I know You are all-powerful. You are mighty and You have a perfect plan for my life. Please help me be humble before You. In Jesus' name. Amen.*

How to Pray (3) by Rachel Burkum   **Today's Reading:** Matthew 6:7-13

"The Lord's Prayer" in Matthew is not only used as an example of how to pray, but it is often memorized and recited. There is nothing wrong with this – but I would like to help us personalize our prayers.

Verse 11 says, *"Give us the food we need for today."* This doesn't only mean actual food. Of course, we need food to survive, and this is a good thing to ask God for. But "food" can also mean anything we need. If my car breaks down, can I ask God to help provide a new part to fix it? Or if my roof leaks, can I ask God to help me find a way to repair it? Of course! If I don't have enough money to pay my bills, is it okay to ask God for money? Absolutely. God cares for all of our daily needs! This includes anything we need in this life on earth. Matthew 10:29-30 says, *"When birds are sold, two small birds cost only a penny. But not even one of those little birds can die without your Father knowing it. God even knows how many hairs are on your head."* God sees the big things in life, and He sees the little things, too. If He knows how many hairs are on your head, you can trust He watches us and knows and pays attention to what you need.

After we have come before the Lord in respect, then we have the opportunity to ask Him for what we need. Don't be afraid to tell Him what is on your heart.

Prayer: *God, thank You for loving me so much. Help me to remember that I can talk to You about all my needs. In Jesus' name. Amen.*

How to Pray (4) by Rachel Burkum   **Today's Reading:** Matthew 6:7-13

Let's move on to verse 12 in our reading today. "*Forgive our sins, just as we have forgiven those who did wrong to us.*" When Jesus prayed, He began with coming before God humbly with respect. Then He asked God to provide for any daily needs. Now Jesus asks God for forgiveness.

Did Jesus need forgiveness? No. Jesus was fully God and fully human, but He did not ever sin. The reason He prays about forgiveness in these verses is because it is an example for *us* – and all of us have sinned. What should we do when we fail to do what God wants? We should ask Him for forgiveness.

God sees everything we do and He knows when we give in to temptation. He also knows when we are sorry and want to repent (change). But we should still confess to Him and ask for forgiveness. This shows we are humble and willing to admit when we did something wrong. Jesus' death on the cross covers all our sins. But God still wants us to talk to Him about it.

We also can't forget to forgive other people who have hurt us. If we are not willing to forgive others, that bitterness separates us from God. We need to forgive others the same way God forgives us. This isn't always easy, but it is the right thing to do, and it will bring us closer to God.

Prayer: *Dear Father, please forgive me for my sins. Thank You! Please also help me forgive other people who have hurt me. In Jesus' name. Amen.*

How to Pray (5) by Rachel Burkum   **Today's Reading:** Matthew 6:7-13

This is the last day we will discuss Jesus' example to us on how to pray. I want to focus on verse 13, which says, "*Don't let us be tempted, but save us from the Evil One.*" Jesus is encouraging us to pray to God to help us avoid temptation.

It can be easy to think, "I can do this on my own." Asking for help goes against human nature. We often want to do things by our own power, and we don't want someone else's help. However, without God, facing temptations will only lead to sin. We need His help through the power of the Holy Spirit. In 1 Corinthians 10:13b, the apostle Paul tells us, "*But when you are tempted, God will also give you a way to escape that temptation.*" We don't need to face the temptations of this world alone. We don't need to face the devil alone. God wants us to ask for His help.

Let's review the last few days. First, we need to know God and have a relationship with Him. We also need to recognize His holiness and come to Him humbly. Third, we can always ask God for what we need in our daily lives – He wants to provide for us. We should forgive others who hurt us, just like God forgives us. And last, we should seek God's help for resisting sinful temptations.

We can pray to God any time, anywhere, out loud, or in our thoughts. No matter how you decide to pray, God simply wants you to communicate with Him!

Prayer: *Dear God, I love You and I want to talk with You every day. Help me to always remember that You listen to my prayers. In Jesus' name. Amen.*

Scars by Jim Godsey

I have a small scar above my right eye from being hit with a toy gun when I was a child. I have a slightly longer scar on my lower stomach from surgery. Several small scars on my hands and fingers tell of accidents I had while learning to use tools and pocket knives, and learning to play sports. I also have several scars on my arms and head from the removal of spots that could have become skin cancer.

Our scars tell stories about us. They are signs – signs of hurt and pain to our bodies but also signs of healing. The story in our Bible reading for today talks about Jesus' scars. When Jesus appeared to His disciples after His death and resurrection, He had scars from being crucified. When the other disciples told Thomas that they had seen Jesus after His resurrection, Thomas did not believe them. He said, *"That's hard to believe. I will have to see the nail holes in his hands, put my finger where the nails were, and put my hand into his side. Only then will I believe it"* (verse 25b).

Jesus' scars proved to Thomas that He truly was the crucified Savior. For us, Jesus' scars tell us the story of salvation and how Jesus endured pain and suffering on the cross. But it is through these scars that our spiritual wounds are healed and that we can have forgiveness and eternal life.

Praise God today for Jesus' scars and for salvation through Him.

Prayer: *Dear God, thank You that Jesus was willing to suffer and die so that my sins could be forgiven. In Jesus' name. Amen.*

God Parted the Waters (1) by Donna Howard

For today and the next three days we will talk about four times in the Bible where God parted waters. We will begin by talking about Moses.

After more than 400 years of holding the Israelite slaves in Egypt, Pharaoh finally agreed to let the people go so they could worship the Lord. However, when Pharaoh realized what he had done, he regretted his decision. He said, *"Why did we let the Israelites leave? Why did we let them run away? Now we have lost our slaves!"*(verse 5b). So Pharaoh changed his mind, and he and all of his army raced after the Israelites to force them to return to Egypt.

When the Israelites saw Pharaoh and his army racing toward them, they were terrified. They cried out to the God to help them. Then God said to Moses, *"Raise the walking stick in your hand over the Red Sea, and the sea will split. Then the people can go across on dry land"* (verse 16). Moses obeyed God and the sea split in two. When the people saw God's great power, they trusted Him and went through the Red Sea on dry land.

This was a great example of God's power. Do you believe in God's power? Do you trust Him to help you every day?

Prayer: *Dear God, help us to always believe in Your great power and to trust in You. In Jesus' name. Amen.*

God Parted the Waters (2) by Donna Howard   **Today's Reading:** Joshua 1:1-2; 3:14-17

Our Bible reading for today tells us that after the death of Moses, God spoke to Joshua, the new leader of the Israelites. God said, *"My servant Moses is dead. Now you and all these people must go across the Jordan River. You must go into the land I am giving to the Israelites"* (Joshua 1:2). Joshua told the people to get ready. In three days they would cross the Jordan River and take the land that God was giving to them. God told the Israelites that He would be with them and that no one would be able to stop them.

The Israelites arrived at the Jordan River early in the morning. God told Joshua to tell the priests who were carrying the Box of the Agreement to go to the edge of the river and stop. *"The priests who were carrying the Box came to the shore of the river. When they stepped into the water, immediately the water stopped flowing and piled up like a wall . . . The people crossed the river near Jericho. The ground at that place became dry, and the priests carried the Box of the Agreement of the Lord to the middle of the river and stopped. They waited there while all the Israelites walked across the Jordan River on dry land"* (Joshua 3:15b-17).

Joshua and the Israelites obeyed God, and He parted the water. Do you obey God when He asks you to do hard things?

Prayer: *Dear God, help me to always obey You and trust You to take care of me. In Jesus' name. Amen.*

God Parted the Waters (3) by Donna Howard   **Today's Reading:** 2 Kings 2:1-14

In 2 Kings, chapter 1, we learn how God protected the prophet Elijah from attacks by three groups of Ahaziah's soldiers. He did this by sending fire from heaven to consume them.

Chapter 2 tells us about the end of Elijah's life. Verse 1 tells us, *"It was near the time for the Lord to take Elijah by a whirlwind up into heaven. Elijah and Elisha started to leave Gilgal."* When they arrived in Gilgal, God told Elijah to go to Bethel. Elijah told Elisha to stay in Gilgal, but when he learned that Elijah was going to die, Elisha insisted on going along. When they arrived in Bethel, God told Elijah to go to Jericho. Again Elijah told Elisha to say where he was, and again Elisha insisted on going with him.

When Elijah and Elisha arrived at the Jordan River, *"Elijah took off his coat, folded it, and hit the water with it. The water separated to the right and to the left. Then Elijah and Elisha crossed the river on dry ground"* (verse 8). God took Elijah into heaven, and Elisha carried on the work of being God's prophet.

Each time God told Elijah to do something, Elijah obeyed and did what God wanted him to do. Elijah trusted God and always obeyed Him. Do you always obey God?

Prayer: *Dear Loving Father, I want to always obey You and do what You want. In Jesus' name. Amen.*

God Parted the Waters (4) by Donna Howard

Today's Reading: 2 Kings 2:1-14

As we closed our devotion yesterday, God was taking Elijah to heaven. *"Elijah and Elisha were walking and talking together. Suddenly, some horses and a chariot came and separated Elijah from Elisha. The horses and the chariot were like fire. Then Elijah was carried up into heaven in a whirlwind"* (verse11).

Elisha was very upset that Elijah, his friend and mentor, was gone and that he would never see him again. So he grabbed his clothes and tore them in two to show his sadness. *"Elijah's coat had fallen to the ground, so Elisha picked it up. He went back and stood at the edge of the Jordan River. He hit the water and said, 'Where is the Lord, the God of Elijah?'" Just as Elisha hit the water, the water separated to the right and to the left! Then Elisha crossed the river"* (verses 13-14).

This was the fourth time that God parted the water so that people could walk across on dry land. Each time it was God who did the miracle. Moses, Joshua, Elijah and Elisha all trusted God to perform these miracles and show His great power so that people would know that He was the one, true God.

These miracles show us that God can do the impossible. When we truly believe that, then we can trust God to help us go through each day. Thank God today for His great power.

Prayer: *Dear Loving Father, please help me to always trust You to do what is best for me. In Jesus' name. Amen.*

Love Protects by Gayle Thorn

Today's Reading: 1 Corinthians 13:6-7

Think about some things and people that you love. If you had a puppy, would you let him run around in the street? If you had a parakeet, would you open the window and let it fly in the backyard? If you had a family member who was allergic to milk, would you give them a big bowl of ice cream to snack on? Of course not!

First, it would be foolish, even dangerous, to do those things. Second, you wouldn't want to endanger or hurt your pet or family member. Why? Because you love them. When you love someone, you do everything that you can to protect them from any harm. Paul said it this way in our Bible verses today. *"Love is never happy when others do wrong, but it is always happy with the truth. Love never gives up on people. It never stops trusting, never loses hope, and never quits."*

Do your words and actions prove your love for the people around you? I hope so. I hope your words and actions show other people that you love them. I hope the things you do and say are done and said to protect people and not harm them.

Take some time today to think about what you say and do. Then make sure that you are following Paul's advice in 1 Corinthians and showing love for your family and friends.

Prayer: *Heavenly Father, thank You for loving me and protecting me. Help me to do the same for those around me. In Jesus' name. Amen.*

Remembering by Bonnie Hall

Today's Reading: Joshua 4:1-24

After my husband died while he was on duty as a firefighter, I received an American flag at a National Fallen Firefighter Memorial Service. I received the flag 18 months after my husband had died. That flag sits in my living room today. Every time I look at that flag, I remember how God gave me the strength and courage to go on with my life after my husband died.

Joshua, chapter 4, tells us what happened after the Israelites crossed the Jordan River on dry land. Verses 1-3 say, *"After all the people had crossed the Jordan River, the Lord said to Joshua, 'Choose twelve men, one from each tribe. Tell them to look in the river where the priests were standing and get twelve rocks from that place. Carry these rocks with you and put them where you stay tonight.'"*

So, according to God's instructions, the 12 Israelite men each chose a rock from the river, and placed them where they set up camp. Those rocks were piled up to help the Israelites and their descendants remember how God had protected them and helped them cross the Jordan River.

How has God protected you and given you strength? It is good for us to always remember how God has helped us. Then when we face times of trouble, we can know that God will continue to be with us.

Prayer: *Loving Father, thank You for helping me through some very difficult times in my life. Help me to always remember Your love and protection. In Jesus' name. Amen.*

Women in Acts (1) by Jo Krueger

Today's Reading: Acts 1:12-14

Women in Bible times were often put down and considered inferior. But God used many women to help start and grow His church. We learn about these women in the book of Acts. Some women had important roles, while others were only mentioned briefly. But all of these women can teach us something about serving and loving God.

One of the first women mentioned in Acts is Mary, the mother of Jesus. Verse 14 of our Bible reading tells us that Mary was one of the women who met with the apostles after Jesus went back to heaven. *"The apostles were all together. They were constantly praying with the same purpose. Some women, Mary the mother of Jesus, and his brothers were there with the apostles."* Why did Mary meet with the apostles? She met to pray with them.

It must have been exciting to be part of that prayer group. Maybe they were not sure they could do God's work without Jesus. Perhaps they wondered how they could share the Good News about Jesus with so many other people.

Mary believed in Jesus and served God through His church. You can serve God through your local church, too. Look for ways God can use you to spread His message of salvation.

Prayer: *Heavenly Father, show me how I can serve You and other Christians today. In Jesus' name. Amen.*

Women in Acts (2) by Jo Krueger   **Today's Reading:** Acts 5:1-11

Our Bible verses for today tell us about a woman named Sapphira. She and her husband, Ananias, were part of the church in Jerusalem. Acts 4: 34b-35 tell us what the people in that church did. *"Everyone who owned fields or houses sold them. They brought the money they got and gave it to the apostles. Then everyone was given whatever they needed."*

Ananias and Sapphira sold some land, but they gave only part of the money to the apostles. They secretly kept some of the money for themselves. It was not wrong for Ananias and Sapphira to only give part of the money to the church. But they lied about how much money they gave. Because of their lies, God punished them, and they both died. *"At that moment Sapphira fell down by his feet and died. The young men came in and saw that she was dead. They carried her out and buried her beside her husband"* (verse 10). This was a lesson for the other people in the church that they needed to always tell the truth.

There are people today in the church who are like Ananias and Sapphira. These people pretend that they give lots of money so that other people will praise them and respect them. But God always wants us to tell the truth. Be sure that everything you say is true and pleasing to God.

Prayer: *Dear God, help me to always please You by being honest and telling the truth. In Jesus' name. Amen.*

Women in Acts (3) by Jo Krueger   **Today's Reading:** Acts 6:1-4

In the Jerusalem church, there were two groups of people. The first group was Jews who read God's Word in the Hebrew language. The second group was people who read God's Word in the Greek language. When the Greek-speaking Jews came to Jerusalem, they heard about Jesus, became Christians and fellowshipped with the church there.

In both groups there were widows – women who husbands had died. The church provided food and other provisions for these widows. But there was a problem. Verse 1 of our Bible reading tells us what that problem was. *"More and more people were becoming followers of Jesus. But during this same time, the Greek-speaking followers began to complain against the other Jewish followers. They said that their widows were not getting their share of what the followers received every day."* So the apostles had a meeting of all the followers. They decided to choose seven men who would make sure that all the widows were taken care of.

It is important today for Christians to take care of each other, too. James 1:27a says, *"The worship that God wants is this: caring for orphans or widows who need help."* Look for ways to serve the widows in your local congregation. God is pleased when you share with your brothers and sisters in Christ.

Prayer: *Dear God, I want to share with people who are in need. Help me to be faithful and generous. In Jesus' name. Amen.*

Women in Acts (4) by Jo Krueger

The early church was composed of both men and women. And soon after the church started, some Jews who did not believe in Jesus started persecuting Christians. Both men and women were arrested or even killed because they followed Jesus.

Our Bible verses for today tell us about a time before Paul (formerly called Saul) became a Christian. He planned to go to the city of Damascus. The Jewish high priest had given him the authority to find people in Damascus who were Jesus' followers and arrest them. If Paul *"found any believers there, men or women, he would arrest them and bring them back to Jerusalem"* (verse 2b).

Paul became a Christian and stopped persecuting Christians. Then as he traveled to share the Gospel throughout the Roman Empire, the Jews persecuted *him*. But Paul always stayed strong in his faith.

People across the globe are being persecuted today. And this persecution is happening more and more in the United States – both to men and women. We need to be ready to experience bad things because we are Christians.

We should be like Paul and always depend on God to give us strength and wisdom as we share the Gospel. No matter what you will face today, stand strong for God and His Word.

Prayer: *Heavenly Father, I want to always stand strong for You and Your Word. In Jesus' name. Amen.*

Women in Acts (5) by Jo Krueger

Our Bible reading today is about another women mentioned in the book of Acts. In the city of Joppa there was a woman named Tabitha. She was also called Dorcas. Tabitha was always doing good things for people. She also gave some of her money to help people in need.

While Peter was teaching in Joppa, Tabitha died. The Christians there were very sad. They asked Peter to come to the room where they had put Tabitha's body. Many people were in the room. They cried and showed Peter some of the clothes that Tabitha had made for them. *"Peter sent all the people out of the room. He knelt down and prayed. Then he turned to Tabitha's body and said, 'Tabitha, stand up!' She opened her eyes. When she saw Peter, she sat up. He gave her his hand and helped her stand up. Then he called the believers and the widows into the room. He showed them Tabitha; she was alive!"* (verses 40-41).

Tabitha was a true servant. She helped other Christians by giving them clothes and money. Maybe you think that your job in God's family is not very important. But God needs all kinds of servants in His kingdom – teachers, nursery workers, musicians, cooks, maintenance people and many more. Thank God today for the ways you can serve Him.

Prayer: *Dear Father, thank You for giving me a job to do in Your kingdom. Help me to serve You faithfully. In Jesus' name. Amen.*

Women in Acts (6) by Jo Krueger

Today's Reading: Acts 12:1-17

Our Bible verses for today tell us that King Herod was persecuting Christians. He had James, the brother of John, killed. And he also had Peter put in jail because he was teaching about Jesus. King Herod had 16 soldiers guarding Peter while he was in jail.

During Peter's imprisonment, God sent an angel to lead him out of jail. When Peter was outside the jail, he thought, *"Now I know that the Lord really sent his angel to me"* (verse 11a). Then Peter went to the home of Mary, where some Christians were meeting. Verse 12 says that these Christians were praying. What were they praying about? They were probably asking God to rescue Peter from jail.

Peter knocked on the door of the house and a servant girl named Rhoda came to answer it. Rhoda knew that it was Peter at the door, and she became excited to see him. But she was so excited that she *"even forgot to open the door!"* (verse 14b). Rhoda ran inside and told the other Christians that Peter was there.

Rhoda was excited because she knew that God had answered their prayers about Peter. When God answers your prayers and does something wonderful in your life, be sure to thank Him. Be excited that God loves you and takes care of you every day.

Prayer: *Thank You, Father, for always answering my prayers and doing what is best for me. In Jesus' name. Amen.*

Women in Acts (7) by Jo Krueger

Today's Reading: Acts 16:1-2

Timothy was a young man who became a Christian. Acts chapter 16, tells us that Timothy's father was a Greek. But Timothy's mother was a Jew who believed in God. After Timothy became a Christian, he traveled and told people about Jesus. Sometimes Timothy traveled with Paul. Verse 2 of our Bible reading tells us what other Christians thought about Timothy. *"The believers in the cities of Lystra and Iconium had only good things to say about him."*

2 Timothy is a letter that Paul wrote to Timothy to encourage him in his ministry. In that letter, Paul talks about Timothy's grandmother and mother. Paul said, *"I remember your true faith. That kind of faith first belonged to your grandmother Lois and to your mother Eunice. I know you now have that same faith"* (2 Timothy 1:5).

Lois and Eunice believed in God. And they taught Timothy to believe and follow God, too. That was the foundation for Timothy later in life to learn about Jesus and to understand that He is God's Son. Timothy became a strong preacher who led many people to Jesus.

Is is important for us to teach our children and grandchildren about Jesus. And it is also important for us to follow Jesus' example of obeying God. Then our children and grandchildren will want to be like Jesus, too.

Prayer: *God, I want to show other people how they can follow Jesus and live for Him. In His name. Amen.*

Women in Acts (8) by Jo Krueger
Today's Reading: Acts 16:13-15

Our Bible verses for today tell us about the time Paul traveled to the city of Philippi, which was a Roman colony in the area of Macedonia. There he met a woman named Lydia. Lydia was a business woman who sold purple cloth. She believed in God and gathered with some women near the river to pray. Paul preached to those women about Jesus. *"Lydia was listening to Paul, and the Lord opened her heart to accept what Paul was saying. She and all the people living in her house were baptized"* (verses 14b-15a).

Lydia gave Paul and his friends a place to stay and food to eat while they were in Philippi. That is called Christian hospitality. In 1 Peter 4:9 Peter encouraged Christians to practice hospitality. He said, *"Open your homes to each other and share your food without complaining."*

Look for ways that you can show hospitality to other Christians. Ask a family to come to your home for a meal. Invite a visiting missionary to stay in your home while they are in your town. Take a meal to an elderly person or someone who is sick or injured.

Look for ways that you can show love and encouragement to your brothers and sisters in Christ today.

Prayer: *God, I want to share with other Christians and encourage them in their walk with You. In Jesus' name. Amen.*

Women in Acts (9) by Jo Krueger
Today's Reading: Acts 16:16-24

One day, Paul and his friends met a servant girl. This girl had a spirit from the devil that gave her the power to tell what would happen in the future. Some men owned this girl and made lots of money when she told people what would happen to them in the future.

The servant girl started following Paul and Silas and their friends. Verse 17b tells us, *"She kept shouting, 'These men are servants of the Most High God! They are telling you how you can be saved!'"* Paul commanded the evil spirit to come out of the girl. The men who owned the girl were very upset because the evil spirit was gone and they couldn't use the girl to make money any more. So, they had Paul and Silas beaten and thrown into jail.

We don't know what happened to the servant girl after this. I am sure she must have been very happy to be free from the evil spirit. I hope that she learned more about Jesus and became a Christian. Maybe she even led other people to follow accept Jesus as their Lord and Savior.

There are many people in the world today who are following the devil. These people need to know about Jesus and His free gift of salvation. Tell someone about Jesus today.

Prayer: *God I love You and want to share Your love with people that I will meet today. In Jesus' name. Amen.*

Women in Acts (10) by Jo Krueger

Today's Reading: Acts 18:1-3

Today is our last day to talk about women in Acts who played an important role in the establishment of the church. Paul went to the city of Athens. There he met Aquila and his wife, Priscilla.

Priscilla and Aquila were Jews who had been forced by the Roman emperor to leave Rome. *"They were tent makers, the same as Paul, so he stayed with them and worked with them"* (verse 3). Priscilla and her husband helped teach a man named Apollos. They *"took him to their home and helped him understand the way of God better"* (Acts 18:26b).

Several times Paul mentioned Priscilla and her husband in the letters he wrote to churches. They must have been very faithful people who helped take care of Paul and other Christians. One time Paul even said that *"they risked their own lives to save mine"* (Romans 16:4a).

Today God will give us opportunities to be like Priscilla and Aquila. We can pray for foreign missionaries and support them financially. We can also go on mission trips to help missionaries do their work. Ask God to show you where you can serve Him best.

Prayer: *God, show me how I can be like Priscilla and Aquila and help other Christians share the news about Jesus. In His name. Amen.*

Obeying God by Bonnie Hall

Today's Reading: Joshua 6:1-27

After Joshua and the Israelites had walked through the Jordan River on dry land, they were in the land that God had given to them. Now it was time for them to take over the cities and remove the people who did not worship God. The first city that they encountered was Jericho.

So God gave Joshua instructions on how the Israelites were to defeat the city of Jericho. *"Then the Lord said to Joshua, 'Look, I will let you defeat the city of Jericho. You will defeat the king and all the fighting men in the city. March around the city with your army once every day for six days. Tell seven of the priests to carry trumpets made from the horns of male sheep and to march in front of the priests who are carrying the Holy Box. On the seventh day march around the city seven times and tell the priests to blow the trumpets while they march. They will make one loud noise from the trumpets. When you hear that noise, tell all the people to begin shouting. When you do this, the walls of the city will fall down and your people will be able to go straight into the city'"* (verse 2-5). Joshua and the people followed God's instructions exactly. Because they obeyed God, they saw the city walls come down and they were able to take the city for God.

It is very important for us to be like the Israelites and obey God's instructions. When we do, He will bless us and what we do will be successful.

Prayer: *Dear Father, I know that it is important to obey You. Help me to study Your Word and do what You say. In Jesus' name. Amen.*

Gratitude by Bob La Forge
Today's Reading: 2 Chronicles 32:20-25

Hezekiah was attacked by a great army, but God destroyed his enemies and delivered him. So Hezekiah became famous, and many gifts were given to him by other rulers. Then he became sick and was ready to die. Hezekiah asked God to heal him, and God answered his prayers and allowed him to live.

But instead of thanking God, Hezekiah became proud and starting bragging. He showed everyone how wealthy he was and became more interested in his success than in being grateful for what God had done for him. Verse 25 of our Bible reading says, *"But Hezekiah's heart was proud, so he did not give God thanks for his kindness. This is why God was angry with Hezekiah and with the people of Judah and Jerusalem."*

Every good thing that we have is a gift from God. These gifts are our houses, cars, jobs, church family, and our friends. But many times we think that we have those things because we are smart or talented.

God wants us to be grateful for what He does for us. When we succeed, we should not show off and tell everyone how clever we are. Instead, He wants us to praise Him and thank Him and remember that we can do nothing without Him.

Be sure to show God your gratitude today!

Prayer: *Thank You, Father, for all the wonderful things You have done for me. In Jesus' name. Amen.*

Time for Bed by Pam Davis
Today's Reading: Luke 9:57-58

Bedtime gives each of us different feelings. Some people can't wait to get comfortable in bed. But some people are restless and toss and turn all night. I enjoy bedtime. First, I rest my head on my pillow. Then I pull up the covers. Bedtime for me is more than rest and relaxation for my body. It is a refuge from my worldly cares.

Many people dread bedtime because they have no home or bed to sleep in. There are many reasons that people live on the streets. Some have mental or addiction problems. Others may have lost their jobs or homes. And sadly, there are also countless refugees in our country. Homeless and helpless, they spend their nights sleeping on sidewalks, under bridges or in abandoned buildings.

Jesus understands these people. Our Bible verses tell us that He had the same problem. *"They were all traveling along the road. Someone said to Jesus, 'I will follow you anywhere you go.' He answered, 'The foxes have holes to live in. The birds have nests. But the Son of Man has no place where he can rest his head.'"*

Jesus left the glory of heaven to come to earth and live among us. Thank Him today that He was willing to give up heaven and come to die for us and give us salvation and eternal life.

Prayer: *Loving Father, thank You that Jesus was willing to give up the comfort of heaven and die for me. In Jesus' name. Amen.*

Mini Prayer Retreat by Gayle Thorn

Today's Reading: Luke 9:28

Our Bible verse for today says, *"About eight days after Jesus said these things, he took Peter, John, and James and went up on a mountain to pray."* Jesus often took time to pray. Let's look at why prayer was important to Jesus.

Prayer can make bad days better and good days great. Prayer clears the mind. It draws us closer to God. Prayer helps us understand God and His plan for our lives better. Prayer is how we confess our sins and ask for forgiveness. Prayer and Bible reading give us strength to resist the temptation to sin. Prayer refreshes and restores us.

Here is how you can have a mini prayer retreat and get closer to God. First, pick a new place to pray, maybe in your backyard or at a park. Second, pause and ask God to join you. Third, take time to admire God. Talk to Him about His goodness, mercy, grace, forgiveness and kindness. Fourth, look around you. Notice what you see, hear, feel and smell. Thank God for all those things and for the blessings He has given to you.

Finally, talk to God about your life and needs and the lives and needs of others. Take your time. Enjoy God's presence in your mini prayer retreat. Let your time with Him refresh and restore you.

Prayer: *Dear God, please refresh and restore me as I take time to talk to You today. In Jesus' name. Amen.*

Help and Guidance by Bonnie Hall

Today's Reading: Joshua 8:1-35

The next city that the Israelites came to after Jericho was Ai. Once again, God told Joshua not to be afraid. He said that He would help the Israelites defeat the people in Ai. So Joshua told his men what to do and that they should follow God's instructions so they would win the battle. The Israelites did exactly as God told them to do, and they were successful.

After the battle was over in Ai, our Bible reading tells us that Joshua built an altar to honor God. *"Then Joshua built an altar for the Lord, the God of Israel. He built the altar on Mount Ebal. The Lord's servant Moses told the Israelites how to build altars. So Joshua built the altar the way it was explained in the Book of the Law of Moses. The altar was made from stones that were not cut. No tool had ever been used on those stones. They offered burnt offerings to the Lord on that altar. They also gave fellowship offerings"* (verses 30-31).

When we find ourselves in the midst of daily challenges and problems, we need to rely on God's help and guidance like Joshua did. That's when we need to turn to God's Word, search it and then do what God wants us to do. When we do that, we will be successful and we will find a peace that can only come from God.

Thank God today for His Word, and rely on it to help you succeed.

Prayer: *Dear Loving God, thank You that I can study and learn from Your Word. In Jesus' name. Amen.*

Not My Home by Rachel Burkum

Today's Reading: John 14:1-6

Recently I had the opportunity to set up my own office. I'm a graphic designer, so this allowed me a place to work without distractions. I was very excited when I was told I could decorate the office. It wasn't long before I had a desk, an extra table and chair, and I even painted the walls. I slowly collected other items too - decorations for my desk, or things to hang on the wall. It has been a lot of fun making the office "my" space. But no matter how much stuff I set up in that room, it's still not my house - my home. I can spend a lot of time in my office, but I can't live there.

Jesus told His followers that He would soon leave them. He talked about His death, resurrection, and return to Heaven. He explained He was going to prepare a place for them. They didn't understand, but we know from reading the Bible that Jesus meant He was preparing Heaven for all of His followers - that means you and me, too. *"I am going there to prepare a place for you. After I go and prepare a place for you, I will come back. Then I will take you with me, so that you can be where I am"* (2b-3). That means this world is not our true home. Heaven is our true home!

Just like my office is not really where I live, this world is not forever. Are you looking forward to spending eternity with Jesus? I am!

Prayer: *Father, I can't wait for Jesus' return! Please help me stay close to You always. In Jesus' name. Amen.*

The Mind of Christ by Gayle Thorn

Today's Reading: 1 Corinthians 2:6-16

Most Christians say they want to become more like Jesus. That includes having "the mind of Christ" or thinking the way He thinks.

In verse 16 of today's Bible reading Paul asked, *"As the Scriptures say, 'Who can know what is on the Lord's mind? Who is able to give him advice?' But we have been given Christ's way of thinking."* So, how can we have "the mind of Christ"? Here are some things each of us can do to begin thinking the way Christ thinks.

Give your mind to Christ just as you gave Him your body and life when you accepted Him as your Savior. *"Love the Lord your God with all your heart, all your soul, all your mind, and all your strength"* (Mark12:30). Recognize that we have a choice. We can choose to think like Christ or to not think like Him. *"Think only about what is up there, not what is here on earth"* (Colossians 3:2). Take control of your mind. Get rid of anything that keeps you from thinking like Christ. Replace those things with Bible verses, Bible study or Christian music. *"So prepare your minds for service. With complete self-control put all your hope in the grace that will be yours when Jesus Christ comes"* (1 Peter 1:13).

Make a lifelong habit of thinking like Christ. It's not a one-time event – it's a way of living.

Prayer: *Heavenly Father, I give You my mind. Help me to fill it with Christ-like thoughts. In His name. Amen.*

Bread by Debbie Klahn

People in almost every culture around the world eat some type of bread. If the people do not have bread, then they will have some kind of other food that is made from wheat or another plant.

As I have traveled and visited countries around the world, I have eaten many different types of bread. Many countries have special stores that only sell different kinds of bread. People will stand in long lines to buy bread. Most of the time the bread does not cost a lot of money. Both rich people and poor people eat bread. Their kinds of bread may look different or taste different, but they are an important food in their diet.

Our Bible verses for today are often called "The Lord's Prayer." This is a prayer that Jesus prayed to show His followers how to pray. In verse 11 Jesus said, *"Give us the food we need for today."* Jesus was teaching people to ask God every day to provide the food that they need. Christians all over the world understand that God will provide for them.

God will provide for our physical need for food. But He will also provide us spiritual food through Jesus, who is the "bread of life." Turn to Jesus – He can satisfy all of our needs.

Prayer: *Lord, thank You for Your promise of providing for us physically and spiritually. In Jesus' name. Amen.*

Sacrifice by Jim Godsey

The Old Testament tells us about the people who lived in Canaan. This was the land that God had given to His people, the Israelites. The Canaanites worshiped the false god, Molech. One thing they did was sacrifice their children to this god. But God said in Leviticus 20:2b, *"Anyone living in Israel who gives one of their children to the false god Molech must be killed! It doesn't matter if they are a citizen of Israel or a foreigner, you must throw stones at them and kill them."*

So some people ask, "If God did not want the Israelites to sacrifice their children, they why did He sacrifice His Son, Jesus?" When we read our Bible verses for today we learn in verse 16 that *"God loved the world so much that he gave his only Son, so that everyone who believes in him would not be lost but have eternal life."* Jesus was not a child being sacrificed to a false god. He chose to give up His life so that we can have eternal life.

Jesus died for all people so that they can have their sins forgiven and then live with Him forever. Not all people will accept Jesus as their Lord and Savior, but it is our job to tell everyone about His love and His willingness to give up His life.

Thank Jesus today for what He did for you!

Prayer: *God, thank You for sending Jesus to die and rise again so that I can become Your child. In Jesus' name. Amen.*

Chili by Jo Krueger

It is a damp, cold day so I decided to make a pot of chili for supper. It has been simmering for over a hour now and it smells so good! I have used several chili recipes through the years, but a few years ago I created my own recipe. My family really likes the way I make chili now. I try very hard each time I make it to follow the recipe exactly, so it will taste the same.

It's not easy to be a Christian and follow Jesus every day. Some days it just seems like we make mistakes and give in to the devil's temptations. But the way we can be consistent in our Christian life is to use the same "recipe" every day. What is the recipe for Christian living? We can find it in the Bible. If we want to avoid sin, we need to read the Bible and follow it every day!

In our Bible reading for the today, the psalmist asks how he can live a pure life. His answer is to obey God's Word. And then in verse 11 he says, *"I study your teachings very carefully so that I will not sin against you."* That's our recipe for living the Christian life – to study God's teachings and live them.

When I make chili, I follow the recipe so that it will always taste the same. If you want to follow and obey God, read the Bible and apply it to your life every day!

Prayer: *Dear Father, show me through Your Word how I can follow You and obey You. In Jesus' name. Amen.*

Cities in Acts (1) by Jo Krueger

The book of Acts tells us that Peter, Paul and other Christian leaders traveled to many cities to tell the people about Jesus. Today we have cell phones, the Internet and television to help us spread the news about something important that has happened. But when the church began, the only way to share the news about Jesus' death and resurrection was by one person telling another person.

If someone wanted a person in another city to know about Jesus, that person had to travel to the city and talk to them. That is exactly how the message about Jesus spread from Jerusalem into many areas of the Roman Empire.

Our Bible reading today is about the day the church started in the city of Jerusalem. Peter preached to a large group of people. *"Peter warned them with many other words; he begged them, 'Save yourselves from the evil of the people who live now!' Then those who accepted what Peter said were baptized. On that day about 3000 believers were added to the group of believers"* (verses 40-41).

For the next few days we will look at some of the cities where Jesus' followers traveled, and we will learn how God's church grew and spread so that the whole world would know about Jesus.

Prayer: *Heavenly Father, thank You for the people in Your church and Your Son, Jesus. In His name. Amen.*

Cities in Acts (2) by Jo Krueger

Today's Reading: Acts 9:1-20

Damascus was a city about 150 miles from Jerusalem. Located northeast of Mount Hermon and about 50 miles from the Mediterranean Sea, Damascus was a leading trade city. Christians from Jerusalem traveled to Damascus and told people about Jesus, and many became Christians.

Saul, who was later called Paul, was a very religious Jew. He did not believe that Jesus was God's Son, and he hated Christians. Saul went to Damascus to arrest Christian men and women and take them back to Jerusalem. Our Bible reading tells us that while Saul was traveling to Damascus, a bright light shone on him, and Jesus spoke to Him. *"Saul, got up from the ground and opened his eyes, but he could not see"* (verse 8a).

In Damascus there was a Christian name Ananias. Ananias went to see Saul and teach him about Jesus. *"Immediately, something that looked like fish scales fell off Saul's eyes. He was able to see! Then he got up and was baptized"* (verse 18). Saul became a new man. He left his old life of sin and started living for Jesus. Later Saul traveled to many places in the Roman Empire to tell people about Jesus and establish Christian churches.

Will you be like Paul today? Who will you tell about Jesus?

Prayer: *Dear Loving God, show me someone today who I can tell about Jesus. In Jesus' name. Amen.*

Cities in Acts (3) by Jo Krueger

Today's Reading: Acts 14:8-20

Lystra was a city in the area that we call Turkey today. Paul and Barnabas traveled together telling people about Jesus. One day they stopped in Lystra so they could share the Gospel message there.

Our Bible reading for today tells us that in Lystra, Paul and Barnabas healed a crippled man. When the people there saw that the man was healed, they thought that Paul and Barnabas were gods. *"The people began to call Barnabas 'Zeus,' and they called Paul 'Hermes,' because he was the main speaker. The temple of Zeus was near the city. The priest of this temple brought some bulls and flowers to the city gates. The priest and the people wanted to offer a sacrifice to Paul and Barnabas"* (verses 12-13).

Paul and Barnabas were very upset about that. They told the people of Lystra that they were not gods. They also told them, *"Turn to the true living God, the one who made the sky, the earth, the sea, and everything that is in them"* (verse 15b). Then the people became angry and tried to kill Paul. So Paul and Barnabas left Lystra and went to another city.

Maybe today you will tell someone about Jesus, but they will refuse to listen. Keep sharing the news about Jesus with people who want to follow Him. Ask God to help you speak boldly for Him.

Prayer: *Dear Father, help me to be bold as I tell other people about Jesus today. In Jesus' name. Amen.*

Cities in Acts (4) by Jo Krueger   **Today's Reading:** Acts 16:20-34

In our Bible verses for today, we learn that Paul and his traveling companion, Silas, went to the city of Philippi. This city was a Roman colony in the area of Macedonia in Greece.

While Paul and Silas were in Philippi they healed a girl who had a spirit from the devil. The people who used the girl to make money were upset so they had Paul and Silas beaten and thrown into jail.

"About midnight Paul and Silas were praying and singing songs to God. The other prisoners were listening to them. Suddenly there was an earthquake so strong that it shook the foundation of the jail. All the doors of the jail opened, and the chains on all the prisoners fell off" (verses 25-26). But Paul and Silas did not leave the jail. Instead they told the jailer and his family about God. *"It was late at night, but the jailer took Paul and Silas and washed their wounds. Then the jailer and all his people were baptized."* (verse 33).

Paul and Silas were in jail – that was a bad situation. But what did they do? Did they complain and blame God. No! They praised God and shared the Good News about Jesus.

No matter what happens to you today, remember to be like Paul and Silas and praise and serve God.

Prayer: *Lord I want to always praise and serve You. In Jesus' name. Amen.*

Cities in Acts (5) by Jo Krueger   **Today's Reading:** Acts 17:10-13

Today our Bible reading tells us about Paul and Silas once again. This time they traveled to the city of Berea. Like Philippi, Berea was also in the area of Macedonia in Greece.

Verse 11 tells us three things about the people in Berea. *"The people in Berea were more open-minded than those in Thessalonica. They were so glad to hear the message Paul told them. They studied the Scriptures every day to make sure that what they heard was really true. The result was that many of them believed, including many important Greek women and men"* (verses 11-12). These verses tell us that these people were open-minded, they were happy to hear Paul's message, and they studied the Scriptures to learn the truth.

These people in Berea are a good example for Christians today. Like them, we should always be open-minded and happy to study the Bible. The world is full of people who will try to get us to believe their false teachings. So whenever someone teaches us something, we should make sure that what they are teaching really agrees with the Bible.

I hope you will decide to be like the Bereans today. Study God's Word, the Bible, and obey it!

Prayer: *Heavenly Father, thank You for Your Word. Help me to learn from it and then share Your message with others. In Jesus' name. Amen.*

Cities in Acts (6) by Jo Krueger **Today's Reading:** Acts 20:7-12

So far we have read in Acts and learned about the cities of Jerusalem, Damascus, Lystra, Philipi and Berea. Troas was a city on the Agean coast of western Asia Minor. Our Bible reading tells us about a wonderful miracle that Paul performed in the city of Troas.

On a Sunday, Paul met together with some Christians. They ate the Lord's Supper, and Paul preached to them. *"Because he was planning to leave the next day, he continued talking until midnight"* (verse 7b). There was a young man named Eutychus in the group. Eutychus was sitting in the window, and *"he went to sleep and fell out of the window. He fell to the ground from the third floor. When the people went down and lifted him up, he was dead"* (verse 9b).

Paul brought Eutychus back to life. *"The Lord's followers took Eutychus home alive, and they were all greatly comforted"* (verse 12). God was with Paul and gave him the power to perform awesome miracles. Many of the people who traveled and spread God's Word were able to do miracles. Those miracles helped people know that God's message was true and that Jesus was truly the Son of God.

You can read about many more miracles in the book of Acts. Thank God for His great power today!

Prayer: *God, thank You for being so powerful. And thank You for helping the early Christians spread the Gospel of Jesus. In His name. Amen.*

Cities in Acts (7) by Jo Krueger **Today's Reading:** Acts 28:10-31

The city we will look at from the book of Acts today is Rome. Rome was a very large city and the center of the Roman Empire. The Roman emperors lived in Rome. The city was filled with people who did not know about Jesus. They worshiped many Roman false gods and goddesses. So Paul wanted to go there and tell them about the one true God.

Paul finally was able to travel to Rome. He was under arrest and in chains, but God gave him the opportunity to preach to the people that he met every day. While Paul was in Rome, he told many people about Jesus. *"Paul and the Jews chose a day for a meeting. On that day many more of these Jews met with Paul at his house. He spoke to them all day long, explaining God's kingdom to them. He used the Law of Moses and the writings of the prophets to persuade them to believe in Jesus"* (verse 23). Paul was in chains, but that did not stop him from using every opportunity to preach the Good News about Jesus.

Sometimes we think that our circumstances prevent us from telling others about Jesus. But no matter what happens to us or where we are, we should continue sharing about Jesus.

I hope you will you be like Paul today and tell someone about Jesus.

Prayer: *Father be with me today and help me to be a witness for You. In Jesus' name. Amen.*

God With Us by Bob La Forge   **Today's Reading:** Matthew 1:18-25

How can I know that someone really exists? I can see a person's name in a telephone book, but maybe it is just someone with the same name. I can interview someone who claims to have spoken with the person, but perhaps they are lying. However, if I actually meet and talk to that person, then I will be convinced.

We cannot see God. So how do we know that He really exists and cares about us? In Exodus, chapter 13, we learn that God showed His presence to the Israelites through pillars of cloud and fire. Then He came to dwell in the Holy Tent that the Israelites set up while traveling. Finally, God's glory was present in the Temple.

Then in God's perfect timing, He chose to come to earth and live among us. But He did not appear as a fire or cloud. Instead He sent His Son, Jesus, to walk and talk with people on earth. Our Bible reading today tells us that God's angel came to Joseph to tell him that Jesus would be born. Matthew adds in verses 22-23, *"All this happened to make clear the full meaning of what the Lord said through the prophet: 'The virgin will be pregnant and will give birth to a son. They will name him Immanuel.' (Immanuel means 'God with us.')"*

We don't need any more proof. God does exist, and He cares about us. The death and resurrection of Jesus show us that God is truly with us!

Prayer: *Dear Father, thank You for sending Your only Son to live among people and show us how to live. In Jesus' name. Amen.*

Holy One from God by Gayle Thorn   **Today's Reading:** John 6:60-71

In John, chapter 6, Jesus spoke to a crowd of people. He told them that if they wanted eternal life, they must believe that He was God. Anyone who chose to follow Him had to believe that Jesus was the Messiah, the one sent by God to save people from their sins.

Many people had followed Jesus only because they were curious. They wanted to see Jesus do a miracle or give them a free meal like when He fed a group of more than 5000 people. Because Jesus told them they must believe He was God, they abandoned Him. After the people left, Jesus turned to His 12 disciples and asked, "Do you want to leave, too?"

In John 6:69 Peter said, *"We believe in you. We know that you are the Holy One from God."* Peter and the other disciples recognized that Jesus was the holy Messiah sent by God. They knew that no one else could give them eternal life. They were determined to remain faithful to Jesus no matter what. Unlike the crowd who had only followed Jesus to be entertained or for other selfish reasons, the 12 disciples followed Jesus because they knew that only Jesus could forgive sins and give them eternal life.

Why are you following Jesus? Do you truly believe that He is God's Son?

Prayer: *Heavenly Father, I believe that You are the Holy One and that I need You to forgive my sins. In Jesus' name. Amen.*

Close to the Master by Jo Krueger   **Today's Reading:** Colossians 3:22-25

My husband has owned many dogs. One was a military dog, several were K-9 police dogs and some have just been family dogs. Several years ago, we were given a K-9 dog that was being retired. He lived with us for several years until he died. Soon after he died, a neighbor brought us a small puppy. They didn't know what kind of dog she was, but she was a darling puppy!

My husband named her Gretchen, and she is now 11 years old. Through the years she has become a constant companion for my husband. Clearly she believes that my husband is her master. She follows him everywhere and obeys him. But Gretchen does one thing that shows me that she thinks he is truly her master. When my husband is sick, Gretchen will lay right beside his bed and not leave him. And I think that sometimes she knows when he is sick even before he does!

Verse 24 of our Bible reading today says, *"Remember that you will receive your reward from the Lord, who will give you what he promised his people. Yes, you are serving Christ. He is your real Master."* As Christians, our master is Jesus. We should want to be close to Him every day – just like Gretchen stays close to my husband.

Stay close to Jesus today. Read the Bible, pray, and tell others how important Jesus is to you.

Prayer: *Dear God, thank You for our Master, Jesus. Help me to stay close to Him every day. In His name. Amen.*

Be Strong and Brave by Bonnie Hall   **Today's Reading:** Joshua 10:1-25

As the Israelites were traveling to a new land, they camped at Gilgal. Nearby, five Amorite kings made plans to attack the city of Gibeon. The people in Gibeon sent a message to Joshua asking for help to fight off the coming attack.

God spoke to Joshua and told him not to be afraid and to help the people of Gibeon fight the five kings. God also said that He would be with them and that no one would be able to defeat the Israelites. During the fight, the five kings ran away and hid in a cave. Finally they were captured, and Joshua prepared to kill them. *"Then Joshua said to his men, 'Be strong and brave! Don't be afraid. I will show you what the Lord will do to all the enemies you will fight in the future'"* (verse 25).

There are times when we find ourselves fighting our own battles in life. Maybe we are facing health challenges. Maybe we are having problems with our neighbors. Maybe we have financial problems. Or maybe we ask someone to help us but they ignore us. Just as Joshua told his men, we must be strong and brave as we depend on God to help us face these situations.

You don't know what you will have to face today. As you start your day, ask God to be with you and give you strength. Then depend on Him to help you in every situation that arises.

Prayer: *Dear God, You are truly amazing. Thank You for always being with me. In Jesus' name. Amen.*

Unchanging Rock by Bob La Forge   **Today's Reading:** Malachi 3:6

When I was growing up, there was an abandoned sandpit that we made into an obstacle course with ropes, ladders and homemade bridges. At one spot, we had to crawl backwards through a drainpipe that ended at an overhang, and then blindly step out onto a ladder. One day, the ladder was missing, and I stepped out in the air. I fell about 10 feet and landed on my back gasping for breath. That sandpit is now a grocery store, and I have grown much older. Everything changes and sometimes the things that we once depended on are gone.

Even though things are always changing around us, there is one thing that never changes – God! Nothing can change God because it is He who controls and holds things together. He cannot change Himself because in all ways He is perfect and in complete harmony. Our Bible verse for today confirms that truth. *"I am the Lord, and I don't change. You are Jacob's children, and you have not been completely destroyed."*

Because God does not change, we can be secure knowing that His attitude is always the same loving faithfulness toward us. His acceptance of us does not vary since it is not based on our moods, but on the fact that He doesn't change. To have a close relationship with God, we need to change our lives and glorify Him. Then He truly becomes our unchanging rock that keeps us strong.

Prayer: *Thank You, Father, for being our unchanging rock and for helping us every day. In Jesus' name. Amen.*

Technology: GPS by Lily Woods   **Today's Reading:** 2 Timothy 3:14-17

I love technology. Some people find it frustrating, but I think it's fascinating. I love learning new programs on my computer, and figuring out how to use new gadgets. That's what this series is going to be about – certain types of technology.

Have you ever used GPS? Most new cars come with it already equipped in their system. All you need is some kind of Internet or satellite connection, and you can have a map at your fingertips! I've used GPS many times to help me figure out where I need to go. It is especially handy when I'm driving in an area that is totally unfamiliar. But GPS isn't always right. Sometimes it miscalculates where I actually am. Sometimes it doesn't include updates about construction or brand new roads. And usually it doesn't tell me when there's been an accident or traffic is moving slowly. GPS is great, but I can't always depend on it 100%.

There *is* one thing we can always depend on though, and that's God's Word, the Bible. In verse 16a of our reading today, Paul tells Timothy, *"All Scripture is given by God."* If it's given by God, we know that it is true. It's not unpredictable, wrong, or half-true. And it doesn't depend on the Internet! GPS is a great tool to help us navigate roads we drive. But we need to also recognize the Bible as our "map" for our spiritual life and follow it.

Prayer: *Dear Lord, please help me remember to look to Your Word for instructions on how I should live. In Jesus' name. Amen.*

Technology: Smart Watches by Lily Woods   **Today's Reading:** Ephesians 2:17-22

When I first learned about smart watches, I was very curious. I imagined a communication device like I'd seen on science fiction shows. Then I was able to purchase one! It was so neat! I was notified whenever I received a call or text message on my cell phone, and I could actually reply with short messages! Later, as this technology progressed, I purchased newer models and different brands. I now own a smart watch that is so "smart" I can ask it questions and it will answer me! I set timers and alarms, it reminds me when I need to exercise, it saves text messages, and even controls my cell phone's music.

My smart watch gives me all the tools I need, right from my wrist. But I have to remember to keep the battery charged. I also need to make sure it's a short distance from my phone so it will work properly. Sometimes I have to restart it if there's a problem. Smart watches are fantastic, but they are limited.

God is not limited, and we are not limited by when or how we can talk to Him. Paul's letter to the Ephesians assures us that, "...*through Christ we all have the right to come to the Father...*" (verse 18). We, as Christians, can go directly before God! We can pray to Him whenever we like, and wherever we are. Nothing needs to be recharged or restarted. God is accessible 24/7.

Prayer: *God, help me remember there are no limitations to You or when I can speak to You. In Jesus' name. Amen.*

Technology: Laptops by Lily Woods   **Today's Reading:** Psalm 136:1-26

I'm old enough to remember when computers were big, heavy and bulky. When I was a child, my father owned a desktop computer, and that was the only computer in our house. He taught me how to play a few games on it, but that's all I really knew how to do until I was older. Now that technology has advanced, I own multiple laptops! Each has a specific purpose, and each is very easy to use and transport. Laptops are so small compared to computers years ago - it's hard to believe how things have changed.

I love my laptop, and it works very well, but there are certain things I need to remember. One of the most important things is the battery. It will last several hours on its own, but if I don't plug in my laptop, it will eventually "die." I have to be careful because if my laptop runs out of power, then I'm out of luck!

One thing that will never run out is God's love. We don't need cords, adapters or electrical outlets. There's no battery that will run out. God's love is forever. In today's Bible reading, we are told 26 times, "*His [God's] faithful love will last forever.*" 26 times! The Bible mentions God's love for us over and over again, not just in this Psalm. Many people question whether or not God really loves them. But if you simply read the Bible, you'll see countless verses that confirm He does love you.

Prayer: *Father, help me to always remember Your love is forever. Thank You! In Jesus' name. Amen.*

Technology: Video Games by Lily Woods   **Today's Reading:** Psalm 46:1-11

Have you every played video games? Maybe you or someone you know is a "gamer" and plays all the time for relaxation or entertainment. I like games where I can pretend to be a fictional character. I can give them a unique name, change their appearance, and maybe even pick their skills. Some games let you shape your character even more as the story progresses. It's fun to be able to forget about the real world for a while, and enjoy a fake world where I can control what happens.

Unfortunately, real life isn't like that. There are many things out of our control. In a video game, if a mistake is made, the player can start over and have another chance, or quit and come back later to try again. But in real life, we often don't get second chances. This world is unpredictable, not always fun, and sometimes cruel.

Thankfully, we have Someone to turn to when we experience struggles: God. Psalm 46 starts out by saying, "*God is our protection and source of strength. He is always ready to help us in times of trouble.*" We don't always know or understand how God will help us through certain situations, but we can be assured that He will. There are things in life we can't control. But one thing we *can* control is how we react to trials. Will you give up and quit? Or will you rest in God and allow Him to help you?

Prayer: *Dear Lord, I know You are there to help me always. Help me to feel Your peace. In Jesus' name. Amen.*

Technology: Identity by Lily Woods   **Today's Reading:** Jeremiah 1:4-8

Have you ever heard of (or experienced) identity theft? That's when someone steals someone else's personal information. They spend money or do wrongful things while pretending to be someone else. It can be very difficult to recover after someone has stolen your identity. The Internet is a fantastic tool, but it can also be dangerous. Thankfully, most good websites use security. For example, when you place an order online, maybe you type your credit card numbers. You should be confident the website is safe so no one else can steal that information. Technology gives us convenience and confidence, both.

While identity theft is a very real concern, there's another identity issue that is even more important: our identity in Christ. In today's Bible verses, Jeremiah talks about how God knew him before he was even born. What's even more amazing is that God knows all of us that well! He made us and knew all of us long before we were born. He knew our names, our personalities, our hearts, and what our lives would be like. John 1:12 says, "*But some people did accept him [Jesus]. They believed in him, and he gave them the right to become children of God.*" We are children of God! That is our true identity, and no one can ever steal it. Make sure today that you find your identity in Christ alone.

Prayer: *Father, thank You for adopting me into Your family! Help me to always remember my true identity is in You. In Jesus' name. Amen.*

Technology: Cameras by Lily Woods   Today's Reading: James 4:1-10

A few days ago, I mentioned I was old enough to remember when computers were big and bulky. That means I also remember when cameras contained physical film. I used to love dropping off film at the store, waiting a few days, then going to pick up my printed pictures. It was always exciting to finally see them. As technology advanced, I later had a digital camera. Then a better one! And now I usually use my cell phone because it has an even better camera on it. Technology has advanced so much that "anyone" can take a good picture. There are so many automatic settings, that the camera itself will find the main target, auto focus, adjust the lighting and color, and even blur the background - all on its own! It's amazing how so little work is required to take a good picture.

I wish everything was that easy. But most things in life take a lot more work - especially things that are most important, like a relationship with Jesus. If someone says they believe in God, but they fail to work at their relationship with Him, it's worthless. James, chapter 4, reminds us to pay attention to our actions and behavior towards God. Verse 8 says, "*Come near to God and he will come near to you. You are sinners, so clean sin out of your lives.*" Being a Christian doesn't mean we can be lazy. We need to work at doing what is right and try to live like Jesus.

Prayer: *Heavenly Father, I want to work at having a better relationship with You! In Your Son's name. Amen.*

Technology: Smart Bulbs by Lily Woods   Today's Reading: John 8:12-20

I absolutely love "smart" light bulbs. If you're not familiar with them, they are light bulbs that use the Internet. They connect to other devices in order to function. My porch light is programmed to come on in the evening and turn off in the morning. My basement has four lights I can turn on all at the same time. My bathroom has several more smart bulbs, and I have a special setting for when I want to relax in a hot bath. Some smart bulbs have a lot of choices for colors or brightness, and other devices, like ones with "Alexa," can control them, too. It's great to come home and simply speak to turn on the lights.

There are drawbacks, though. If the Internet fails, so do the bulbs. Sometimes they disconnect for unknown reasons and won't turn on at all. Sometimes they are reset or don't show the proper brightness. Smart bulbs are great, but not always reliable.

The Bible often refers to Jesus as "light." Today's reading starts out in verse 12a saying, "*He said, 'I am the light of the world. Whoever follows me will never live in darkness.'*" He didn't say "you will only sometimes be in darkness," or "my light turns on and off." He said if we follow Him, we will *never* live in darkness! That means He is reliable. His light will always be there for us, and will last forever. Are you walking in His light?

Prayer: *Dear Lord, I want to always be in Jesus' light, and to live like You want me to. In Jesus' name. Amen.*

Fear of God by Gayle Thorn

Today's Reading: Psalm 112:1

Psalm 112:1 says, *"Praise the Lord! Great blessings belong to those who fear and respect the Lord, who are happy to do what he commands."* What does it mean to fear the Lord? Fearing the Lord is not an "Oh, I am so scared" kind of fear. This kind of fear shouldn't make us want to hide from God. It shouldn't give us nightmares.

To fear the Lord means that we are afraid that we might hurt or disappoint God. It means that we love God so much that we are afraid we might let Him down if we disobey Him. It means we are afraid of doing or saying anything that might dishonor God.

When we genuinely love God, we should be afraid of doing anything that could hurt God, offend Him or make Him sad. We should also be afraid of not doing the things that we know please Him and make Him happy.

How can we know what we can do or not do to make God happy? Read the Bible. God gave us a whole book to help us live to please Him. Pray. Ask God to teach you how to live in a way that makes Him happy.

Do you have a healthy fear of God? God will give great blessings to people who fear and respect Him.

Prayer: *Heavenly Father, help me to obey You. I want to always please and honor You. In Jesus' name. Amen.*

Ready for Thanksgiving by Jennifer Forrester

Today's Reading: Ezra 3:1-11

The turkey is thawing, and the pies are baked. It will be good to gather as a family to share a Thanksgiving meal, times of laughter and a few memories from the past. When most Americans think about "thanksgiving," they think about the national holiday in November. But the Israelites had many days of thanksgiving to God. Whenever God helped them accomplish something great, they would gather together and thank God for what He had done.

After the Israelites were allowed to return home from captivity, one of the first things they wanted to do was rebuild the Temple. Our Bible verses tell us that they set up a new altar where the altar in the old Temple had been, and they began making sacrifices to God. This was a reason for the Israelites to celebrate and give thanks. Verse 11 says, *"They sang songs of praise and thanksgiving, taking turns in singing each part. They sang, 'The Lord is good. His faithful love will last forever.' Then all the people cheered — they gave a loud shout and praised the Lord because the foundation of the Lord's Temple had been laid."*

As you get ready for a day of thanksgiving, don't forget to stop and celebrate what God has done in your life. Praise Him for how He works in your life and thank Him for His love and promise of eternal life.

Prayer: *Lord, thank You today and every day for what You do for me. I look forward to celebrating with You in heaven. In Jesus' name. Amen.*

Thank You, God by Gayle Thorn   **Today's Reading:** 2 Corinthians 9:12-15

"Thanks be to God for his gift that is too wonderful to describe." Those words of praise are found in 2 Corinthians 9:15. What is the gift that this verse is talking about? It is talking about salvation through faith in Jesus Christ.

Salvation certainly is an indescribable gift. There is no way that we can put a price on it. We can never repay God for it. There is no gift that is worth more to us. However, we can thank God for our salvation and show Him that we appreciate His love and generosity.

Since we can't send God a "thank you" note, we need to find other ways of showing Him our gratefulness. Here are a few ideas: We could give a little extra in the Sunday morning offering at church. We could volunteer a few hours or a day to help a Christian non-profit organization. We could offer to help a neighbor with some work around their house. We could send an appreciation card to our pastor. We could spend five extra minutes each morning reading our Bible. We could smile at a stranger as we pass by.

Probably the easiest way to thank God for His wonderful gift – and often the most overlooked – is simply to take a moment every day to say, "Thank You, God, for saving me."

Prayer: *Heavenly Father, thank You for saving me and giving me eternal life. In Jesus' name. Amen.*

"Thank You" Card for God by Gayle Thorn   **Today's Reading:** Psalm 119:41-48

I'm so thankful that God sent Jesus to rescue me from sin. If you've accepted Jesus as your Savior, I suspect you are thankful to God, too. Verse 48 of our Bible reading to today beautifully sums up how we can show our thankfulness to God. *"Not only do I love your commands, but I also honor them. I will study your laws."*

First, we can pause in our busy life and spend time talking to God and listening for His voice. Speaking to and listening to God is probably the best way we can thank God for Jesus' sacrifice.

Second, we can read, study, memorize and think about God's Word. We can continually learn more about what pleases God and then find ways to put what we've learned into action. Doing what makes God happy is a wonderful way to show Him that we appreciate what Jesus did for us on the cross.

Third, our hands can be busy doing the actions that He expects of us so that our lives will make Him happy. God doesn't want us to learn His ways and then keep them to ourselves. He wants us to go out and live what we've learned by helping and serving other people.

I hope you are a living "thank you" card to God.

Prayer: *Dear Father, I want my whole life — everything I think, say and do — to be one big "thank you" card to You. In Jesus' name. Amen.*

Cup of Thanks by Gayle Thorn **Today's Reading:** Psalm 116:12-14

Verse 13 of our Bible reading for today says, *"He saved me, so I will give him a drink offering, and I will call on the Lord's name."* This verse is talking about the drink offerings in the Old Testament law that were given by the people as a way of saying, "Thank You," to God.

Jesus came to earth and lived as a man. He faced many struggles while on earth. Then He willingly allowed Himself to be arrested, beaten, ridiculed and nailed to a rough wooden cross where He died. Jesus allowed those things to happen to Him although He had not sinned or committed a crime. He allowed those things to happen to Him so that we would not have to suffer eternal punishment for the crimes and sins that we have committed. Jesus was punished in our place.

Jesus then defeated death by rising from the dead and returning to heaven, alive and well. In doing so, He showed that death can't keep us away from God. Jesus did all that because He loves us.

Because Jesus did all those wonderful things for us, we need to accept the free gift of salvation that He offers us and raise our "cup" in thanks. Have you accepted the salvation that Jesus offers you? If not, please do! Then you can truly say, "Thank You," to God.

Prayer: *Thank You, Father, that Jesus was willing to suffer and die in my place. In His name. Amen.*

Inconceivable by Rachel Burkum **Today's Reading:** 1 John 3:11-18

One of my favorite movies includes a character who likes to say, "Inconceivable!" whenever something amazing happens. It's a funny quote, and whenever it's said around other people who also like the movie, we always laugh. Inconceivable is a big word. But it really just means "unbelievable" or unable to understand.

"Inconceivable" though, really is a good word to describe God's love. His love is so great that we, as humans, cannot understand it. In verse 16a of our Bible reading today, it says, *"This is how we know what real love is: Jesus gave his life for us."* He gave His life! Think about that for a moment. Romans 5:8 says, *"But Christ died for us while we were still sinners, and by this God showed how much he loves us."* Not only did Jesus die for us, He died for us even though we are all sinners. He didn't just die for "good" people or people who have great lives. He died for each and every one of us, in spite of our sins.

We also have to realize that God knew when He sent Jesus to earth that the purpose was for Jesus to be a sacrifice. God didn't have to do this for us. But He did because He loves us that much. He sent His very own Son. Jesus also could have said, "No." But He didn't. He willingly went to the cross and endured a brutal death. For us. For me. For you. God's love is truly inconceivable! Have you thanked Him today?

Prayer: *Dear God, I don't understand how You could love me so much. Thank You for sending Jesus! In His name. Amen.*

Honesty is the Best Policy by Gayle Thorn   **Today's Reading:** Psalm 7:1-9

There's an old saying that goes, "Honesty is the best policy." Why is being honest the best way to handle every situation that we face in life? Psalm 7:8 gives us the main reason for being honest in all of our thoughts and actions. This verse says, *"Lord, judge the people. Lord, judge me. Prove that I am right and that I am innocent."* God will someday judge our words as well as our actions. When the time comes, I hope we are all found to be pleasing in God's eyes. If God is pleased with us, He will reward us with eternal life.

What are the benefits of being honest? God delights and blesses honest people (Psalm 24:5). People respect honest people (1 Thessalonians 4:11-12). God rewards honest people, and they will live with Him (Psalm 15). Honest people can know with certainty the direction of their life (Proverbs 11:5). Honest people avoid doing evil and have inner peace (Proverbs 21:15). Honest people attract good friends (Proverbs 22:11). And God blesses the children of honest people (Proverbs 20:7).

As you can see, the Bible shows us that there are many benefits to being honest. We benefit greatly by being honest. And God benefits from our honesty, too. When we are honest, God is glorified.

Is honesty the policy that you follow in life?

Prayer: *Dear Heavenly Father, help me to live a life filled with honesty and integrity. In Jesus' name. Amen.*

Sweet Smells by Rachel Burkum   **Today's Reading:** 2 Corinthians 2:14-15

It's December 1st, so it is getting close to Christmas. That means I can get out my Christmas decorations. I especially love my Christmas candles. I'm talking about the ones that really *smell* like "Christmas" to me. I like the scent of pine, or apple and cinnamon. Those are my favorites, and they remind me of happy Christmas memories from when I was growing up. These candles fill my house with good smells. I especially like burning them when I have visitors because they can enjoy them, too.

Today's Bible verses compare us sharing the Good News with others to something that smells good. *"God uses us to spread his knowledge everywhere like a sweet-smelling perfume"* (verse 14b). Some versions of the Bible use the words, "pleasing aroma." When we smell something good, it can help us relax and feel good. When we do things that please God, that is the kind of feeling we give to Him. And when we share Jesus with others, it can give them this good feeling as well.

During this Christmas season, let's all remember to be fragrant "candles" to others. Not everyone will believe or want to follow God. But that should never stop us from talking about Jesus. No matter what the world says, it's our job to do what pleases God.

Prayer: *Father, thank You for today's lesson. Please help my actions be "sweet-smelling" to You and others. In Jesus' name. Amen.*

Jesus (1) by Jo Krueger   **Today's Reading:** 1 Timothy 1:15-17

In a few weeks, Christians around the world will celebrate Jesus' birth. Many activities this month will be centered around the Good News of Jesus coming to live among people. So today and for the next few days, we will talk about Jesus and His special purpose for coming to earth.

At Christmastime some people only think about Jesus as a baby being born in a manger in Bethlehem. They do not think about His ministry, His death, His burial or His resurrection. Verse 15a of our Bible reading for today tells us the reason Jesus came to earth: *"Here is a true statement that should be accepted without question: Christ Jesus came into the world to save sinners."*

Jesus' special purpose in coming to earth was to die for our sins. We are all sinners, so without His death and resurrection, Jesus' life here on earth would be meaningless. God sent Jesus to die on the cross and be the final perfect sacrifice for our sins.

Tomorrow we will begin talking about Jesus' death and what its importance is to us. I hope you will think about these things as you celebrate Christmas this month.

Praise God today for sending Jesus to be your Savior!

Prayer: *God, thank You for Your wonderful plan of salvation for us through Jesus. In His name. Amen.*

Jesus (2) by Jo Krueger   **Today's Reading:** Matthew 21:1-9

Have you ever watched a royal ceremony from England on TV? For these special events, the king and queen always wear crowns. A crown is a sign of authority and power and wealth. Crowns like English royalty wear are usually made of gold and decorated with expensive jewels.

In our Bible verses, Jesus entered the city of Jerusalem a few days before He was crucified. The people there were excited to see Him. *"On the way to Jerusalem, many people spread their coats on the road for Jesus. Others cut branches from the trees and spread them on the road"* (verse 8). They worshiped and praised Him. But these people did not really understand the reason why Jesus came to earth. They expected Him to overthrow the Romans and establish an earthly kingdom where He would sit on a throne and wear a crown. But that was not God's plan for His Son.

Jesus is truly a king. The book of Revelation describes how Jesus is the king of a heavenly kingdom. If we obey Jesus and allow Him to rule our lives, we will share in His kingdom and live with Him forever. In that kingdom, there will be no pain, sorrow, sickness or sin. Won't that be wonderful?

Is Jesus the king of your life? Think about what it will be like to live with Him forever. Then thank God for His plan of sending Jesus to be our Lord and Savior.

Prayer: *Dear Father, thank You for Jesus who is the king of my life. Help me to serve Him every day. In His name. Amen.*

Jesus (3) by Jo Krueger

In Bible times, people did not wear shoes like we wear today. Their shoes were made from leather and similar to our sandals today. Roads were not paved, so when they walked on dusty roads, their feet became very dirty. It was a custom to wash people's feet when they came to visit. I am sure that washing people's feet was not a pleasant job!

In our verses today, Jesus washed the feet of His disciples. He knew He would soon die, rise again and leave the earth. Jesus wanted to teach His disciples important things for them to remember when He was gone. Jesus did not wash their feet just to get their feet clean. He did it to show them that they should be humble like a servant. Jesus is God's Son, but He was willing to do a dirty job like washing feet!

Sometimes we may be tempted to act proud and think we are better than other people. Then we need to remember Jesus' example of humility. We need to serve others like Jesus did. In verse 15 of our Bible reading Jesus said, *"I did this as an example for you. So you should serve each other just as I served you."* When we serve people, God will be pleased with us and know that we are truly following Jesus.

Think of ways you can be a servant today. Then go out and serve the people in your family and your neighborhood.

Prayer: *Dear Loving God, I want to be a humble servant like Jesus and serve others. In His name. Amen.*

Jesus (4) by Jo Krueger

The Bible tells us about many different Jewish ceremonies. Some of these ceremonies required people to drink a cup of wine. Accepting and drinking a cup of wine was their way of showing their commitment or making a promise to do something important.

In our Bible reading today, Jesus shared the Passover meal with His disciples. Jesus knew that He was going to die soon and that this was the last time He would celebrate this meal with them. In verse 29 Jesus said, *"I want you to know, I will not drink this wine again until that day when we are together in my Father's kingdom and the wine is new. Then I will drink it again with you."* When Jesus took the cup and drank from it, He was promising to follow God's plan for Him to go to the cross and die a horrible death for you and me!

What does God have planned for your life? Are you willing to serve as part of a ministry in your local church? Are you willing to be a faithful marriage partner and a good parent to your children? Are you willing to share the Good News about Jesus with your neighbors?

Think about Jesus and that He was willing to do whatever God wanted Him to do. Then promise to serve and obey God every day of your life.

Prayer: *Dear God, show me how I can serve and obey You today and every day. In Jesus' name. Amen.*

Jesus (5) by Jo Krueger   **Today's Reading:** Matthew 27:15-26

Many years ago, on a sunny day in December, I was shopping in a mall in a nearby state. Very suddenly it started snowing hard. They announced on the mall speaker system that it was snowing heavily and that they would soon be closing the mall. Immediately everyone rushed toward the doors to get to their cars. In the crowd, people were jostled and shoved. Some people were even pushed to the ground.

Maybe the crowd in our Bible reading today was like that. They were pushing people and shouting angry words. Probably some people in the crowd didn't even know who Jesus was. But they became excited and started shouting along with the rest of the angry mob. In the end, this group of people chose to kill Jesus.

Have you ever wanted to follow the crowd? Have you ever been tempted to do something wrong just because those around you were doing it and you wanted to fit in? Paul talks about this in Romans 12:2. *"Don't change yourselves to be like the people of this world, but let God change you inside with a new way of thinking. Then you will be able to understand and accept what God wants for you. You will be able to know what is good and pleasing to him and what is perfect."*

We should not be doing what everyone else is doing. Instead, we should think and act like Jesus.

Prayer: *Loving Father, please help me to do what You want me to do today and not follow the crowd. In Jesus' name. Amen.*

Jesus (6) by Jo Krueger   **Today's Reading:** Matthew 27:27-44

I remember a Christmas gift exchange at school when I was in the sixth grade. One boy received a pair of mittens as his gift. The boy was from a very poor family, and he probably needed a new pair of mittens, but the rest of the students in the class got toys, games or books. Some of the children started making fun of the boy and his mittens. They teased him and called him names. Finally he started crying and ran out of the classroom.

Have you ever felt ashamed or embarrassed like that little boy? Today's Bible verses tell us about a time when people made fun of Jesus. *"They took off Jesus' clothes and put a red robe on him. Then they made a crown from thorny branches and put it on his head, and they put a stick in his right hand. Then they bowed before him, making fun of him"* (verses 28-29a). These people mocked Jesus and spit on Him. Finally, they took Him outside the city and crucified Him.

Jesus suffered more than any embarrassment we might face here on earth. He did that for us. Why? Because He loves us so much! Jesus was willing to endure pain so that we can have our sins forgiven. He died on the cross so that we can live forever with Him.

Praise God that Jesus was willing to be our perfect sacrifice.

Prayer: *Father, please help me to remember how much Jesus suffered for me on the cross. In Jesus' name. Amen.*

Jesus (7) by Jo Krueger
Today's Reading: Matthew 27:57-66

I used to live in a place where the soil was very rocky. We always had to work hard to clear the land so we could plant a garden. Often we would see a small stone on the surface of the ground. When we tried to remove it, we would discover that it really was a huge stone. Most of the stone was buried under the ground.

A large stone covered the entrance to the tomb where Jesus was buried. It was so large that it couldn't be lifted – it had to be rolled in front of the opening. The Roman governor, Pilate, ordered the guards to stay at the tomb. He knew that people had said Jesus would rise again. Pilate wanted to make sure that no one would come and steal Jesus' body. *"So they all went to the tomb and made it safe from thieves. They did this by sealing the stone in the entrance and putting soldiers there to guard it"* (verse 66).

But nothing could keep Jesus in the tomb! Not a huge stone! Not even Pilate's guards! It was God's plan for Jesus to rise from the dead. This showed the world that Jesus has power over death. Only the Son of God could give up His life and then rise from the dead.

Because Jesus has power over death, we, too, will rise someday and live forever with Him. Thank God today for Jesus and His power over death!

Prayer: *God, thank You for Jesus' great power and His miraculous resurrection. In Jesus' name. Amen.*

Jesus (8) by Jo Krueger
Today's Reading: Luke 24:1-12

You may have heard the expression, "It's just too good to be true!" People often say this when something wonderful happened, but they just can't believe that it really happened. For example, a person might win the lottery or receive an unexpected inheritance and they say, "It's just too good to be true!"

When Jesus' followers heard that He was risen from the dead, I think they might have said, "It's just too good to be true!" Jesus had been telling His disciples for a long time that He would die and rise again, but when the women came from the tomb and told them about the resurrection, they didn't believe it. *"But the apostles did not believe what they said. It sounded like nonsense"* (verse 11). But soon, the disciples saw Jesus and believed. That must have been a wonderful time of rejoicing and celebration when they knew for sure that Jesus was alive again!

It has been almost 2000 years since Jesus died and rose again. We cannot see Jesus today. We cannot sit and talk with Him. We cannot touch the nail prints in His hands. But we do have the Bible and the eyewitness testimony of people who were with Him. We can know that the Bible is true and that Jesus really rose from the dead.

Take time to celebrate this wonderful miracle today!

Prayer: *Thank You, God, for the miracle of Jesus' resurrection. I want to celebrate it every day. In Jesus' name. Amen.*

Jesus (9) by Jo Krueger
Today's Reading: Acts 1:6-11

When I was 10 years old I went to a week-long Christian summer camp for the first time. I had a great time at camp except for one thing – I was so homesick for my family! When my mom and dad arrived on Friday to pick me up, I remember running to the car and hugging them again and again. I had missed them so much!

After Jesus' resurrection, He was on earth for only a short time before He returned to heaven to be with God. But before He left, He promised them that He would come back again someday. The disciples knew that they would miss Jesus, but He told them what they should do when He was gone. *"But the Holy Spirit will come on you and give you power. You will be my witnesses. You will tell people everywhere about me – in Jerusalem, in the rest of Judea, in Samaria, and in every part of the world"* (verse 8). Then two angels appeared and told the disciples that at some time in the future, Jesus would come back to earth in the same way they had seen Him leave.

I am very excited to see Jesus someday! It will be so good to talk with Him face to face and thank Him for all He has done for me. I hope you are excited, too, about seeing Jesus. But until He returns, we need to continue to serve Him faithfully every day.

Make today a special day of service for Jesus!

Prayer: *Heavenly Father, I look forward to the time when Jesus will return. Help me stay faithful to Him. In His name. Amen.*

Twinkling Lights by Lily Woods
Today's Reading: James 1:17-18

One of my very favorite things about Christmastime is looking at all the lights. White lights, colored lights, blue lights – all the lights! I love houses that are so bright they light up their yards. There are lights that look like icicles, lights that line the sidewalks, and lights that blink on and off. In my own house, my Christmas tree has a lot of lights, and I even string lights around my living room! Christmas lights bring me a feeling of happiness and make me smile.

Some people feel stress around Christmastime. But it's also the perfect time to remember all that God has given to us. Our Bible reading for today reminds us that all good things come from God. He's given us life – eternal life, if we accept it – and hope through sending His Son, Jesus, to die and rise again. My favorite part is the end of verse 17. *"But God never changes like the shadows from those lights. He is always the same."*

Christmas lights twinkle and blink and turn on and off. But God? He is always the same. Always constant. Never-ending. Always loving. His love doesn't turn on and off. When He sent Jesus as a baby, it was His way of saying, "I love you!" to the world. And that never has and never will change.

I'm going to let Christmas lights be a reminder to me of God's love this year!

Prayer: *Dear God, thank You so much for sending Jesus! I love Him and want to honor Him this Christmas and always. In Jesus' name. Amen.*

Christmas Freedoms (1) by Gayle Thorn   **Today's Reading:** Matthew 28:9

Today we will begin a devotional series that talks about Christmas as a time to remember the freedoms that we have as Christians. We will look at things that the Bible says we are free to do because of Jesus' birth and death and our faith in Him. Then when the new year arrives, we will be ready to live God's way.

Let's begin with our Bible verse for today. *"Suddenly, Jesus was there in front of them. He said, 'Hello!' The women went to him and, holding on to his feet, worshiped him."* Jesus had risen from the dead. He was seen by some of His disciples. The moment they realized Jesus was alive, they fell down on their knees, held onto Jesus' feet and worshiped Him.

We should follow the example of these women. Let's focus on worshiping Jesus. We can worship as a group with other believers in a local church, in Bible study groups or in prayer groups. We need to focus on private worship by spending time every day reading, studying, memorizing and meditating on God's Word. Let's also take time to pray.

We can worship Jesus anywhere and at any time. Worshiping Jesus is how we get to know Him and how our faith grows strong. So let's worship Jesus as we celebrate this Christmas season and all through the new year!

Prayer: *Heavenly Father, teach me to worship and honor Jesus throughout my day. In His name. Amen.*

Christmas Freedoms (2) by Gayle Thorn   **Today's Reading:** Proverbs 11:24-25

Giving isn't only about sharing money. We can give of our material possessions. We can give of our time. We can give by using our skills and abilities to help people. We can give by sharing our thoughts with others. We can give by sharing the needs of other people with God through prayer.

The Bible talks about at least two kinds of givers: Givers who don't really want to give and givers who give freely, generously and with love. God wants us to be the second kind of giver.

Jesus was born as a baby and then later died on the cross to free us from our sins, including greed and selfishness. So we are free to be the generous loving and cheerful givers that God wants us to be.

Verse 24 of our Bible reading for today says, *"Some people give freely and gain more; others refuse to give and end up with less."* If we give freely and generously, God will bless us freely and generously. If we choose to be greedy or selfish and give little or nothing, God will give us little or no blessing.

Let's encourage each other to give freely and generously of all our many resources. That will bless others and open the doors for God's blessings on our lives this Christmas and in the days ahead.

Prayer: *Heavenly Father, help me to find ways to give freely and generously to others. In Jesus' name. Amen.*

Christmas Freedoms (3) by Gayle Thorn   **Today's Reading:** John 15:9-12

The yearly celebration of Jesus' birth gives us hope. That hope, and the promise that our sins are forgiven and that we will have eternal life with God in heaven fills us with joy. Joy isn't the same as happiness. Happiness is how we feel when we like something or something pleases us. When good things happen we're happy. When bad or sad things happen we are not happy.

Joy is feeling content and confident that God is in control and that He loves us. Joy is knowing that God is working out all our circumstances for our best on good days and on bad days. Joy doesn't go away when bad or sad things happen. As long as we trust and hope in Jesus and His love for us, we have joy and we are free to share that joy with other people.

In our Bible verses, Jesus said these things. *"I have loved you as the Father has loved me"* (verse 9a). *"I have told you these things so that you can have the true happiness that I have"* (verse 11a). And *"This is what I command you: Love each other as I have loved you"* (verse 12).

This Christmas let's obey Jesus and celebrate the joy we have through our faith in Him. Then let's share that joy by telling someone about Jesus and what He has done for us.

Prayer: *Heavenly Father, thank You for the joy that comes from my salvation and hope in Jesus. Remind me to share that joy with the people around me today. In Jesus' name. Amen.*

Christmas Freedoms (4) by Gayle Thorn   **Today's Reading:** Psalm 55:1-14

So far in our series we have talked about several things that we are free to do because of Jesus' birth. We are free to worship Jesus, give generously, and we are free to share the joy that He gives us.

In Psalm 55 David is talking to God about the hard things he and the Jewish people were experiencing. He talks about the threats and the danger posed by their enemies. In verses 12-14 David remembers the good days of the past saying, *"If it were an enemy insulting me, I could bear it. If it were my enemies attacking me, I could hide. But it is you, the one so close to me, my companion, my good friend, who does this. We used to share our secrets with one another as we walked through the crowds together in God's Temple."* David's friend was Ahithophel who had betrayed him. David was remembering the good times they had together in God's Temple.

We can use David's memory as a reminder of how good and meaningful it is to be with Christian friends especially in God's house.

Thankfully, as Christians, we are free to spend time with our church families. I hope we will take advantage of that freedom by attending church this Christmas and throughout the coming year so we can build relationships with other believers and worship with them.

Prayer: *Heavenly Father, thank You for my church family. Help me to make meeting with them a priority this Christmas season and in the new year. In Jesus' name. Amen.*

Christmas Freedoms (5) by Gayle Thorn   **Today's Reading:** 2 Corinthians 8:10-15

At Christmastime, people often spend too much money. They may buy many unnecessary items on credit. Maybe we would be wiser to keep our Christmas purchases simpler and smaller and use our money to help people who are really in need.

In verse 14 of our Bible reading for today, Paul advised the people in Corinth to do something similar saying, *"At this time you have plenty and can provide what they need. Then later, when they have plenty, they can provide what you need. Then everyone will have an equal share."* What a simple but wonderful plan! If we have more than we need we should give some of our extra to someone who doesn't have enough. If that person has more than he needs, he should share of his abundance with someone. When we all share our abundance with each other, we will all have enough. None of us will be needy.

Because Jesus was born on that first Christmas and died for our sins, He has made us free from our natural greed and selfishness and free to share with each other. Jesus made it possible for us to be free to be generous.

I hope this Christmas we will look at all the good things God has given to us and then share some of our abundance with those in need.

Prayer: *Father, thank You for all the wonderful things You have given to me. Give me a generous heart and help me to freely share my blessing with others. In Jesus' name. Amen.*

Christmas Freedoms (6) by Gayle Thorn   **Today's Reading:** Luke 2:1-14

Luke, chapter 2, tells us about the angel who announced Jesus' birth to the shepherds, told them where to find the baby, and how to know they had found the right baby.

Then in verses 13 and 14, we read that *"a huge army of angels from heaven joined the first angel, and they were all praising God, saying, 'Praise God in heaven, and on earth let there be peace to the people who please him.'"* These verses say we are free to receive God's peace. God's peace is the calm assurance that no matter our circumstances, we can know that God accepts us, God is with us, God loves us and God is in control. Nothing will surprise or fool God. We can rest easy and trust Him.

We are also free to receive and share God's good will with others. Some Bible translations say in verse 14, *"good will toward men."* Good will is God's kindness and grace. When we choose to allow Jesus to be our Lord and Savior, this pleases God. When we choose to obey God's Word, this pleases God. When we please God, He promises to show us His kindness and grace. God wants us to share His good will with others.

You are free to share God's kindness, peace and grace with other people this Christmas season.

Prayer: *Dear Loving Father, thank You for Your peace and good will. Help me to share those gifts freely with others. In Jesus' name. Amen.*

Christmas Freedoms (7) by Gayle Thorn   **Today's Reading:** James 1:17

We all enjoy receiving gifts, especially at Christmas. But the best gifts can't be found under a Christmas tree or in a Christmas stocking. They are given to us by God. James 1:17 says, *"Everything good comes from God. Every perfect gift is from him. These good gifts come down from the Father who made all the lights in the sky. But God never changes like the shadows from those lights. He is always the same."*

What are some of these good and perfect gifts? Some of them are love, joy, peace, hope, forgiveness and eternal life. This Christmas we can remember that we are free to accept these wonderful gifts. And the good thing is that God gives us these gifts every day of the year – not just on Christmas Day!

How can we receive these gifts from God?

We need to ask and believe. It's that simple! All we need to do is ask God to give us the good and perfect gifts that He has for us and then believe that He wants to give us those gifts.

The best thing about God's good and perfect gifts is that they are eternal. God's gifts never wear out, never break and never get lost or stolen. God's good and perfect gifts will last forever!

Prayer: *Dear Heavenly Father, please fill my life with Your good and perfect gifts every day of the year. In Jesus' name. Amen.*

Christmas Freedoms (8) by Gayle Thorn   **Today's Reading:** Matthew 5:14-16

Christmas lights are beautiful! It is fun to drive around and look at the lights people have displayed on their houses and in their yards. Many towns have contests to see who has the best light display.

How can we know where to find houses that have Christmas lights? Just look around! The lights are bright and colorful. When you look across the countryside, you can't miss seeing any house that has lights strung on it. Those lights guide us right to them!

Our Bible verses for today tell us that, as Christians, we are light, too. *"You are the light that shines for the world to see. You are like a city built on a hill that cannot be hidden. People don't hide a lamp under a bowl. They put it on a lampstand. Then the light shines for everyone in the house. In the same way, you should be a light for other people. Live so that they will see the good things you do and praise your Father in heaven."* With Jesus as our Lord and Savior, and His Holy Spirit in our hearts, we are free to be lights that show the way to Jesus. When people look at the way you live or listen to the things you say, they should see right through you to Jesus.

I hope we all choose to let our lights shine for Jesus this Christmastime and all throughout the year.

Prayer: *Dear Father, help me to let Jesus shine brightly through my actions and my words. In His name. Amen.*

Christmas Freedoms (9) by Gayle Thorn   **Today's Reading:** Matthew 18:1-5

Today's Christmas freedom is found in Matthew 18:4. *"The greatest person in God's kingdom is the one who makes himself humble like this child."* Jesus is Lord of your life so you are free to be humble like a child.

How are children humble? Think about an infant or a toddler. Very small children can't provide their own food, clothing or shelter. They can't defend themselves. They don't have the ability to go from place to place on their own. These small children must depend on their parents for everything. They must trust their parents to know what is best for them and do that for their child. Even Jesus as a baby and small child was totally dependent on His earthly parents, Mary and Joseph, to provide for His needs.

We Christians should have that same total dependence on our Heavenly Father. We should recognize our inability to do anything without Him. We should be willing to trust Him without question in every situation. We should trust God to know what is best for us and to do what is best for us.

This Christmastime, let's thank God that we are free to be humble like a young child. Then let's go and live in humble dependence on our heavenly Father every day of the year.

Prayer: *Heavenly Father, we are grateful that, through faith in Jesus, we are Your children. Help us to completely trust and depend on You. In Jesus' name. Amen.*

Christmas Freedoms (10) by Gayle Thorn   **Today's Reading:** Colossians 3:23

Another Christmas freedom we have is the freedom to love the Lord with our whole heart and obey Him in every part of our life.

Wow! It's hard to imagine being so free from our own self-love, arrogance, greed, selfishness and other forms of pride that we can trust, love and obey God completely. But with Jesus in our lives, we really are free to love and obey God with our whole mind, body and soul.

One of the ways we can put this whole-hearted love and obedience into action is to follow the instructions found in our Bible verse for today. *"In all the work you are given, do the best you can. Work as though you are working for the Lord, not any earthly master."* Everything we do, everything we say and everything we think, we should think, do and say for Jesus. That means we should always do our best work, speak the best words and think the best thoughts. We should never think, speak or act carelessly.

This Christmas and all though the coming months, let's start doing our best in everything we do so God will see that we really do love Him and cheerfully obey Him with every part of our lives.

Prayer: *Heavenly Father, teach us to do our best, speak our best, and think our best so that our lives will show everyone that we truly do love You with our whole heart and life. In Jesus' name. Amen.*

Christmas Freedoms (11) by Gayle Thorn   **Today's Reading:** 1 Peter 3:15

We live in a sad and broken world. Many people have no hope and no purpose. They struggle to try to do something to give their life meaning because they believe that all they have is this lifetime. They believe that when they die, everything ends. They cease to exist. All is lost.

But Christians think differently. Christians have hope. Jesus is the God of hope and He gives this hope to us. This hope is the assurance that God is with us, even in bad times. His Holy Spirit guides, helps, comforts, teaches us how to pray and so much more! This hope knows that God has a plan and a purpose for our lives. This hope gives our life meaning. It is the confidence that God always works out every situation for our best. It is the assurance that God keeps all of His promises to us, including the promise to give us eternal life with Him in heaven.

How are we to respond when we have this amazing hope?

We need to remember the message of our Bible verse for today. *"But keep the Lord Christ holy in your hearts. Always be ready to answer anyone who asks you to explain about the hope you have."* Remember on Christmas day and every day of the year that we have the freedom to tell everyone about the hope we have through Jesus, the Giver of hope!

Prayer: *Dear Father, thank You for the hope we have because of our faith in Jesus. Help us to tell others about that hope. In Jesus' name. Amen.*

Christmas Freedoms (12) by Gayle Thorn   **Today's Reading:** 2 Thessalonians 3:16

Peace is more than just getting away from the noise and stress of the workplace or home. Peace is a sense of completeness and a soundness or quietness of mind and spirit. Peace is a sense of total well-being. We can never have true peace without Jesus. Jesus is our source of peace. With Jesus as our Lord and Savior, we have the freedom to live in His unequaled peace every moment of every day, no matter what our circumstances are.

We are also free to tell people about the perfect peace that comes from being in a personal relationship with Jesus. We can tell them that they can have the peace of Jesus, too. We can pray that other people will want Jesus and experience His peace. That's what Paul did for the people of Thessalonica in today's Bible verse. *"We pray that the Lord of peace will give you peace at all times and in every way. The Lord be with you all."*

This Christmas, let's ask Jesus to fill us with His peace each day. Let's also ask Him to remind us that His peace is plentiful and that we have the freedom to tell others how they, too, can receive and experience God's peace for themselves.

Finally, let's go into the new year determined to live in Jesus' peace and tell everyone about it.

Prayer: *Dear Heavenly Father, thank You for Your peace. Thank You that I can have that peace through faith in Jesus. In His name. Amen.*

Christmas Freedoms (13) by Gayle Thorn   **Today's Reading:** John 15:12-15

We have talked about the Christmas freedoms that we have in Jesus. Today we will talk about another freedom. Did you know that loving other people isn't an option for Christians? Jesus didn't say "It would be nice if you would love one another." Jesus said in verses 12-14 of our Bible reading for today, *"This is what I command you: Love each other as I have loved you. The greatest love people can show is to die for their friends. You are my friends if you do what I tell you to do."*

When we have Jesus in our lives, we don't have to struggle to love other people. When we ask Jesus to be our Savior, He gives us His Holy Spirit. The Holy Spirit loves everyone. Our job is to allow His love to flow through us to other people.

When the Holy Spirit's love flows through us and into the lives of other people, we stop loving the human way. The human way of loving is conditional. It says "I will love you if..." God's way of loving is unconditional. It says "I love you no matter what." We have the freedom to love people God's way because of Jesus' birth and sacrificial death.

I hope that we will all begin loving each other God's way this Christmas season. I also hope that we will choose to keep loving each other throughout the days and weeks ahead.

Prayer: *Father, thank You for Your unconditional love for me. Help me to love others in the same way. In Jesus' name. Amen.*

Christmas Freedoms (14) by Gayle Thorn   **Today's Reading:** Romans 5:10-15

Some people love to shop for the perfect Christmas gift. Other people think gift shopping is stressful. A recent poll said that 69% of Americans would like to stop Christmas gift exchanges. They would prefer to save money and spend time with their families.

Our heavenly Father loves to give us gifts. He is the perfect gift-giver. He always gives perfect gifts. Our Bible reading describes the best gift God has given to us. Verse 10 says, *"I mean that while we were God's enemies, he made friends with us through his Son's death."*

God gave us the gift of friendship. He did this by sending Jesus to die in our place and be punished for our sins. When we believe and accept Jesus' death as our punishment, God forgives our sin and makes us His friend.

This Christmas Day, and every day we have the freedom to thank God for His gifts of forgiveness and friendship.

I hope that you have enjoyed this Christmas freedoms series. I also hope that you will take all these freedoms from God and live as the person God created you to be in Jesus Christ. Merry Christmas!

Prayer: *Dear Heavenly Father, thank You for forgiving me, rescuing me from my sin and making me Your friend. In Jesus' name. Amen.*

Christmas Clutter by Donna Howard   **Today's Reading:** Luke 2:1-7

Today is the day after Christmas. The living room is still cluttered with torn wrapping paper, empty boxes and colorful bows of all sizes. I groan as I look around me. Where should I start cleaning up this mess? I pick up the box that had held our two-year-old great granddaughter's first baby doll. That was a gift that she loved. Another box held a gift for our 18-year-old grandson – a book about robotics. I smile as I revel in the love and happiness that created the mess as our family came together to celebrate the birthday of our Lord.

My husband Lynn's deep voice still resonates through my mind as I remember his reading the Christmas story from Luke, chapter 2. *"While Joseph and Mary were in Bethlehem, the time came for her to have the baby. She gave birth to her first son. She wrapped him up well and laid him in a box where cattle are fed. She put him there because the guest room was full"* (verses 6-7).

I am smiling now. The mess can wait. All I want to do is spend the day in quiet reflection on God's greatest gift. That precious baby in the manger was a special gift to me and my family, too.

I think I will sink into my easy chair, close my eyes and praise God for the awe and wonder of Christmas.

Prayer: *Dear God, thank You for the greatest gift ever – Your only Son, Jesus. In Jesus' name. Amen.*

Perfect Planning by Suzanne Austin-Hill   **Today's Reading:** Proverbs 16:9

I noticed a friend always had a decorative, pocket-sized holder for hand sanitizer hanging on her purse. So I ordered one for her that was shaped like a colorful cartoon lion. When you press the button on the holder, the lion roars. Her birthday was months away, so I had no idea when I was going to give it to her.

The package arrived at my house on Thursday. Then I found out on the next Sunday my friend was scheduled to interpret the song, "The Lion and the Lamb," in American Sign Language. I immediately knew I would surprise her with my little gift on Sunday morning.

When I try to control my life, sometimes my plan seems to work. But sometimes my plan must change. And sometimes I don't even have a plan! Has this ever happened to you?

Today's Bible verse reminds us, *"People can plan what they want to do, but it is the Lord who guides their steps."* As believers, we give God control of everything in our lives, including little things like when to give a gift. God has a plan for us. It's always the best and it always works!

You can depend on God's plan for your life today.

Prayer: *Dear Loving Lord, I am so thankful that when I don't know what to do, You do! In Jesus' name. Amen.*

Come Worship Him by Donna Howard

Today's Reading: Matthew 2:1-12

Our Bible reading for today tells us about wise men who came from the East to worship Jesus. These men had studied the Old Testament prophecies that told about the birth of a king. When they arrived in Jerusalem, it was probably months or even years after Jesus had been born in Bethlehem. The wise men asked people, *"Where is the child who has been born to be the king of the Jews? We saw the star that shows he was born. We saw it rise in the sky in the east and have come to worship him"* (verse 2b).

We have probably all heard the phrase that is repeated at Christmastime – "Wise men still seek Him." I like that! And I try to seek Jesus every day of the year. But I hope that I will never forget that the main reason I seek Jesus is to worship Him. I want to give Him my love and praise. I want to glorify Him. I want to feel the joy that the wise men felt when they found Jesus. *"The wise men came to the house where the child was with his mother Mary. They bowed down and worshiped him. Then they opened the boxes of gifts they had brought for him. They gave him treasures of gold, frankincense, and myrrh"* (verse 11).

If I am wise, I will worship and honor Jesus every day of the year. Please join me in bowing down and worshiping our Savior and King!

Prayer: *Dear Loving Father, I want to worship and praise Jesus every day of the year. In His name. Amen.*

Forgiveness by Gayle Thorn

Today's Reading: Proverbs 19:11

It's not easy to forgive someone who has hurt us, but wise King Solomon tells us in today's Bible verse, *"Experience makes you more patient, and you are most patient when you ignore insults."* Forgiving people for doing or saying hurtful things about us starts in our own minds.

Here are five tips to help you forgive others and receive God's healing for your heart. First, put aside your pride. Remind yourself of the careless, hurtful words and actions that you have said and done in the past. Second, give the person who hurt you, his attitudes, and his behavior to God. Let God deal with that person.

Third, give the specific words or actions that hurt you to God. Let God give you comfort, peace and healing in their place. Fourth, trust God. Accept His timing in dealing with the person and your hurt. Fifth, ask God to replace the anger and hurt you feel toward the person who hurt you with love for that person.

We have hurt Jesus terribly because of our sin. But He forgave us. The least we can do is follow His example by forgiving other people. *"Don't be angry with each other but forgive each other. If you feel someone has wronged you, forgive them. Forgive others because the Lord forgave you"* (Colossians 3:13).

Prayer: *Dear Loving Father, help me to forgive and show love for people who have hurt me in the past. I trust You to deal with them in Your own way and in Your own time. In Jesus' name. Amen.*

Good-bye Old Year! by Jo Krueger   **Today's Reading:** Ecclesiastes 12:1-14

Well, this year is almost over. I hope it has been a good year for you. I know for me this year has flown by so fast. The older I get, the faster the days pass. It seems that January 1st was just yesterday!

Today I want to encourage you to look back over your year. Then stop and give thanks to God. Thank Him for the good times you have had with your family and friends. Thank Him for the ways He has blessed you materially and spiritually throughout the year. And praise Him for the opportunities that you had this year to serve and honor Him.

Our Bible verses for today were written by King Solomon. Through the book of Ecclesiastes, he shard his wisdom about things he experienced in life. Then in verses 13-14 of his closing chapter, Solomon looked back over his life and shared what is really important. *"Now, what should we learn from everything that is written in this book? The most important thing a person can do is to respect God and obey his commands, because he knows about everything people do – even the secret things. He knows about all the good and all the bad, and he will judge people for everything they do."*

Thank God today for this past year and the many ways He has helped you obey and serve Him.

Prayer: *Dear God, thank You for being with me throughout this year. Help me to continue to respect and obey You. In Jesus' name. Amen.*

Good-bye Old Year! (2) by Jo Krueger   **Today's Reading:** Philippians 3:12-14

I hope you enjoyed looking back over the past year yesterday. Today we will look ahead to the new year.

Have you noticed some new TV ads the past couple of weeks? Businesses like Peloton and Weight Watchers are getting their message out – "You need to work at being healthier in the new year!" People on talk shows are sharing what their New Year's resolutions will be. Some want to become wealthier or more famous during the coming year.

Paul knew that he was not perfect. He knew that he was not yet all that God wanted him to be. And Paul knew that he should not worry about his past mistakes and failures. That's why he wrote our Bible verses for today. In verse 14 he said, *"I keep running hard toward the finish line to get the prize that is mine because God has called me through Christ Jesus to life up there in heaven."*

That's what our goal should be in the new year. We need to focus on the prize that is waiting for us in heaven. If we do, our thoughts and actions will please God and we will be doing the work of sharing the Good News about Jesus with others.

As you go into a new year, I pray that you will keep your eyes on the prize!

Prayer: *Dear Lord, I am looking forward to another year of loving and serving You. Help me to keep my life focused on living with You forever. In Jesus' name. Amen.*

Be sure to check out all books in this series!

Search on Amazon for "Every Day in God's Word by Jo Krueger"

| Volume 1 | Volume 2 | Volume 3 |

Made in the USA
Coppell, TX
24 November 2023